D1518815

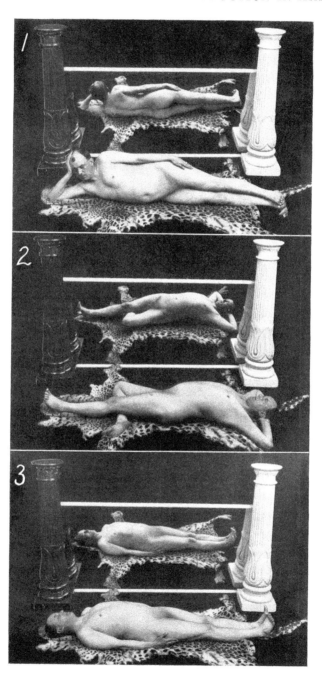

1. The Dying Buddha   {   These three recumbent positions are
2. The Hanged Man.   {   more suitable for repose after medi-
3. The Corpse.   {   tation than for meditation itself.

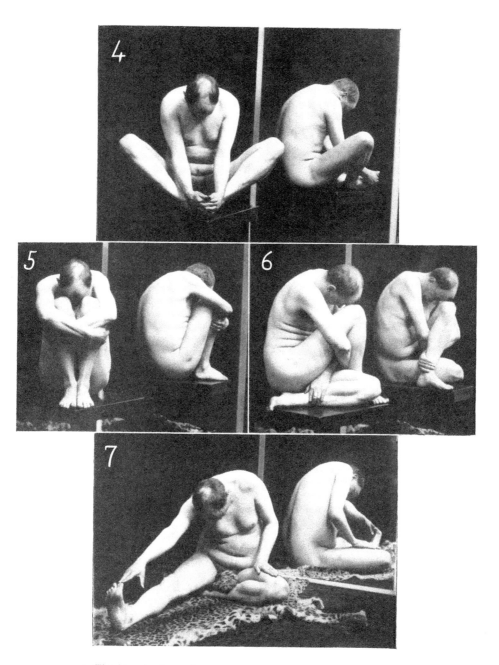

4. The Arrowhead.
5. The Bear.
6. The Ivy.
7. The Parallelogram.

These positions with bowed head are suitable for Asana and for meditation, but not for Pranayama.

Owing to the unnecessary strain thrown upon Neophytes by unprepared persons totally ignorant of the groundwork taking the Oath of a Probationer, the Imperator of A∴A∴, under the seal and by the authority of V.V.V.V.V., ordains that every person wishing to become a Probationer of A∴A∴ must first pass three months as a Student of the Mysteries.

He must possess the following books:—

1. The EQUINOX, from No. 1 to the current number.
2. "Raja Yoga," by Swami Vivekananda.
3. "The Shiva Sanhita," or "The Hathayoga Pradipika."
4. "Konx Om Pax."
5. "The Spiritual Guide," by Miguel de Molinos.
6. "777."
7. "Rituel et Dogme de la haute Magie," par Eliphaz Levi, or its translation, by A. E. Waite.
8. "The Goetia of the Lemegeton of Solomon the King."
9. "Tannhäuser," by A. Crowley.
10. "The Sword of Song," by A. Crowley.
11. "Time," by A. Crowley.
12. "Eleusis," by A. Crowley.
    [These four last items are to be found in his Collected Works.]
13. "The Book of the Sacred Magic of Abra-melin the Mage."

An examination in these books will be made. The Student is expected to show a thorough acquaintance with them, but not necessarily to understand them in any deeper sense. On passing the examination he may be admitted to the grade of Probationer.

Persons wishing for information, assistance, further interpretation, etc., are requested to communicate with

THE CHANCELLOR OF THE A∴ A∴
c/o THE EQUINOX,
3 Great James Street,
W.C.

Telephone: CITY 8987,

or to call at that address by appointment. A representative will be there to meet them.

Probationers are reminded that the object of Probations and Ordeals is one: namely, to select Adepts. But the method appears twofold: (i) to fortify the fit; (ii) to eliminate the unfit.

The Chancellor of the A∴ A∴ views without satisfaction the practice of Probationers working together. A Probationer should work with his Neophyte, or alone. Breach of this rule may prove a bar to advancement.

Some of the weaker brethren having found the postures in Liber E too difficult, the pitiful heart of the Præmonstrator of A∴ A∴ has been moved to authorise the publication of additional postures, which will be found facing this page. An elderly, corpulent gentleman of sedentary habit has been good enough to pose, so that none need feel debarred from devoting himself to the Great Work on the ground of physical infirmity.

THE EQUINOX

THE EQUINOX

THE OFFICIAL ORGAN OF THE A∴A∴

THE REVIEW OF SCIENTIFIC ILLUMINISM

EDITED BY MARY D'ESTE STURGES

SUB-EDITOR: VICTOR B. NEUBURG

An VIII   VOL. I.   No. VII   ☉ in ♈

MARCH MCMXII
O. S.

"THE METHOD OF SCIENCE—THE AIM OF RELIGION"

WIELAND & CO.
3 GREAT JAMES STREET, GRAY'S INN
LONDON, W.C.

The Equinox
The Review of Scientific Illuminism
Vol. I.   No. VII.

First published in London in 1912

An CXIV   ☉ in ♏

Digital edition available at:
https://keepsilence.org/the-equinox

Contents of this page
in the first edition:

*Preliminaries, pages 1-248, and
pages 355-400a of this Volume
printed by Turnbull & Spears,
Edinburgh; the remainder by the
Chiswick Press, London*

CONTENTS

LIST OF ILLUSTRATIONS

John 1911

ALEISTER CROWLEY. A LITHOGRAPH BY AUGUSTE CLOT
FROM THE SKETCH MADE BY AUGUSTUS JOHN.

EDITORIAL

It is with no light heart that I take the reins of the government of this magazine from the hand of our beloved Editor, Aleister Crowley, a reproduction of whose portrait by Augustus John faces this page.

For this Seventh Number of the Equinox is the most important that has hitherto appeared. It contains the Account of the Revelation made in Egypt to Frater P... at The Equinox of the Gods, with facsimiles of Liber Legis and of the Stele of Revealing, the base of all our Work.

Yet it behoves our Editor, our Brother, our Friend, and our Father, to enter upon that Magical Retirement which has been so wonderfully ushered in by our Seven Times Blessed Soror Virakam.

And so let us leave Him, seated upon the Immortal Lily, his body fixed as the Earth, his Spirit freer and as boundless as the Air, his Soul a piercing Flame of Fire; what new wonder, what further Unveiling he may bring, let us not ask; let us await with that eager Scepticism which is his own unsullied sword.

      *   *   *   *   *   *   *

Coincident with the retirement of Aleister Crowley, who always pays for everything, comes a rise in the price of this Magazine, to meet the great expense of the coloured plates and other illustrations, and the Great Hebrew Dictionary in No. VIII.

3

THE EQUINOX

*   *   *   *   *   *   *

The American market having absorbed nearly all unsold copies of back numbers, the price of all copies of Nos. I. and II. is advanced to one guinea, that of Nos. III.-VI. to half-a-guinea. There are still a few sets of the Edition de Luxe at ten guineas; single numbers, two guineas each. We shall be glad to buy saleably undamaged copies at a small discount on these prices.

*   *   *   *   *   *   *

FRATER PERDVRABO has now written a complete Illustrated Treatise on Mysticism and Magick at the request, and by the hand, of SOROR VIRAKAM. It is written to suit those who as yet know nothing of the subject. It will be published shortly at a popular price, under the title of BOOK FOUR.

MARY D'ESTE.

LIBER B

MAGI

SVB FIGVRÂ

I

A∴A∴
Publication in Class B.
Imprimatur:
N. Fra A∴A∴

LIBER B

VEL MAGI

SVB FIGVRÂ I

00. One is the Magus: twain His forces: four His weapons. These are the Seven Spirits of Unrighteousness; seven vultures of evil. Thus is the art and craft of the Magus but glamour. How shall He destroy Himself?

0. Yet the Magus hath power upon the Mother both directly and through Love. And the Magus is Love, and bindeth together That and This in His Conjuration.

1. In the beginning doth the Magus speak Truth, and send forth Illusion and Falsehood to enslave the soul. Yet therein is the Mystery of Redemption.

2. By His Wisdom made He the Worlds; the Word that is God is none other than He.

3. How then shall He end His speech with Silence? For He is Speech.

4. He is the First and the Last. How shall He cease to number Himself?

5. By a Magus is this writing made known through the mind of a Magister. The one uttereth clearly, and the other understandeth; yet the Word is falsehood, and the Understanding darkness. And this saying is Of All Truth.

6. Nevertheless it is written; for there be times of darkness, and this as a lamp therein.

7. With the Wand createth He.

8. With the Cup preserveth He.

9. With the Dagger destroyeth He.

10. With the Coin redeemeth He.

11. His weapons fulfil the wheel; and on What Axle that turneth is not known unto Him.

12. From all these actions must He cease before the curse of His Grade is uplifted from Him. Before He attain to That which existeth without Form.

13. And if at this time He be manifested upon earth as a Man, and therefore is this present writing, let this be His method, that the curse of His grade, and the burden of His attainment, be uplifted from Him.

14. Let Him beware of abstinence from action. For the curse of His grade is that He must speak Truth, that the Falsehood thereof may enslave the souls of men. Let Him then utter that without Fear, that the Law may be fulfilled. And according to His Original Nature will that law be shapen, so that one may declare gentleness and quietness, being an Hindu; and another fierceness and servility, being a Jew; and yet another ardour and manliness, being an Arab. Yet this matter toucheth the mystery of Incarnation, and is not here to be declared.

15. Now the grade of a Magister teacheth the Mystery of Sorrow, and the grade of a Magus the Mystery of Change, and the grade of Ipsissimus the Mystery of Selflessness, which is called also the Mystery of Pan.

16. Let the Magus then contemplate each in turn, raising

it to the ultimate power of Infinity. Wherein Sorrow is Joy, and Change is Stability, and Selflessness is Self. For the interplay of the parts hath no action upon the whole. And this contemplation shall be performed not by simple meditation—how much less then by reason? but by the method which shall have been given unto Him in His initiation to the Grade.

17. Following which method, it shall be easy for Him to combine that trinity from its elements, and further to combine Sat-Chit-Ananda, and Light, Love, Life, three by three into nine that are one, in which meditation success shall be That which was first adumbrated to Him in the grade of Practicus (which reflecteth Mercury into the lowest world) in Liber XXVII., " Here is Nothing under its three Forms."

18. And this is the Opening of the Grade of Ipsissimus, and by the Buddhists it is called the trance Nerodha-Samapatti.

19. And woe, woe, woe, yea woe, and again woe, woe, woe unto seven times be His that preacheth not His law to men !

20. And woe also be unto Him that refuseth the curse of the grade of a Magus, and the burden of the Attainment thereof.

21. And in the word CHAOS let the Book be sealed; yea, let the Book be sealed.

LIBER NV

SVB FIGVRÂ

XI

A∴A∴
Publication in Class D
(for Winners of the Ordeal X.).
Imprimatur:

ᆿᆿᆿ · · ·
V.V.V.V.V. . . .
N. Fra A∴A∴
O.M. 7°=4°.

LIBER NV

ooo. This is the Book of the Cult of the Infinite Without.

oo. The Aspirant is Hadit. Nuit is the infinite expansion of the Rose; Hadit the infinite concentration of the Rood. (*Instruction of V.V.V.V.V.*)

o. First let the Aspirant learn in his heart the First Chapter of the Book of the Law. (*Instruction of V.V.V.V.V.*)

1. Worship, *i.e.* identify thyself with, the Khabs, the secret Light within the Heart. Within this, again, unextended, is Hadit.

This is the first practice of Meditation (ccxx. I. 6 and 21).

2. Adore and understand the Rim of the Stélé of Revealing.

> " Above, the gemmed azure is
>   The naked splendour of Nuit;
> She bends in ecstasy to kiss
>   The secret ardours of Hadit."

This is the first practice of Intelligence (ccxx. I. 14).

3. Avoid any act of choice or discrimination.

This is the first practice of Ethics (ccxx. I. 22).

4. Consider of six and fifty that $50 \div 6 = 0.12$.

o the circumference, Nuit.

. the centre, Hadit.

1 the unity proceeding, Ra-Hoor-Khuit.

2 the world of illusion.

Nuit thus comprehends All in None.

Also $50 + 6 = 56 = 5 + 6 = 11$, the key of all Rituals.

And $50 \times 6 = 300$, the Spirit of the Child within.

(Note $N_{Fts} = 72$, the Shemhamphorash and the Quinaries of the Zodiac, etc.)

This is the second practice of Intelligence (ccxx. I. 24, 25).

5. The Result of this Practice is the Consciousness of the Continuity of Existence, the Omnipresence of the Body of Nuit.

In other words, the Aspirant is conscious only of the Infinite Universe as a single Being. (Note for this the importance of Paragraph 3. ED.)

This is the first Indication of the Nature of the Result (ccxx. I. 26).

6. Meditate upon Nuit as the Continuous One resolved into None and Two as the phases of her being.

[For the Universe being self-contained must be capable of expression by the formula $(n - n) = 0$. For if not, let it be expressed by the formula $n - m = p$. That is, the Infinite moves otherwise than within itself, which is absurd. ED.]

This is the second practice of Meditation (ccxx. I. 27).

7. Meditate upon the facts of Samadhi on all planes, the liberation of heat in chemistry, joy in natural history, Ananda

in religion, when two things join to lose themselves in a third.

This is the third practice of Meditation (ccxx. I. 28, 29, 30).

8. Let the Aspirant pay utmost reverence to the Authority of the A∴ A∴ and follow Its instructions, and let him swear a great Oath of Devotion unto Nuit.

This is the second practice of Ethics (ccxx. I. 32).

9. Let the Aspirant beware of the slightest exercise of his will against another being. Thus, lying is a better posture than sitting or standing, as it opposes less resistance to gravitation. Yet his first duty is to the force nearest and most potent; *e.g.* he may rise to greet a friend.

This is the third practice of Ethics (ccxx. I. 41).

10. Let the Aspirant exercise his will without the least consideration for any other being. This direction cannot be understood, much less accomplished, until the previous practice has been perfected.

This is the fourth practice of Ethics (ccxx. I. 42, 43, 44).

11. Let the Aspirant comprehend that these two practices are identical.

This is the third practice of Intelligence (ccxx. I. 45).

12. Let the Aspirant live the Life Beautiful and Pleasant. For this freedom hath he won. But let each act, especially of love, be devoted wholly to his true mistress, Nuit.

This is the fifth practice of Ethics (ccxx. I. 51, 52, 61, 63).

13. Let the Aspirant yearn toward Nuit under the stars of Night, with a love directed by his Magical Will, not merely proceeding from the heart.

This is the first practice of Magick Art (ccxx. I. 57).

14. The Result of this Practice in the subsequent life of the Aspirant is to fill him with unimaginable joys : to give him certainty concerning the nature of the phenomenon called death ; to give him peace unalterable, rest, and ecstasy.

This is the second Indication of the Nature of the Result (ccxx. I. 58).

15. Let the Aspirant prepare a perfume of resinous woods and gums, according to his inspiration.

This is the second practice of Magick Art (ccxx. I. 59).

16. Let the Aspirant prepare a Pantacle, as follows.

Inscribe a circle within a Pentagram, upon a ground square or of such other convenient shape as he may choose. Let the circle be scarlet, the Pentagram black, the ground royal blue studded with golden stars.

Within the circle, at its centre, shall be painted a sigil that shall be revealed to the Aspirant by Nuit Herself.

And this Pentacle shall serve for a Telismatic Image, or as an Eidolon, or as a Focus for the mind.

This is the third practice of Magick Art (ccxx. I. 60).

17. Let the Aspirant find a lonely place, if possible a place in the Desert of Sand, or if not, a place unfrequented, and without objects to disturb the view. Such are moorlands, fens, the open sea, broad rivers, and open fields. Also, and especially, the summits of mountains.

There let him invoke the Goddess as he hath Wisdom and Understanding so to do. But let this Invocation be that of a pure heart, *i.e.* a heart wholly devoted to Her, and let him remember that it is Hadit Himself in the most secret place thereof that invoketh. Then let this serpent Hadit burst into flame.

LIBER NV

This is the fourth practice of Magick Art (ccxx. I. 61.

18. Then shall the Aspirant come a little to lie in Her bosom.

This is the third Indication of the Nature of the Result (ccxx. I. 61).

19. Let the Aspirant stand upon the edge of a precipice in act or in imagination. And let him imagine and suffer the fear of falling.

Next let him imagine with this aid that the Earth is falling, and he with it, or he from it; and considering the infinity of space, let him excite the fear within him to the point of ecstasy, so that the most dreadful dream of falling that he hath ever suffered be as nothing in comparison.

This is the fourth practice of Meditation. (Instruction of V.V.V.V.V.)

20. Thus having understood the nature of this Third Indication, let him in his Magick Rite fall from himself into Nuit, or expand into Her, as his imagination may compel him.

And at that moment, desiring earnestly the Kiss of Nuit, let him give one particle of dust, *i.e.* let Hadit give himself up utterly to Her.

This is the fifth practice of Magick Art (ccxx. I. 61).

21. Then shall he lose all in that hour.

This is the fourth Indication of the Nature of the Result (ccxx. I. 61).

22. Let the Aspirant prepare a lovesong of rapture unto the Goddess, or let him be inspired by Her unto this.

This is the sixth practice of Magick Art (ccxx. 63).

23. Let the Aspirant be clad in a single robe. An

"abbai" of scarlet wrought with gold is most suitable. (The abbai is not unlike the Japanese kimono. It must fold simply over the breast without belt or other fastening. ED.)

This is the seventh practice of Magick Art (ccxx. I. 61).

24. Let the Aspirant wear a rich head-dress. A crown of gold adorned with sapphires or diamonds with a royal blue cap of maintenance, or nemmes, is most suitable.

This is the eighth practice of Magick Art (ccxx. I. 61).

25. Let the Aspirant wear many jewels such as he may possess.

This is the ninth practice of Magick Art (ccxx. I. 63).

26. Let the Aspirant prepare an Elixir or libation as he may have wit to do.

This is the tenth practice of Magick Art (ccxx. I. 63).

27. Let the Aspirant invoke, lying supine, his robe spread out as it were a carpet.

This is the eleventh practice of Magick Art. (Instruction of V.V.V.V.V.)

28. Summary. Preliminaries.

These are the necessary possessions.

1. The Crown or head-dress.
2. The Jewels.
3. The Pantacle.
4. The Robe.
5. The Song or Incantation.
6. The Place of Invocation.
7. The Perfume.
8. The Elixir.

29. Summary continued.   Preliminaries.

These are the necessary comprehensions.

    1. The Natures of Nuit and Hadit, and their relation.

    2. The Mystery of the Individual Will.

30. Summary continued.   Preliminaries.

These are the meditations necessary to be accomplished.

    1. The discovery of Hadit in the Aspirant, and indentification with Him.

    2. The Continuous One.

    3. The value of the Equation $n + (-n)$.

    4. Cremnophobia.

31. Summary continued.   Preliminaries.

These are the Ethical Practices to be accomplished.

    1. Assertion of Kether-point-of-view.

    2. Reverence to the Order.

    3. Abolition of human will.

    4. Exercise of true will.

    5. Devotion to Nuit throughout a beautified life.

32. Summary continued.   The Actual Rite.

    1. Retire to desert with crown and other insignia and implements.

    2. Burn perfume.

    3. Chant incantation.

    4. Drink unto Nuit of the Elixir.

    5. Lying supine, with eyes fixed on the stars, practice the sensation of falling into nothingness.

    6. Being actually within the bosom of Nuit, let Hadit surrender Himself.

33. Summary concluded.   The Results.
  1. Expansion of consciousness to that of the Infinite.
  2. " Loss of all" the highest mystical attainment.
  3. True Wisdom and Perfect Happiness.

LIBER ISRAFEL

SVB FIGVRÂ

LXIV

A∴A∴
Publication in Class B.
Imprimatur:
N. Fra A∴A∴

LIBER ISRAFEL

SVB FIGVRÂ LXIV

[This book was formerly called " Anubis," and is referred to the 20th key,
" The Angel."]

o. The Temple being in darkness, and the Speaker
ascended into his place, let him begin by a ritual of the
Enterer, as followeth.

1. ˋ Procul, O procul este profani.

2. Bahlasti! Ompehda!

3. In the name of the Mighty and Terrible One, I proclaim
that I have banished the Shells unto their habitations.

4. I invoke Tahuti, the Lord of Wisdom and of Utterance,
the God that cometh forth from the Veil.

5. O Thou! Majesty of Godhead! Wisdom-crowned
Tahuti ! Lord of the Gates of the Universe ! Thee, Thee, I
invoke.

O Thou of the Ibis Head ! Thee, Thee I invoke.

Thou who wieldest the Wand of Double Power ! Thee,
Thee I invoke !

Thou who bearest in Thy left hand the Rose and Cross
of Light and Life: Thee, Thee, I invoke.

Thou, whose head is as an emerald, and Thy nemmes
as the night-sky blue ! Thee, Thee I invoke.

23

THE EQUINOX

Thou, whose skin is of flaming orange as though it burned in a furnace! Thee, Thee I invoke.

6. Behold! I am Yesterday, To-Day, and the Brother of To-Morrow!

I am born again and again.

Mine is the Unseen Force, whereof the Gods are sprung! Which is as Life unto the Dwellers in the Watch-Towers of the Universe.

I am the Charioteer of the East, Lord of the Past and of the Future.

I see by mine own inward light: Lord of Resurrection; Who cometh forth from the Dusk, and my birth is from the House of Death.

7. O ye two Divine Hawks upon your Pinnacles!

Who keep watch over the Universe!

Ye who company the Bier to the House of Rest!

Who pilot the Ship of Ra advancing onwards to the heights of heaven!

Lord of the Shrine which standeth in the Centre of the Earth!

8. Behold, He is in me, and I in Him!

Mine is the Radiance, wherein Ptah floateth over the firmament!

I travel upon high!

I tread upon the firmament of Nu!

I raise a flashing flame, with the lightning of Mine Eye!

Ever rushing on, in the splendour of the daily glorified Ra: giving my life to the Dwellers of Earth.

9. If I say "Come up upon the mountains!" the Celestial Waters shall flow at my Word.

LIBER ISRAFEL

For I am Ra incarnate!

Khephra created in the Flesh!

I am the Eidolon of my father Tmu, Lord of the City of the Sun!

10. The God who commands is in my mouth!

The God of Wisdom is in my Heart!

My tongue is the Sanctuary of Truth!

And a God sitteth upon my lips.

11. My Word is accomplished every day!

And the desire of my heart realises itself, as that of Ptah when He createth!

I am Eternal; therefore all things are as my designs; therefore do all things obey my Word.

12. Therefore do Thou come forth unto me from Thine abode in the Silence: Unutterable Wisdom! All-Light! All-Power!

Thoth! Hermes! Mercury! Odin!

By whatever name I call Thee, Thou art still nameless to Eternity: Come Thou forth, I say, and aid and guard me in this work of Art.

13. Thou, Star of the East, that didst conduct the Magi!

Thou art The Same all-present in Heaven and in Hell!

Thou that vibratest between the Light and the Darkness!

Rising, descending! Changing ever, yet ever The Same!

The Sun is Thy Father!

Thy Mother the Moon!

THE EQUINOX

The Wind hath borne Thee in its bosom; and Earth hath ever nourished the changeless Godhead of Thy Youth!

14. Come Thou forth, I say, come Thou forth!
And make all Spirits subject unto Me:
So that every Spirit of the Firmament
And of the Ether,
And of the Earth,
And under the Earth,
On dry land
And in the Water,
Of whirling Air
And of rushing Fire,
And every Spell and Scourge of God the Vast One, may be obedient unto Me!

15. I invoke the Priestess of the Silver Star, Asi the Curved One, by the ritual of Silence.

16. I make open the gate of Bliss; I descend from the Palace of the Stars; I greet you, I embrace you, O children of earth, that are gathered together in the Hall of Darkness.

17. (A pause.)

18. The Speech in the Silence.
The Words against the Son of Night.
The Voice of Tahuti in the Universe in the Presence of the Eternal.
The Formulas of Knowledge.
The Wisdom of Breath.
The Root of Vibration.
The Shaking of the Invisible.
The Rolling Asunder of the Darkness.
The Becoming Visible of Matter.

LIBER ISRAFEL

The Piercing of the Scales of the Crocodile.

The Breaking Forth of the Light!

19. (Follows the Lection.)

20. There is an end of the speech; let the Silence of darkness be broken; let it return into the silence of light.

21. The speaker silently departs; the listeners disperse unto their homes; yea, they disperse unto their homes.

LIBER STELLÆ RUBEÆ

A secret ritual of Apep, the Heart of IAO-OAI, delivered unto V.V.V.V.V. for his use in a certain matter of Liber Legis, and written down under the figure

LXVI

A∴A∴
Publication in Class A.
Imprimatur:
N. Fra A∴A∴

LIBER STELLÆ RUBEÆ

1. Apep deifieth Asar.

2. Let excellent virgins evoke rejoicing, son of Night!

3. This is the book of the most secret cult of the Ruby Star. It shall be given to none, save to the shameless in deed as in word.

4. No man shall understand this writing—it is too subtle for the sons of men.

5. If the Ruby Star have shed its blood upon thee; if in the season of the moon thou hast invoked by the Iod and the Pe, then mayst thou partake of this most secret sacrament.

6. One shall instruct another, with no care for the matters of men's thought.

7. There shall be a fair altar in the midst, extended upon a black stone.

8. At the head of the altar gold, and twin images in green of the Master.

9. In the midst a cup of green wine.

10. At the foot the Star of Ruby.

11. The altar shall be entirely bare.

12. First, the ritual of the Flaming Star.

13. Next, the ritual of the Seal.

14. Next, the infernal adorations of OAI.

> Mu pa telai,
> Tu wa melai
> ā, ā, ā.
> Tu fu tulu !
> Tu fu tulu
> Pa, Sa, Ga.
>
> Qwi Mu telai
> Ya Pu melai ;
> ū, ū, ū.
> 'Se gu malai ;
> Pe fu telai,
> Fu tu lu.
>
> O chi balae
> Wa pa malae :—
> Ūt ! Ūt ! Ūt !
> Ge ; fu latrai,
> Le fu malai
> Kūt ! Hūt ! Nūt !
>
> Al Ōāī
> Rel moai
> Ti—Ti—Ti !
> Wa la pelai
> Tu fu latai
> Wi, Ni, Bi.

15. Also thou shalt excite the wheels with the five wounds and the five wounds.

16. Then thou shalt excite the wheels with the two and

the third in the midst; even ♄ and ♃, ☉ and ☋, ♂ and ♀, and ☿.

17. Then the five—and the sixth.

18. Also the altar shall fume before the master with incense that hath no smoke.

19. That which is to be denied shall be denied; that which is to be trampled shall be trampled; that which is to be spat upon shall be spat upon.

20. These things shall be burnt in the outer fire.

21. Then again the master shall speak as he will soft words, and with music and what else he will bring forward the Victim.

22. Also he shall slay a young child upon the altar, and the blood shall cover the altar with perfume as of roses.

23. Then shall the master appear as He should appear— in His glory.

24. He shall stretch himself upon the altar, and awake it into life, and into death.

25. (For so we conceal that life which is beyond.)

26. The temple shall be darkened, save for the fire and the lamp of the altar.

27. There shall he kindle a great fire and a devouring.

28. Also he shall smite the altar with his scourge, and blood shall flow therefrom.

29. Also he shall have made roses bloom thereon.

30. In the end he shall offer up the Vast Sacrifice, at the moment when the God licks up the flame upon the altar.

31. All these things shalt thou perform strictly, observing the time.

32. And the Beloved shall abide with Thee.

33. Thou shalt not disclose the interior world of this rite unto any one : therefore have I written it in symbols that cannot be understood.

34. I who reveal the ritual am IAO and OAI ; the Right and the Averse.

35. These are alike unto me.

36. Now the Veil of this operation is called Shame, and the Glory abideth within.

37. Thou shalt comfort the heart of the secret stone with the warm blood. Thou shalt make a subtle decoction of delight, and the Watchers shall drink thereof.

38. I, Apep the Serpent, am the heart of IAO. Isis shall await Asar, and I in the midst.

39. Also the Priestess shall seek another altar, and perform my ceremonies thereon.

40. There shall be no hymn nor dithyramb in my praise and the praise of the rite, seeing that it is utterly beyond.

41. Thou shalt assure thyself of the stability of the altar.

42. In this rite thou shalt be alone.

43. I will give thee another ceremony whereby many shall rejoice.

44. Before all let the Oath be taken firmly as thou raisest up the altar from the black earth.

45. In the words that Thou knowest.

46. For I also swear unto thee by my body and soul that shall never be parted in sunder that I dwell within thee coiled and ready to spring.

47. I will give thee the kingdoms of the earth, O thou Who hast mastered the kingdoms of the East and of the West.

48. I am Apep, O thou slain One. Thou shalt slay thyself upon mine altar : I will have thy blood to drink.

49. For I am a mighty vampire, and my children shall suck up the wine of the earth which is blood.

50. Thou shalt replenish thy veins from the chalice of heaven.

51. Thou shalt be secret, a fear to the world.

52. Thou shalt be exalted, and none shall see thee ; exalted, and none shall suspect thee.

53. For there are two glories diverse, and thou who hast won the first shalt enjoy the second.

54. I leap with joy within thee ; my head is arisen to strike.

55. O the lust, the sheer rapture, of the life of the snake in the spine !

56. Mightier than God or man, I am in them, and pervade them.

57. Follow out these my words.

58. Fear nothing.
Fear nothing.
Fear nothing.

59. For I am nothing, and me thou shalt fear, O my virgin, my prophet within whose bowels I rejoice.

60. Thou shalt fear with the fear of love : I will overcome thee.

61. Thou shalt be very nigh to death.

62. But I will overcome thee ; the New Life shall illumine thee with the Light that is beyond the Stars.

63. Thinkest thou ? I, the force that have created all, am not to be despised.

64. And I will slay thee in my lust.

65. Thou shalt scream with the joy and the pain and the fear and the love—so that the ΛΟΓΟΣ of a new God leaps out among the Stars.

66. There shall be no sound heard but this thy lion-roar of rapture ; yea, this thy lion-roar of rapture.

ASTARTÉ

VEL

LIBER BERYLLI

SVB FIGVRÂ

CLXXV

7

A∴A∴
Publication in Class B.
Imprimatur:
N. Fra A∴A∴

LIBER ASTARTÉ

VEL BERYLLI

SVB FIGVRÂ CLXXV

0. This is the book of Uniting Himself to a particular Deity by devotion.

1. *Considerations before the Threshold.* First, concerning the choice of a particular Deity. This matter is of no import, sobeit that thou choose one suited to thine own highest nature. Howsoever, this method is not so suitable for gods austere as Saturn, or intellectual as Thoth. But for such deities as in themselves partake in anywise of love it is a perfect mode.

2. *Concerning the prime method of this Magick Art.* Let the devotee consider well that although Christ and Osiris be one, yet the former is to be worshipped with Christian, and the latter with Egyptian rites. And this although the rites themselves are ceremonially equivalent. There should, however, be *one* symbol declaring the transcending of such limitations; and with regard to the Deity also, there should be some *one* affirmation of his identity both with all other similar gods of other nations, and with the Supreme of whom all are but partial reflections.

3. *Concerning the chief place of devotion.* This is the Heart of the devotee, and should be symbolically represented

by that room or spot which he loves best. And the dearest spot therein shall be the shrine of his temple. It is most convenient if this shrine and altar should be sequestered in woods, or in a private grove, or garden. But let it be protected from the profane.

4. *Concerning the Image of the Deity.* Let there be an image of the Deity; first, because in meditation there is mindfulness induced thereby; and second, because a certain power enters and inhabits it by virtue of the ceremonies; or so it is said, and We deny it not. Let this image be the most beautiful and perfect which the devotee is able to procure; or if he be able to paint or to carve the same, it is all the better. As for Deities with whose nature no Image is compatible, let them be worshipped in an empty shrine. Such are Brahma and Allah. Also some post-captivity conceptions of Jehovah.

5. *Further concerning the shrine.* Let this shrine be furnished appropriately as to its ornaments, according to the book 777. With ivy and pine-cones, that is to say, for Bacchus, and let lay before him both grapes and wine. So also for Ceres let there be corn, and cakes; or for Diana moon-wort and pale herbs, and pure water. Further, it is well to support the shrine with talismans of the planets, signs and elements appropriate. But these should be made according to the right Ingenium of the Philosophus by the light of the Book 777 during the course of his Devotion. It is also well, nevertheless, if a magick circle with the right signs and names be made beforehand.

6. *Concerning the ceremonies.* Let the Philosophus prepare a powerful Invocation of the particular Deity, according to his Ingenium. But let it consist of these several parts:

40

First, an Imprecation, as of a slave unto his Lord.

Second, an Oath, as of a vassal to his Liege.

Third, a Memorial, as of a child to his Parent.

Fourth, an Orison, as of a Priest unto his God.

Fifth, a Colloquy, as of a Brother with his Brother.

Sixth, a Conjuration, as of a Friend with his Friend.

Seventh, a Madrigal, as of a Lover to his Mistress.

And mark well that the first should be of awe, the second of fealty, the third of dependence, the fourth of adoration, the fifth of confidence, the sixth of comradeship, the seventh of passion.

7. *Further concerning the ceremonies*. Let then this Invocation be the principal part of an ordered ceremony. And in this ceremony let the Philosophus in no wise neglect the service of a menial. Let him sweep and garnish the place, sprinkling it with water or with wine as is appropriate to the particular Deity, and consecrating it with oil, and with such ritual as may seem him best. And let all be done with intensity and minuteness.

8. *Concerning the period of devotion, and the hours thereof.* Let a fixed period be set for the worship; and it is said that the least time is nine days by seven, and the greatest seven years by nine. And concerning the hours, let the Ceremony be performed every day thrice, or at least once, and let the sleep of the Philosophus be broken for some purpose of devotion at least once in every night.

Now to some it may seem best to appoint fixed hours for the ceremony, to others it may seem that the ceremony should be performed as the spirit moves them so to do : for this there is no rule.

9. *Concerning the Robes and Instruments.* The Wand and Cup are to be chosen for this Art; never the Sword or Dagger, never the Pantacle, unless that Pantacle chance to be of a nature harmonious. But even so it is best to keep the Wand and Cup; and if one must choose, the Cup.

For the Robes, that of a Philosophus, or that of an Adept Within is most suitable; or, the robe best fitted for the service of the particular Deity, as a bassara for Bacchus, a white robe for Vesta. So also, for Vesta, one might use for instrument the Lamp; or the sickle, for Chronos.

10. *Concerning the Incense and Libations.* The incense should follow the nature of the particular Deity; as, mastic for Mercury, dittany for Persephone. Also the libations, as, a decoction of nightshade for Melancholia, or of Indian hemp for Uranus.

11. *Concerning the harmony of the ceremonies.* Let all these things be rightly considered, and at length, in language of the utmost beauty at the command of the Philosophus, accompanied, if he have skill, by music, and interwoven, if the particular Deity be jocund, with dancing. And all being carefully prepared and rehearsed, let it be practised daily until it be wholly rhythmical with his aspiration, and as it were, a part of his being.

12. *Concerning the variety of the ceremonies.* Now, seeing that every man differeth essentially from every other man, albeit in essence he is identical, let also these ceremonies assert their identity by their diversity. For this reason do We leave much herein to the right Ingenium of the Philosophus.

13. *Concerning the life of the devotee.* First, let his way of life be such as is pleasing to the particular Deity. Thus to

invoke Neptune, let him go a-fishing; but if Hades, let him not approach the water that is hateful to Him.

14. *Further, concerning the life of the devotee.* Let him cut away from his life any act, word, or thought, that is hateful to the particular Deity; as, unchastity in the case of Artemis, evasions in the case of Ares. Besides this, he should avoid all harshness or unkindness of any kind in thought, word, or deed, seeing that above the particular Deity is One in whom all is One. Yet also he may deliberately practise cruelties, where the particular Deity manifests His love in that manner; as in the case of Kali, and of Pan. And therefore, before the beginning of his period of devotion, let him practise according to the rules of Liber Jugorum.

15. *Further concerning the life of the devotee.* Now, as many are fully occupied with their affairs, let it be known that this method is adaptable to the necessities of all.

And We bear witness that this which followeth is the Crux and Quintessence of the whole Method.

First, if he have no Image, let him take anything soever, and consecrate it as an Image of his God. Likewise with his robes and instruments, his suffumigations and libations: for his Robe hath he not a night-dress; for his instrument a walking-stick; for his suffumigation a burning match, for his libation a glass of water?

But let him consecrate each thing that he useth to the service of that particular Deity, and not profane the same to any other use.

16. *Continuation.* Next, concerning his time, if it be short. Let him labour mentally upon his Invocation, concentrating it, and let him perform this Invocation in his heart whenever

he hath the leisure. And let him seize eagerly upon every opportunity for this.

17. *Continuation.* Third, even if he have leisure and preparation, let him seek ever to bring inward the symbols, so that even in his well-ordered shrine the whole ceremony revolve inwardly in his heart, that is to say in the temple of his body, of which the outer temple is but an image.

For in the brain is the shrine, and there is no Image therein ; and the breath of man is the incense and the libation.

18. *Continuation.* Further concerning occupation. Let the devotee transmute within the alembic of his heart every thought, or word, or act into the spiritual gold of his devotion.

As thus: eating. Let him say: " I eat this food in gratitude to my Deity that hath sent it to me, in order to gain strength for my devotion to Him."

Or : sleeping. Let him say : " I lie down to sleep, giving thanks for this blessing from my Deity, in order that I may be refreshed for new devotion to Him."

Or : reading. Let him say : " I read this book that I may study the nature of my Deity, that further knowledge of Him may inspire me with deeper devotion to Him."

Or : working. Let him say : " I drive my spade into the earth that fresh flowers (fruit, or what not) may spring up to His glory, and that I, purified by toil, may give better devotion to Him."

Or, whatever it may be that he is doing, let him reason it out in his own mind, drawing it through circumstance and circumstance to that one end and conclusion of the matter. And let him not perform the act until he hath done this.

44

LIBER ASTARTÉ

As it is written : Liber VII. cap. v.—

22. " Every breath, every word, every thought, is an act of love with thee.

23. " The beat of my heart is the pendulum of love.

24. " The songs of me are the soft sighs :

25. " The thoughts of me are very rapture :

26. " And my deeds are the myriads of Thy children, the stars and the atoms."

And Remember Well, that if thou wert in truth a lover, all this wouldst thou do of thine own nature without the slightest flaw or failure in the minutest part thereof.

19. *Concerning the Lections.* Let the Philosophus read solely in his copies of the holy books of Thelema, during the whole period of his devotion. But if he weary, then let him read books which have no part whatever in love, as for recreation.

But let him copy out each verse of Thelema which bears upon this matter, and ponder them, and comment thereupon. For therein is a wisdom and a magic too deep to utter in any other wise.

20. *Concerning the Meditations.* Herein is the most potent method of attaining unto the End, for him who is thoroughly prepared, being purified by the practice of the Transmutation of deed into devotion, and consecrated by the right performance of the holy ceremonies. Yet herein is danger, for that the Mind is fluid as quicksilver, and bordereth upon the Abyss, and is beset by many sirens and devils that seduce and attack it to destroy it. Therefore let the devotee beware, and precise accurately his meditations, even as a man should build a canal from sea to sea.

21. *Continuation.* Let then the Philosophus meditate

upon all love that hath ever stirred him. There is the love of David and of Jonathan, and the love of Abraham and Isaac, and the love of Lear and Cordelia, and the love of Damon and Pythias, and the love of Sappho and Atthis, and the love of Romeo and Juliet, and the love of Dante and Beatrice, and the love of Paolo and Francesca, and the love of Cæsar and Lucrezia Borgia, and the love of Aucassin and Nicolette, and the love of Daphnis and Chloe, and the love of Cornelia and Caius Gracchus, and the love of Bacchus and Ariadne, and the love of Cupid and Psyche, and the love of Endymion and Artemis, and the love of Demeter and Persephone, and the love of Venus and Adonis, and the love of Lakshmi and Vishnu, and the love of Siva and Bhavani, and the love of Buddha and Ananda, and the love of Jesus and John, and many more.

Also there is the love of many saints for their particular deity, as of St Francis of Assisi for Christ, of Sri Sabhapaty Swami for Maheswara, of Abdullah Haji Shirazi for Allah, of St Ignatius Loyola for Mary, and many more.

Now do thou take one such story every night, and enact it in thy mind, grasping each identity with infinite care and zest, and do thou figure thyself as one of the lovers and thy Deity as the other. Thus do thou pass through all adventures of love, not omitting one; and to each do thou conclude: How pale a reflection is this of my love for this Deity!

Yet from each shalt thou draw some knowledge of love, some intimacy with love, that shall aid thee to perfect thy love. Thus learn the humility of love from one, its obedience from another, its intensity from a third, its purity from a fourth, its peace from yet a fifth.

So then thy love being made perfect, it shall be worthy of that perfect love of His.

22. *Further concerning meditation.* Moreover, let the Philosophus imagine to himself that he hath indeed succeeded in his devotion, and that his Lord hath appeared to him, and that they converse as may be fitting.

23. *Concerning the Mysterious Triangle.* Now then as three cords separately may be broken by a child, while those same cords duly twisted may bind a giant, let the Philosophus learn to entwine these three methods of Magic into a Spell.

To this end let him understand that as they are One, because the end is one, so are they One because the method is One, even the method of turning the mind toward the particular Deity by love in every act.

And lest thy twine slip, here is a little cord that wrappeth tightly round and round all, even the Mantram or Continuous Prayer.

24. *Concerning the Mantram or Continuous Prayer.* Let the Philosophus weave the Name of the Particular Deity into a sentence short and rhythmical; as, for Artemis: ἐπελθον, ἐπελθον, Ἀρτεμις; or, for Shiva: Namo Shivaya namaha Aum; or, for Mary: Ave Maria; or, for Pan, χαιρε Σωτηρ κοσμου Ἰω Παν Ἰω Παν; or, for Allah: Hua Allahu alazi lailaha illa Hua.

Let him repeat this day and night without cessation mechanically in his brain, which is thus made ready for the Advent of that Lord, and armed against all other.

25. *Concerning the Active and the Passive.* Let the Philosophus change from the active love of his particular Deity to a state of passive awaiting, even almost a repulsion, the repulsion not of distaste, but of a sublime modesty.

47

As it is written, Liber LXV. ii. 59. I have called unto Thee, and I have journeyed unto Thee, and it availed me not. 60. I waited patiently, and Thou wast with me from the beginning.

Then let him change back to the Active, until a veritable rhythm is established between the states, as it were the swinging of a Pendulum. But let him reflect that a vast intelligence is required for this; for he must stand as it were almost without himself to watch those phases of himself. And to do this is a high Art, and pertaineth not altogether to the grade of Philosophus. Neither is it of itself helpful, but rather the reverse, in this especial practice.

26. *Concerning Silence.* Now there may come a time in the course of this practice when the outward symbols of devotion cease, when the soul is as it were dumb in the presence of its God. Mark that this is not a cessation, but a transmutation of the barren seed of prayer into the green shoot of yearning. This yearning is spontaneous, and it shall be left to grow, whether it be sweet or bitter. For often times it is as the torment of hell in which the soul burns and writhes unceasingly. Yet it ends, and at its end continue openly thy Method.

27. *Concerning Dryness.* Another state wherein at times the soul may fall is this dark night. And this is indeed purifying in such depths that the soul cannot fathom it. It is less like pain than like death. But it is the necessary death that comes before the rising of a body glorified.

This state must be endured with fortitude; and no means of alleviating it may be employed. It may be broken up by the breaking up of the whole Method, and a return to the world without. This cowardice not only destroys the value

48

of all that has gone before, but destroys the value of the Oath of Fealty that thou hast sworn, and makes thy Will a mockery to men and gods.

28. *Concerning the Deceptions of the Devil.* Note well that in this state of dryness a thousand seductions will lure thee away; also a thousand means of breaking thine oath in spirit without breaking it in letter. Against this thou mayst repeat the words of thine oath aloud again and again until the temptation be overcome.

Also the devil will represent to thee that it were much better for this operation that thou do thus and thus, and seek to affright thee by fears for thy health or thy reason.

Or he may send against thee visions worse than madness.

Against all this there is but one remedy, the Discipline of thine Oath. So then thou shalt go through ceremonies meaningless and hideous to thee, and blaspheme shalt thou against thy Deity and curse Him. And this mattereth little, for it is not thou, so be that thou adhere to the Letter of thine Obligation. For thy Spiritual Sight is closed, and to trust it is to be led unto the precipice, and hurled therefrom.

29. *Further of this matter.* Now also subtler than all these terrors are the Illusions of Success. For one instant's self-satisfaction or Expansion of thy Spirit, especially in this state of dryness, and thou art lost. For thou mayst attain the False Union with the Demon himself. Beware also of even the pride which rises from having resisted the temptations.

But so many and so subtle are the wiles of Choronzon that the whole world could not contain their enumeration.

The answer to one and all is the persistence in the literal fulfilment of the routine. Beware, then, last, of that devil who shall whisper in thine ear that the letter killeth, but the spirit giveth life, and answer : Except a corn of wheat fall into the ground and die, it abideth alone ; but if it die, it bringeth forth much fruit.

Yet shalt thou also beware of disputation with the devil, and pride in the cleverness of thine answers to him. Therefore, if thou hast not lost the power of silence, let it be first and last employed against him.

30. *Concerning the Enflaming of the Heart.* Now learn that thy methods are dry one and all. Intellectual exercises, moral exercises, they are not Love. Yet as a man, rubbing two dry sticks together for long, suddenly found a spark, so also from time to time will true love leap unasked into thy meditation. Yet this shall die and be reborn again and again. It may be that thou hast no tinder near.

In the end shall come suddenly a great flame and a devouring, and burn thee utterly.

Now of these sparks, and of these splutterings of flame, and of these beginnings of the Infinite Fire, thou shalt thus be aware. For the sparks thy heart shall leap up, and thy ceremony or meditation or toil shall seem of a sudden to go of its own will ; and for the little flames this shall be increased in volume and intensity ; and for the beginnings of the Infinite Fire thy ceremony shall be caught up unto ravishing song, and thy meditation shall be ecstasy, and thy toil shall be a delight exceeding all pleasure thou hast ever known.

And of the Great Flame that answereth thee it may not be spoken ; for therein is the End of this Magick Art of Devotion.

31. *Considerations with regard to the use of symbols.* It

is to be noted that persons of powerful imagination, will, and intelligence have no need of these material symbols. There have been certain saints who are capable of love for an idea as such without it being otherwise than degraded by *idolising* it, to use this word in its true sense. Thus one may be impassioned of beauty, without even the need of so small a concretion of it as "the beauty of Apollo," "the beauty of roses," "the beauty of Attis." Such persons are rare; it may be doubted whether Plato himself attained to any vision of absolute beauty without attaching to it material objects in the first place. A second class is able to contemplate ideals through this veil; a third class need a double veil, and cannot think of the beauty of a rose without a rose before them. For such is this Method of most use; yet let them know that there is this danger therein, that they may mistake the gross body of the symbol for the idea made concrete thereby.

32. *Considerations of further danger to those not purged of material thought.* Let it be remembered that in the nature of the love itself is danger. The lust of the satyr for the nymph is indeed of the same nature as the affinity of Quicklime for water on the one hand, and of the love of Ab for Ama on the other; so also is the triad Osiris, Isis, Horus like that of a horse, mare, foal, and of red, blue, purple. And this is the foundation of Correspondences.

But it were false to say "Horus is a foal" or "Horus is purple." One may say "Horus resembles a foal in this respect, that he is the offspring of two complementary beings."

33. *Further of this matter.* So also many have said truly that all is one, and falsely that since earth is That One, and

51

ocean is That One, therefore earth is ocean. Unto Him good is illusion, and evil is illusion ; therefore good is evil. By this fallacy of logic are many men destroyed.

Moreover, there are those who take the image for the God ; as who should say, my heart is in Tiphereth, and an Adeptus is in Tiphereth ; I am therefore an adept.

And in this practice the worst danger is this, that the love which is its weapon should fail in one of two ways.

First, if the love lack any quality of love, so long is it not ideal love. For it is written of the Perfected One : " There is no member of my body which is not the member of some god." Therefore let not the Philosophus despise any form of love, but harmonise all. As it is written : Liber LXI. 32. " So therefore Perfection abideth not in the Pinnacles or in the Foundation, but in the harmony of One with all."

Second, if any part of this love exceed, there is disease therein. As, in the love of Othello for Desdemona, love's jealousy overcame love's tenderness, so may it be in this love of a particular Deity. And this is more likely, since in this divine love no element may be omitted.

It is by virtue of this completeness that no human love may in any way attain to more than to forthshadow a little part thereof.

34. *Concerning Mortifications.* These are not necessary to this method. On the contrary, they may destroy the concentration, as counter-irritants to, and so alleviations of, the supreme mortification which is the Absence of the Deity invoked.

Yet as in mortal love arises a distaste for food, or a pleasure in things naturally painful, this perversion should be endured and allowed to take its course. Yet not to the interference with natural bodily health, whereby the instrument of the soul might be impaired.

And concerning sacrifices for love's sake, they are natural to this Method, and right.

But concerning voluntary privations and tortures, without use save as against the devotee, they are generally not natural to healthy natures, and wrong. For they are selfish. To scourge one's self serves not one's master; yet to deny one's self bread that one's child may have cake is the act of a true mother.

35. *Further concerning Mortifications.* If thy body, on which thou ridest, be so disobedient a beast that by no means will he travel in the desired direction, or if thy mind be baulkish and eloquent as Balaam's fabled Ass, then let the practice be abandoned. Let the shrine be covered in sackcloth, and do thou put on habits of lamentation, and abide alone. And do thou return most austerely to the practice of Liber Jugorum, testing thyself by a standard higher than that hitherto accomplished, and punishing effractions with a heavier goad. Nor do thou return to thy devotion until that body and mind are tamed and trained to all manner of peaceable going.

36. *Concerning minor methods adjuvant in the ceremonies.* *I. Rising on the planes.* By this method mayst thou assist the imagination at the time of concluding thine Invocation. Act as taught in Liber O, by the light of Liber 777.

37. *Concerning minor methods adjuvant in the ceremonies.* *II. Talismanic magic.* Having made by thine Ingenium a talisman or pantacle to represent the particular Deity, and

consecrated it with infinite love and care, do thou burn it ceremonially before the shrine, as if thereby giving up the shadow for the substance. But it is useless to do this unless thou do really in thine heart value the talisman beyond all else that thou hast.

38. *Concerning minor methods adjuvant in the ceremonies. III. Rehearsal.* It may assist if the traditional history of the particular Deity be rehearsed before him; perhaps this is best done in dramatic form. This method is the main one recommended in the " Exercitios Espirituales " of St Ignatius, whose work may be taken as a model. Let the Philosophus work out the legend of his own particular Deity, and apportioning days to events, live that life in imagination, exercising the five senses in turn, as occasion arises.

39. *Concerning minor matters adjuvant in the ceremonies. IV. Duresse.* This method consists in cursing a deity recalcitrant; as, threatening ceremonially "to burn the blood of Osiris, and to grind down his bones to powder." This method is altogether contrary to the spirit of love, unless the particular Deity be himself savage and relentless; as, Jehovah or Kali. In such a case the desire to perform constraint and cursing may be the sign of the assimilation of the spirit of the devotee with that of his God, and so an advance to the Union with Him.

40. *Concerning the value of this particular form of Union or Samadhi.* All Samadhi is defined as the ecstatic union of subject and object in consciousness, with the result that a third thing arises which partakes in no way of the nature of the two.

It would seem at first sight that it is of no importance

54

whatever to choose an object of meditation. For example, the Samadhi called Atmadarshana might arise from simple concentration of the thought on an imagined triangle, or on the heart.

But as the union of two bodies in chemistry may be endothermic or exothermic, the combination of Oxygen with Nitrogen is gentle, while that of Oxygen with Hydrogen is explosive; and as it is found that the most heat is disengaged as a rule by the union of bodies most opposite in character, and that the compound resulting from such is most stable, so it seems reasonable to suggest that the most important and enduring Samadhi results from the contemplation of the Object most opposite to the devotee. [On other planes, it has been suggested that the most opposed types make the best marriages and produce the healthiest children. The greatest pictures and operas are those in which violent extremes are blended, and so generally in every field of activity. Even in mathematics, the greatest parallelogram is formed if the lines composing it are set at right angles. ED.]

41. *Conclusions from the foregoing.* It may then be suggested to the Philosophus, that although his work will be harder his reward will be greater if he choose a Deity most remote from his own nature. This method is harder and higher than that of Liber E. For a simple object as there suggested is of the same nature as the commonest things of life, while even the meanest Deity is beyond uninitiated human understanding. On the same plane, too, Venus is nearer to man than Aphrodite, Aphrodite than Isis, Isis than Babalon, Babalon than Nuit.

Let him decide therefore according to his discretion on the

one hand and his aspiration on the other : and let not one outrun his fellow.

42. *Further concerning the value of this Method.* Certain objections arise. Firstly, in the nature of all human love is illusion, and a certain blindness. Nor is there any true love below the Veil of the Abyss. For this reason We give this Method to the Philosophus, as the reflection of the Exempt Adept, who reflects the Magister Templi and the Magus. Let then the Philosophus attain this method as a foundation of the higher Methods to be given to him when he attains those higher grades.

Another objection lies in the partiality of this Method. This is equally a defect characteristic of the Grade.

43. *Concerning a notable danger of Success.* It may occur that owing to the tremendous power of the Samadhi, over-coming all other memories as it should and does do, that the mind of the devotee may be obsessed, so that he declare his particular Deity to be sole God and Lord. This error has been the foundation of all dogmatic religions, and so the cause of more misery than all other errors combined.

The Philosophus is peculiarly liable to this because from the nature of the Method he cannot remain sceptical ; he must for the time believe in his particular Deity. But let him (1) consider that this belief is only a weapon in his hands, (2) affirm sufficiently that his Deity is but an emanation or reflection or eidolon of a Being beyond him, as was said in Paragraph 2. For if he fail herein, since man cannot remain permanently in Samadhi, the memorised Image in his mind will be degraded, and replaced by the corresponding Demon, to his utter ruin.

56

LIBER ASTARTÉ

Therefore, after Success, let him not delight overmuch in his Deity, but rather busy himself with his other work, not permitting that which is but a step to become a goal. As it is written also, Liber CLXXXV.: "remembering that Philosophy is the Equilibrium of him that is in the House of Love."

44. *Concerning secrecy, and the rites of Blood.* During this practice it is most wise that the Philosophus utter no word concerning his working, as if it were a Forbidden Love that consumeth him. But let him answer fools according to their folly; for since he cannot conceal his love from his fellows, he must speak to them as they may understand.

And as many Deities demand sacrifices, one of men, another of cattle, a third of doves, let these sacrifices be replaced by the true sacrifices in thine own heart. Yet if thou must symbolise them outwardly for the hardness of thine heart, let thine own blood, and not another's, be spilt before that altar.[1]

Nevertheless, forget not that this practice is dangerous, and may cause the manifestation of evil things, hostile and malicious, to thy great hurt.

45. *Concerning a further sacrifice.* Of this it shall be understood that nothing is to be spoken; nor need anything be spoken to him that hath wisdom to comprehend the number of the paragraph. And this sacrifice is fatal beyond all, unless it be a sacrifice indeed. Yet there are those who have dared and achieved thereby.

46. *Concerning yet a further sacrifice.* Here it is spoken of actual mutilation. Such acts are abominable; and while

---

[1] The exceptions to this rule pertain neither to this practice, nor to this grade. N. Fra. A∴A∴

they may bring success in this Method, form an absolute bar to all further progress.

And they are in any case more likely to lead to madness than to Samadhi. He indeed who purposeth them is already mad.

47. *Concerning human affection.* During this practice thou shalt in no wise withdraw thyself from human relations, only figuring to thyself that thy father or thy brother or thy wife is as it were an image of thy particular Deity. Thus shall they gain, and not lose, by thy working. Only in the case of thy wife this is difficult, since she is more to thee than all others, and in this case thou mayst act with temperance, lest her personality overcome and destroy that of thy Deity.

48. *Concerning the Holy Guardian Angel.* Do thou in no wise confuse this invocation with that.

49. *The Benediction.* And so may the Love that passeth all Understanding keep your hearts and minds through Iaω Aδωnai Cabaω and through Babalon of the City of the Pyramids, and through Astarté the Starry One green-girdled in the name Ararita. Amn.

LIBER RV

VEL

SPIRITÛS

SVB FIGVRÂ

CCVI

A ∴ A ∴
Publication in Class B.
Imprimatur:
N. Fra A ∴ A ∴

LIBER RV

VEL SPIRITÛS

SVB FIGVRÂ CCVI

2. Let the Zelator observe the current of his breath.

3. Let him investigate the following statements, and prepare a careful record of research.

> (*a*) Certain actions induce the flow of the breath through the right nostril (Pingala); and, conversely, the flow of the breath through Pingala induces certain actions.

> (*b*) Certain other actions induce the flow of the breath through the left nostril (Ida), and conversely.

> (*c*) Yet a third class of actions induce the flow of the breath through both nostrils at once (Sushumna), and conversely.

> (*d*) The degree of mental and physical activity is interdependent with the distance from the nostrils at which the breath can be felt by the back of the hand.

4. *First practice.* Let him concentrate his mind upon the act of breathing, saying mentally " The breath flows in," " The breath flows out," and record the results. (This practice may resolve itself into Mahasatipatthana (*vide* Liber

61

XXV.) or induce Samadhi. Whichever occurs should be followed up as the right Ingenium of the Zelator, or the advice of his Practicus, may determine.)

5. *Second practice.* Pranayama. This is outlined in Liber E. Further, let the Zelator accomplished in those practices endeavour to master a cycle of 10. 20. 40 or even 16. 32. 64. But let this be done gradually and with due caution. And when he is steady and easy both in Asana and Pranayama, let him still further increase the period.

Thus let him investigate these statements which follow:

    (*a*) If Pranayama be properly performed, the body will first of all become covered with sweat. This sweat is different in character from that customarily induced by exertion. If the Practitioner rub this sweat thoroughly into his body, he will greatly strengthen it.

    (*b*) The tendency to perspiration will stop as the practice is continued, and the body become automatically rigid.

Describe this rigidity with minute accuracy.

    (*c*) The state of automatic rigidity will develop into a state characterised by violent spasmodic movements of which the Practitioner is unconscious, but of whose result he is aware. This result is that the body hops gently from place to place. After the first two or three occurrences of this experience Asana is not lost. The body appears (on another theory) to have lost its weight almost completely, and to be moved by an unknown force.

PRAMAYAMA PROPERLY PERFORMED.

[It has been found necessary to show this because students were trying to do it without exertion, and in other ways incorrectly.—ED.].

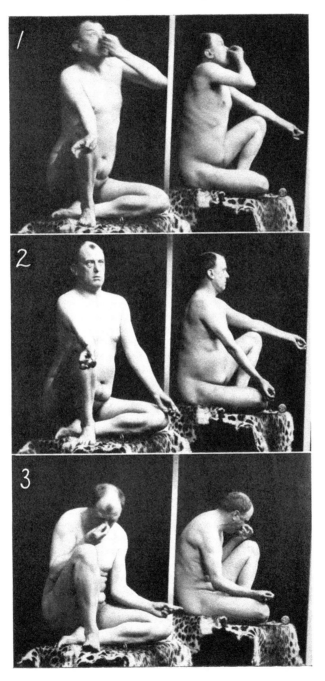

1. The end of Purakam. The bad definition of the image is due to the spasmodic trembling which accompanies the action.

2. Kunbhakam.   3. The end of Rekakam.

(*d*) As a development of this stage, the body rises into the air, and remains there for an appreciably long period, from a second to an hour or more.

Let him further investigate any mental results which may occur.

6. *Third practice.* In order both to economize his time and to develop his powers, let the Zelator practise the deep full breathing which his preliminary exercises will have taught him during his walks. Let him repeat a sacred sentence (mantra), or let him count, in such a way that his footfall beats accurately with the rhythm thereof, as is done in dancing. Then let him practise Pranayama, at first without the Kumbakham, and paying no attention to the nostrils otherwise than to keep them clear. Let him begin by an indrawing of the breath for 4 paces, and a breathing out for 4 paces. Let him increase this gradually to 6.6, 8.8, 12.12, 16.16, and 24.24, or more if he be able. Next let him practise in the proper proportion 4.8, 6.12, 8.16, 12.24 and so on. Then, if he choose, let him recommence the series, adding a gradually increasing period of Kumbhakham.

7. *Fourth practice.* Following on this third practice, let him quicken his mantra and his pace, until the walk develops into a dance. This may also be practised with the ordinary waltz step, using a mantra in three-time, such as ἐπελθον, ἐπελθον, Ἀρτεμις; or Iao; Iao Sabao; in such cases the practice may be combined with devotion to a particular deity; see Liber CLXXV. For the dance as such it is better to use a mantra of a non-committal character, such as το εἰναι, το καλον, το ᾽γαθον, or the like.

8. *Fifth practice.* Let him practise mental concentration during the dance, and investigate the following statements :

(*a*) The dance becomes independent of the will.

(*b*) Similar phenomena to those described in 5 (*a*) (*b*) (*c*) (*d*) occur.

(*c*) Certain important mental results occur.

9. A note concerning the depth and fulness of the breathing. In all proper expiration, the last possible portion of air should be expelled. In this the muscles of the throat, chest, ribs, and abdomen must be fully employed, and aided by the pressing of the upper arms into the flanks, and of the head into the thorax.

In all proper inspiration, the last possible portion of air must be drawn into the lungs.

In all proper holding of the breath, the body must remain absolutely still.

Ten minutes of such practice is ample to induce profuse sweating in any place of a temperature of 17° C. or over.

The progress of the Zelator in acquiring a depth and fulness of breath should be tested by the respirometer.

The exercises should be carefully graduated to avoid overstrain and possible damage to the lungs.

This depth and fulness of breath should be kept as much as possible, even in the rapid exercises, with the exception of the sixth practice following.

10. *Sixth practice.* Let the Zelator breathe as shallowly and rapidly as possible. He should assume the attitude of his moment of greatest expiration, and breathe only with the muscles of his throat. He may also practise lengthening the period between each shallow breathing.

64

LIBER RV

(This may be combined when acquired with concentration on the Visuddhi chakra, *i.e.* let him fix his mind unwaveringly upon a point in the spine opposite the larynx. ED.)

11. *Seventh practice.* Let the Zelator breathe as deeply and rapidly as possible.

12. *Eighth practice.* Let the Zelator practise restraint of breathing in the following manner.

At any stage of breathing let him suddenly hold the breath, enduring the need to breathe until it passes, returns, and passes again, and so on until consciousness is lost, either rising to Samadhi or similar supernormal condition, or falling into oblivion.

13. *Ninth practice.* Let him practise the usual forms of Pranayama, but let Kumbhakham be used after instead of before expiration. Let him gradually increase the period of this Kumbhakham as in the case of the other.

14. A note concerning the conditions of these experiments.

The conditions favourable are dry and bracing air, a warm climate, absence of wind, absence of noise, insects, and all other disturbing influences,[1] a retired situation, simple food eaten in great moderation at the conclusion of the practices of morning and afternoon and on no account before practising. Bodily health is almost essential, and should be most carefully guarded. (See Liber CLXXXV., Task of a Neophyte.) A diligent and tractable disciple, or the Practicus of the Zelator, should aid him in his work. Such a disciple should be noiseless, patient, vigilant, prompt, cheerful, of gentle manner and reverent to his master, intelligent to anticipate

---

[1] Note that in the early stages of concentration of the mind, such annoyances become negligible.

his wants, cleanly and gracious, not given to speech, devoted and unselfish. With all this he should be fierce and terrible to strangers and all hostile influences, determined and vigorous, unceasingly vigilant, the guardian of the threshold.

It is not desirable that the Zelator should employ any other creature than a man, save in cases of necessity. Yet for some of these purposes a dog will serve, for others a woman. There are also others appointed to serve, but these are not for the Zelator.

15. *Tenth practice.* Let the Zelator experiment if he will with inhalations of oxygen, nitrous oxide, carbon dioxide, and other gases mixed in small proportion with his air during his practices. These experiments are to be conducted with caution in the presence of a medical man of experience, and they are only useful as facilitating a simulacrum of the results of the proper practices, and thereby enheartening the Zelator.

16. *Eleventh practice.* Let the Zelator at any time during the practices, especially during periods of Kumbhakham, throw his will utterly toward his Holy Guardian Angel, directing his eyes inward and upward, and turning back his tongue as if to swallow it.

(This latter operation is facilitated by severing the fraenum linguæ, which, if done, should be done by a competent surgeon. We do not advise this or any similar method of cheating difficulties. This is, however, harmless.)

In this manner the practice is to be raised from the physical to the spiritual plane, even as the words Ruh, Ruach, Pneuma, Spiritus, Geist, Ghost, and indeed words of almost all languages, have been raised from their physical meaning of wind, air, breath, or movement, to the spiritual plane.

LIBER RV

(RV is the old root meaning yoni, and hence Wheel (Fr. roue, Lat. rota, wheel), and the corresponding Semitic root means " to go." Similarly Spirit is connected with " spiral."—Ed.)

17. Let the Zelator attach no credit to any statements that may have been made throughout the course of this instruction, and reflect that even the counsel which We have given as suitable to the average case may be entirely unsuitable to his own.

LIBER

ARCANORVM τῶν
ATV τοῦ TAHVTI
QUAS VIDIT
ASAR IN
AMENNTI
SVB FIGVRÂ
CCXXXI

LIBER

CARCERORVM τῶν
QLIPHOTH
CVM SVIS
GENIIS

ADDVNTVR SIGILLA ET
NOMINA EORVM

A ∴ A ∴
Publication in Class A.
Imprimatur:
N. Fra A ∴ A ∴

LIBER XXII CARCERORUM QLIPHOTH CUM SUIS GENIIS

LIBER XXII DOMARUM MERCURII CUM SUIS GENIIS

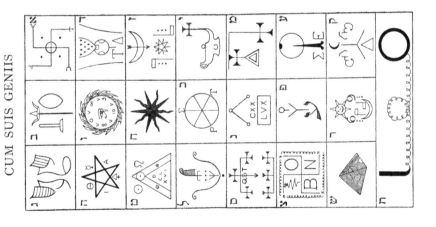

Compare with

LIBER CCXXXI

(This book is true up to the grade of Adeptus Exemptus. V.V.V.V.V. 8°, 3□.)

0. A, the heart of IAO, dwelleth in ecstasy in the secret place of the thunders. Between Asar and Asi he abideth in joy.

1. The lightnings increased and the Lord Tahuti stood forth. The Voice came from the Silence. Then the One ran and returned.

2. Now hath Nuit veiled herself, that she may open the gate of her sister.

3. The Virgin of God is enthroned upon an oyster-shell; she is like a pearl, and seeketh Seventy to her Four. In her heart is Hadit the invisible glory.

4. Now riseth Ra-Hoor-Khuit, and dominion is established in the Star of the Flame.

5. Also is the Star of the Flame exalted, bringing benediction to the universe.

6. Here then beneath the winged Eros is youth, delighting in the one and the other.

He is Asar between Asi and Nepthi; he cometh forth from the veil.

7. He rideth upon the chariot of eternity; the white and the black are harnessed to his car. Therefore he reflecteth the Fool, and the sevenfold veil is reveiled.

8. Also came forth mother Earth with her lion, even Sekhet, the lady of Asi.

9. Also the Priest veiled himself, lest his glory be profaned, lest his word be lost in the multitude.

10. Now then the Father of all issued as a mighty wheel; the Sphinx, and the dog-headed god, and Typhon, were bound on his circumference.

11. Also the lady Maat with her feather and her sword abode to judge the righteous.

For Fate was already established.

12. Then the holy one appeared in the great water of the North; as a golden dawn did he appear, bringing benediction to the fallen universe.

13. Also Asar was hidden in Amennti; and the Lords of Time swept over him with the sickle of death.

14. And a mighty angel appeared as a woman, pouring vials of woe upon the flames, lighting the pure stream with her brand of cursing. And the iniquity was very great.

15. Then the Lord Khem arose, He who is holy among the highest, and set up his crowned staff for to redeem the universe.

16. He smote the towers of wailing; he brake them in pieces in the fire of his anger, so that he alone did escape from the ruin thereof.

17. Transformed, the holy virgin appeared as a fluidic fire, making her beauty into a thunderbolt.

18. By her spells she invoked the Scarab, the Lord Kheph-Ra, so that the waters were cloven and the illusion of the towers was destroyed.

72

LIBER

19. Then the sun did appear unclouded, and the mouth of Asi was on the mouth of Asar.

20. Then also the Pyramid was builded so that the Initiation might be complete.

21. And in the heart of the Sphinx danced the Lord Adonai, in His garlands of roses and pearls making glad the concourse of things ; yea, making glad the concourse of things.

THE GENII OF THE 22 SCALES OF THE SERPENT AND OF THE QLIPHOTH

א Aϛu-iao-uϛa[ϛ =y]	Amprodias
ב Beϛθaoooabitom	Baratchial
ג Gitωnosapφωllois	Gargophias
ד Dηnaᴣartarωθ [ᴣ =st]	Dagdagiel
ה Hoo-oorω-iᴣ	Hemethterith
ו Vuaretza—[a secret name follows] . . .	Uriens
ז Zooωasar	Zamradiel
ח Chiva-abrahadabra-cadaxviii	Characith
ט θalϛᴣer-ā-dekerval	Temphioth
י Iehuvahaᴣanϛθatan	Yamatu
כ Kerugunaviel	Kurgasiax
ל Lusanaherandraton	Lafcursiax
מ Malai	Malkunofat
נ Nadimraphoroiozϛθalai	Niantiel
ס Salaθlala-amrodnaθϛiᴣ	Saksaksalim
ע Oaoaaaoooϛ-iᴣ	A'ano'nin
פ Puraθmetai-apηmetai	Parfaxitas
צ Xanθaᴣeranϛϙ-iᴣ [ϛϙ =sh, q] . . .	Tzuflifu
ק Qani∆nayx-ipamai	Qulielfi
ר Ra-a-gioselahladnaimawa-iᴣ	Raflifu
ש Shabnax-odobor	Shalicu
ת Thath'th'thithϛthuth-thiᴣ	Thantifaxath

73

THE EQUINOX

Note by H. Fra. P. 4°=7⁰ (1899) on the R.O.T.A. by the
Qabalah of Nine Chambers

Units are divine—The upright Triangle.
Tens reflected—The averse Triangle.
Hundreds equilibrated—The Hexagram their combination.

1. *Light.*—[Here can be no evil.] א The hidden light—the "wisdom of God
foolishness with men."
י The Adept bearing Light.
ק The Light in darkness and illusion.
[Khephra about to rise.]

2. *Action.*—ב Active and Passive—dual current, etc.—the Alternating Forces
in Harmony.
כ The Contending Forces—fluctuation of earth-life.
ר The Twins embracing — eventual glory of harmonised life
under ☉.

3. *The Way.*—[Here also no evil.] ג The Higher Self.
ל The severe discipline of the Path.
ש The judgment and resurrection
[0°=0⁰ and 5°=6⁰ rituals.]

4. *Life.*—ד The Mother of God.   Aima.
מ The Son Slain.
ת The Bride.

5. *Force* (Purification).—ה The Supernal Sulphur purifying by fire.
נ The Infernal Water ♏ purifying by putrefaction.
This work is not complete; therefore is there
no equilibration.

6. *Harmony.*—ו The Reconciler [ו of יהוה] above.
ס The Reconciler below [lion and eagle, etc.].
This work also unfinished.

7. *Birth.*—ז The Powers of Spiritual Regeneration.
[The Z.A.M. as Osiris risen between Isis and Nephthys.   The
path of ג, Diana, above his head.]
ע The gross powers of generation.

8. *Rule.*—ח The Orderly Ruling of diverse forces.
פ The Ruin of the Unbalanced Forces.

9. *Stability.*—ט The Force that represses evil.
צ The Force that restores the world ruined by evil.

LIBER TAV

VEL

KABBALÆ TRIVM LITERARUM

SVB FIGVRÂ

CD

A∴A∴
Publication in Class A.
Imprimatur:
N. Fra∴A∴A∴

Top row: א ב ג ד ה ו ז

Middle row: ח ט י כ ל מ נ

Bottom row: ס ע פ צ ק ר ש

The Magister Templi, the Adeptus, the Neophyte [8° = 3□, 5° = 6□, 0° = 0□].

The Ultimate Illusion, the Illusion of Force, the Illusion of Matter.

The Functions of the 3 Orders: Silence in Speech; Speech in Silence: Construction, Preservation, Destruction.

The Supreme Unveiling (or Unveiling of Light), the Unveiling of Life, the Unveiling of Love.

Equilibrium; on the Cubic Stone, on the Path, and among the Shells.

The Rituals of Initiation, 8° = 3□, 5° = 6□, 0° = 0□: Asar, as Bull, as Man, as Sun.

The Ordeals of Initiation, 8° = 3□, 5° = 6□, 0° = 0□: Birth, Death, Resurrection.

[This analysis may be checked by adding the columns vertically, 69, 81, 93, 114, 135, 246, 357. Dividing by 3 we get 23, 27, 31, 38, 45, 82, 119, which in the Sepher Sephiroth mean respectively Life, Purity, Negation, "38 × 11 = 418," Innocent, Formation, Prayer, Weeping. The analogies are obvious.]

LIBER OS ABYSMI

VEL

DAATH

SVB FIGVRÂ

CDLXXIV

A∴A∴
Publication in Class B.
Imprimatur:
N. Fra A∴A∴

LIBER OS ABYSMI

VEL DAATH

SVB FIGVRÂ CDLXXIV

1. This book is the Gate of the Secret of the Universe.

2. Let the Exempt Adept procure the Prolegomena of Kant, and study it, paying special attention to the Antinomies.

3. Also Hume's doctrine of Causality in his " Enquiry."

4. Also Herbert Spencer's discussion of the three theories of the Universe in his " First Principles," Part I.

5. Also Huxley's Essays on Hume and Berkeley.

6. Also Crowley's Essays : Berashith, Time, The Soldier and the Hunchback, et cetera.

7. Also the "Logik" of Hegel.

8. Also the " Questions of King Milinda" and the Buddhist Suttas which bear on Metaphysic.

9. Let him also be accomplished in Logic. (Formal Logic, Keynes.) Further let him study any classical works to which his attention may be sufficiently directed in the course of his reading.

10. Now let him consider special problems, such as the Origin of the World, the Origin of Evil, Infinity, the Absolute, the Ego and the non-Ego, Freewill and Destiny, and such others as may attract him.

11. Let him subtly and exactly demonstrate the fallacies of every known solution, and let him seek a true solution by his right Ingenium.

12. In all this let him be guided only by clear reason, and let him forcibly suppress all other qualities such as Intuition, Aspiration, Emotion, and the like.

13. During these practices all forms of Magick Art and Meditation are forbidden to him. It is forbidden to him to seek any refuge from his intellect.

14. Let then his reason hurl itself again and again against the blank wall of mystery which will confront him.

15. Thus also following is it said, and we deny it not.

At last automatically his reason will take up the practice, suâ sponte, and he shall have no rest therefrom.

16. Then will all phenomena which present themselves to him appear meaningless and disconnected, and his own Ego will break up into a series of impressions having no relation one with the other, or with any other thing.

17. Let this state then become so acute that it is in truth Insanity, and let this continue until exhaustion.

18. According to a certain deeper tendency of the individual will be the duration of this state.

19. It may end in real insanity, which concludes the activities of the Adept during this present life, or by his rebirth into his own body and mind with the simplicity of a little child.

20. And then shall he find all his faculties unimpaired, yet cleansed in a manner ineffable.

21. And he shall recall the simplicity of the Task of the Adeptus Minor, and apply himself thereto with fresh energy in a more direct manner.

22. And in his great weakness it may be that for awhile the new Will and Aspiration are not puissant, yet being undisturbed by those dead weeds of doubt and reason which he hath uprooted, they grow imperceptibly and easily like a flower.

23. And with the reappearance of the Holy Guardian Angel he may be granted the highest attainments, and be truly fitted for the full experience of the destruction of the Universe. And by the Universe We mean not that petty Universe which the mind of man can conceive, but that which is revealed to his soul in the Samadhi of Atmadarshana.

24. Thence may he enter into a real communion with those that are beyond, and he shall be competent to receive communication and instruction from Ourselves directly.

25. Thus shall We prepare him for the Confrontation of Choronzon and the Ordeal of the Abyss, when we have received him into the City of the Pyramids.

26. So, being of Us, let the Master of the Temple accomplish that Work which is appointed.

(In Liber CDXVIII. is an adequate account of this Ordeal and Reception. See also Liber CLVI. for the preparation.)

27. Also concerning the Reward thereof, of his entering into the Palace of the King's Daughter, and of that which shall thereafter befall, let it be understood of the Master of the Temple. Hath he not attained to Understanding? Yea, verily, hath he not attained to Understanding?

LIBER H A D

SVB FIGVRÂ

DLV

A∴ A∴
Publication in Class D
(for Winners of the Ordeal X).
Imprimatur:

ק ק ק · · ·
V.V.V.V.V. . . .
N. Fra A∴ A∴.
O.M. 7°=4°.

LIBER H A D

SVB FIGVR̂A DLV

ooo. This is the Book of the Cult of the Infinite Within.

oo. The Aspirant is Nuit. Nuit is the infinite expansion of the Rose; Hadit the infinite concentration of the Rood. (*Instruction of V.V.V.V.V.*)

o. First let the Aspirant learn in his heart the Second Chapter of the Book of the Law. (*Instruction of V.V.V.V.V.*)

1. Worship, *i.e.* identify thyself with, Nuit, as a lambent flame of blue, all-touching, all-penetrant, her lovely hands upon the black earth, and her lithe body arched for love, and her soft feet not hurting the little flowers, even as She is imaged in the Stélé of Revealing.

This is the first practice of Meditation (ccxx. I. 26).

2. Let him further identify himself with the heart of Nuit, whose ecstasy is in that of her children, and her joy to see their joy, who sayeth : I love you ! I yearn to you. Pale or purple, veiled or voluptuous, I who am all pleasure and purple, and drunkenness of the innermost sense, desire you. Put on the wings, and arouse the coiled splendour within you. Come unto me ! . . . Sing the rapturous love-song unto me ! Burn to me perfumes ! Wear to me jewels ! Drink to me, for I love you ! I love you ! I am the blue-lidded daughter of

Sunset; I am the naked brilliance of the voluptuous night-sky. To me! To me!

This is the second practice of Meditation (ccxx. I. 13, 61, 63, 64, 65).

3. Let the Aspirant apply himself to comprehend Hadit as an unextended point clothed with Light ineffable. And let him beware lest he be dazzled by that Light.

This is the first practice of Intelligence (ccxx. II. 2).

4. Let the Aspirant apply himself to comprehend Hadit as the ubiquitous centre of every sphere conceivable.

This is the second practice of Intelligence (ccxx. II. 3).

5. Let the Aspirant apply himself to comprehend Hadit as the soul of every man, and of every star, conjoining this in his Understanding with the Word *(ccxx. I.* 2). " Every man and every woman is a star." Let this conception be that of Life, the giver of Life, and let him perceive that therefore the knowledge of Hadit is the knowledge of death.

This is the third practice of Intelligence (ccxx. II. 6).

6. Let the Aspirant apply himself to comprehend Hadit as the Magician or maker of Illusion, and the Exorcist or destroyer of Illusion, under the figure of the axle of the Wheel, and the cube in the circle. Also as the Universal Soul of Motion.

(This conception harmonises Thoth and Harpocrates in a very complete and miraculous manner. Thoth is both the Magus of Taro (see Lib. 418) and the Universal Mercury; Harpocrates both the destroyer of Typhon and the Babe on the Lotus. Note that the " Ibis position " formulates this conception most exactly. ED.)

This is the fourth practice of Intelligence (ccxx. II. 7).

LIBER H A D

7. Let the Aspirant apply himself to comprehend Hadit as the perfect, that is Not, and solve the mystery of the numbers of Hadit and his components by his right Ingenium.

This is the fifth practice of Intelligence (ccxx. II. 15, 16).

8. Let the Aspirant, bearing him as a great King, root out and destroy without pity all things in himself and his surroundings which are weak, dirty, or diseased, or otherwise unworthy. And let him be exceeding proud and joyous.

This is the first practice of Ethics (ccxx. II. 18, 19, 20, 21).

9. Let the Aspirant apply himself to comprehend Hadit as the Snake that giveth Knowledge and Delight and bright glory, who stirreth the hearts of men with drunkenness. This snake is blue and gold; its eyes are red, and its spangles green and ultra-violet.

(That is, as the most exalted form of the Serpent Kundalini.)

This is the sixth practice of Intelligence (ccxx. II. 22, 50, 51).

10. Let him further identify himself with this Snake.

This is the second practice of Meditation (ccxx. II. 22).

11. Let the Aspirant take wine and strange drugs, according to his knowledge and experience, and be drunk thereof.

(The Aspirant should be in so sensitive a condition that a single drop, perhaps even the smell, should suffice. ED.)

This is the first practice of Magick Art (ccxx. II. 22).

12. Let the Aspirant concentrate his consciousness in the Rood Cross set up upon the Mountain, and identify himself with It. Let him be well aware of the difference between Its

own soul, and that thought which it habitually awakes in his own mind.

This is the third practice of Meditation, and as it will be found, a comprehension and harmony and absorption of the practices of Intelligence (ccxx. II. 22).

13. Let the Aspirant apply himself to comprehend Hadit as the Unity which is the Negative. (Ain Elohim. ED.)

This is the seventh practice of Intelligence (ccxx. II. 23).

14. Let the Aspirant live the life of a strong and beautiful being, proud and exalted, contemptuous of and fierce toward all that is base and vile.

This is the second practice of Ethics (ccxx. II. 24, 25, 45-49, 52, 56-60).

15. Let the Aspirant apply himself to comprehend Hadit according to this 26th verse of the Second Chapter of the Book of the Law. And this shall be easy for him if he have well accomplished the Third Practice of Meditation.

This is the eighth practice of Intelligence (ccxx. II. 26).

16. Let the Aspirant destroy Reason in himself according to the practice in Liber CDLXXIV.

This is the fourth practice of Meditation (ccxx. II. 27-33).

17. Let the Aspirant observe duly the Feasts appointed by the A.·.A.·. and perform such rituals of the elements as he possesseth, invoking them duly in their season.

This is the second practice of Magick Art (ccxx. II. 35-43).

18. Let the Aspirant apply himself to comprehend Hadit as a babe in the egg of the Spirit (Akasha. ED.) that is invisible within the 4 elements.

This is the ninth practice of Intelligence (ccxx. II. 49).

LIBER H A D

19. The Aspirant seated in his Asana will suddenly commence to breathe strangely, and this without the Operation of his will; the Inspiration will be associated with the thought of intense excitement and pleasure, even to exhaustion; and the Expiration very rapid and forceful, as if this excitement were suddenly released.

This is the first and last Indication of the Sign of the Beginning of this Result (ccxx. II. 63).

20. A light will appear to the Aspirant, unexpectedly. Hadit will arise within him, and Nuit concentrate Herself upon him from without. He will be overcome, and the Conjunction of the Infinite Without with the Infinite Within will take place in his soul, and the One be resolved into the None.

This is the first Indication of the Nature of the Result (ccxx. II. 61, 62, 64).

21. Let the Aspirant strengthen his body by all means in his power, and let him with equal pace refine all that is in him to the true ideal of Royalty. Yet let his formula, as a King's ought, be Excess.

This is the third practice of Ethics (ccxx. II. 70, 71).

22. To the Aspirant who succeeds in this practice the result goes on increasing until its climax in his physical death in its due season. This practice should, however, prolong life.

This is the second Indication of the Nature of the Result (ccxx. II. 66, 72-74).

23. Let the Adept aspire to the practice of Liber XI. and preach to mankind.

This is the fourth Practice of Ethics (ccxx. II. 76).

THE EQUINOX

24. Let the Adept worship the Name, foursquare, mystic, wonderful, of the Beast, and the name of His house; and give blessing and worship to the prophet of the lovely Star.

This is the fifth practice of Ethics (ccxx. II. 78, 79).

25. Let the Aspirant expand his consciousness to that of Nuit, and bring it rushing inward. It may be practised by imagining that the Heavens are falling, and then transferring the consciousness to them.

This is the fifth practice of Meditation. (Instruction of V.V.V.V.V.)

26. Summary. Preliminaries.

These are the necessary possessions.

   1. Wine and strange drugs.

27. Summary continued. Preliminaries.

These are the necessary comprehensions.

   1. The nature of Hadit (and of Nuit, and the relations between them.)

28. Summary continued. Preliminaries.

These are the meditations necessary to be accomplished.

   1. Identification with Nuit, body and spirit.

   2. Identification with Hadit as the Snake.

   3. Identification with Hadit as the Rood Cross.

   4. Destruction of Reason.

   5. The Falling of the Heavens.

29. Summary continued. Preliminaries.

These are the Ethical Practices to be accomplished.

   1. The destruction of all unworthiness in one's self and one's surroundings.

   2. Fulness, almost violence, of life.

30. Summary continued.   Preliminaries.

These are the Magick Arts to be practised.

   1. During the preparation, perform the Invocations of the Elements.

   2. Observe the Feasts appointed by the A∴ A∴

31. Summary continued.   The actual Practice.

   1. Procure the suitable intoxication.

   2. As Nuit, contract thyself with infinite force upon Hadit.

32. Summary continued.   The Results.

   1. Peculiar automatic breathing begins.

   2. A light appears.

   3. Samadhi of the two Infinites within aspirant.

   4. Intensification of 3 on repetition.

   5. Prolongation of life.

   6. Death becomes the climax of the practice.

33. Summary concluded.

These are the practices to be performed in token of Thanksgiving for success.

   1. Aspiration to Liber XI.

   2. Preaching of Θελημα to mankind.

   3. Blessing and Worship to the prophet of the lovely Star.

LIBER TAV

SVB FIGVRÂ

DCCCXXXI

A ∴ A ∴
Publication in Class B.
Imprimatur:
N. Fra A ∴ A ∴

LIBER TAV

SVB FIGVRÂ DCCCXXXI

(This book was formerly called VESTA. It is referred to the path of Virgo and the letter Yod.)

I.

1. This is the Book of drawing all to a point.

2. Herein are described three methods whereby the consciousness of the Many may be melted to that of the One.

II

FIRST METHOD

0. Let a magical circle be constructed, and within it an upright Tau drawn upon the ground. Let this Tau be divided into 10 squares (see Liber CMLXIII., Illustration 1).

1. Let the Magician be armed with the Sword of Art.[1]

2. Let him wear the black robe of a Neophyte.

3. Let a single small flame of camphor burn at the top of the Tau, and let there be no other light or ornament.[1]

4. Let him "open" the Temple as in DCLXXI., or in any other convenient manner.

---

[1] This ritual is preferably performed by the Adept as an Hermit armed with wand and lamp, instead of as in text.—N.

5. Standing at the appropriate quarters, at the edge of the circle, let him banish the 5 elements by the appropriate rituals.

6. Standing at the edge of the circle, let him banish the 7 planets by the appropriate rituals. Let him face the actual position of each planet in the heavens at the time of his working.

7. Let him further banish the twelve signs of the Zodiac by the appropriate rituals, facing each sign in turn.

8. Let him at each of these 24 banishings make three circuits widdershins, with the signs of Horus and Harpocrates in the East as he passes it.

9. Let him advance to the square of Malkuth in the Tau, and perform a ritual of banishing Malkuth. But here let him not leave not the square to circumambulate the circle, but use the formula and God-form of Harpocrates.

10. Let him advance in turn to the squares Jesod, Hod, Netzach, Tiphereth, Geburah, Chesed, and banish each by appropriate rituals.

11. And let him know that such rituals include the pronunciation of the appropriate names of God backwards, and also a curse against the Sephira in respect of all that which it is, for that it is that which distinguishes and separates it from Kether.

12. Advancing to the squares of Binah and Chokmah in turn, let him banish these also. And for that by now an awe and trembling shall have taken hold upon him, let him banish these by a supreme ritual of inestimable puissance. And let him beware exceedingly lest his will falter, or his courage fail.

13. Finally, let him, advancing to the square of Kether,

banish that also by what means he may. At the end whereof let him set his foot upon the light, extinguishing it;[1] and, as he falleth, let him fall within the circle.

SECOND METHOD

1. Let the Hermit be seated in his Asana, robed, and let him meditate in turn upon every several part of his body until that part is so unreal to him that he no longer includes it in his comprehension of himself. For example, if it be his right foot, let him touch that foot, and be alarmed, thinking, " A foot! What is this foot? Surely I am not alone in the Hermitage!"

And this practice should be carried out not only at the time of meditation, but during the day's work.

2. This meditation is to be assisted by reasoning; as, " This foot is not I. If I should lose my foot, I should still be I. This foot is a mass of changing and decaying flesh, bone, skin, blood, lymph, etc., while I am the Unchanging and Immortal Spirit, uniform, not made, unbegotten, formless, self-luminous," etc.

3. This practice being perfect for each part of the body, let him combine his workings until the whole body is thus understood as the non-Ego and as illusion.

4. Let then the Hermit, seated in his Asana, meditate upon the Muladhara cakkra and its correspondence as a power of the mind, and destroy it in the same manner as aforesaid. Also by reasoning: " This emotion (memory, imagination, intellect, will, as it may be) is not I. This emotion is

---

[1] If armed with wand and lamp, let him extinguish the light with his hand.—N.

transient : I am immovable. This emotion is passion ; I am peace." And so on.

Let the other Cakkrams in their turn be thus destroyed, each one with its mental or moral attribute.

5. In this let him be aided by his own psychological analysis, so that no part of his conscious being be thus left undestroyed. And on his thoroughness in this matter may turn his success.

6. Lastly, having drawn all his being into the highest Sahasrara Cakkra, let him remain eternally fixed in meditation thereupon.

7. Aum.

THIRD METHOD

1. Let the Hermit stimulate each of the senses in turn, concentrating upon each until it ceases to stimulate.

[The senses of sight and touch are extremely difficult to conquer. In the end the Hermit must be utterly unable by any effort to see or feel the object of those senses. O. M.]

2. This being perfected, let him combine them two at a time.

For example, let him chew ginger (taste and touch), and watch a waterfall (sight and hearing), and watch incense (sight and smell), and crunch sugar in his teeth (taste and hearing), and so on.

3. These twenty-five practices being accomplished, let him combine them three at a time, then four at a time.

4. Lastly, let him combine all the senses in a single object.

And herein may a sixth sense be included. He is then to withdraw himself entirely from all these stimulations, perinde ac cadaver, in spite of his own efforts to attach himself to them.

5. By this method it is said that the demons of the Ruach,

that is, thoughts and memories, are inhibited, and We deny it not. But if so be that they arise, let him build a wall between himself and them according to the method.

6. Thus having stilled the voices of the Six, may he sense the subtlety of the Seventh.

7. Aum.

[We add the following, contributed by a friend at that time without the A ∴ A ∴ and its dependent orders. He worked out the method himself, and we think it may prove useful to many. O. M.]

(1) The beginner must first practise breathing regularly through the nose, at the same time trying hard to imagine that the breath goes to the Ajna and not to the lungs.

The prana yama exercises described in the EQUINOX, Vol. I., No. 4, p. 101, must next be practised, always with the idea that Ajna is breathing.

Try to realise that *power*, not air, is being drawn into the Ajna, is being concentrated there during Kumbhaka, and is vivifying the Ajna during expiration. Try rather to increase the force of concentration in Ajna than to increase excessively the length of Kumbhaka, as this is dangerous if rashly undertaken.

(2) Walk slowly in a quiet place; realise that the legs are moving, and study their movements. Understand thoroughly that these movements are due to nerve messages sent down from the brain, and that the controlling power lies in the Ajna. The legs are automatic, like those of a wooden monkey: the power in Ajna is that which does the work, is that which walks. This is not hard to realise, and should be grasped firmly, ignoring all other walking sensations.

Apply this method to every other muscular movement.

(3) Lie flat on the back with the feet under a heavy piece of furniture. Keeping the spine straight and the arms in a line with the body, rise slowly to a sitting posture, by means of the force residing in the Ajna (*i.e.* try to prevent the mind dwelling on any other exertion or sensation).

Then let the body slowly down to its original position. Repeat this two or three times every night and morning, and slowly increase the number of repetitions.

(4) Try to transfer all bodily sensations to the Ajna : *e.g.*, " I am cold " should mean " I feel cold," or, better still, " I am aware of a sensation of cold "—transfer this to the Ajna, " The Ajna is aware," etc.

(5) Pain if very slight may easily be transferred to the Ajna after a little practice. The best method for a beginner is to *imagine* he has a pain in the body and then imagine that it passes directly into the Ajna. It does not pass through the intervening structures, but goes direct. After continual practice even severe pain may be transferred to the Ajna.

(6) Fix the mind on the base of the spine and then gradually move the thoughts upwards to the Ajna.

(In this meditation Ajna is the Holy of Holies, but it is dark and empty.)

Finally, strive hard to drive anger and other obsessing thoughts into the Ajna. Try to develop a tendency to think hard of Ajna when these thoughts attack the mind, and let Ajna conquer them.

Beware of thinking of " *my* Ajna." In these meditations and practices, Ajna does not belong to you ; Ajna is the master and worker, you are the wooden monkey.

LIBER VIARVM VIÆ

SVB FIGVRÂ

DCCCLXVIII

A∴A∴
Publication in Class B.
Imprimatur:
N. Fra A∴A∴

LIBER VIARVM VIÆ

SVB FIGVRÂ DCCCLXVIII

Nine locks of the Inferior Beard.	**Nine paths below Adeptus.**	21. ה The Formulation of the Body of Light. Liber O.
		20. ש The Passage of the King's Chamber. Liber H H H.
		19. ר The Illumination of the Sphere. Liber H H H.
		18. ק The Divining of Destiny. Liber Memoriæ Viæ CMXIII.
		17. צ The Adoration under the Starry Heaven. Liber XI., NV (from Liber CCXX.).
		16. פ The Destruction of the House of God. Liber XVI.
		15. ע The Sabbath of the Adepts. Liber CCCLXX.
		14. ס Skrying in the Spirit Vision: The Ladder of Jacob. Liber O.
		13. נ The Preparation of the Corpse for the Tomb. Liber XXV.

Thirteen locks of the Superior Beard.	**Seven paths below M. T.**	12. מ The Sleep of Siloam. Liber CDLI.
		8. ט The Protection of the Sphere. Liber O.
		10. כ The Evocation of the Mighty Ones. Liber
		9. י The Absorbion of the Emanations. Liber DCCCXI.
		11. ל The Passing of the Hall of the Balances. Liber XXX.
		7. ח The Ritual of the Holy Graal. Liber CLVI.
		6. ז The Utterance of the Pythoness. Liber MCXXXIX.
	Three below M.	5. ו The Forthcoming of the Hierophant. Liber VIII. (8th Æthyr in Liber 418).
		4. ה The Formulation of the Flaming Star. Liber V.
		3. ד The Incarnation of the Inmost Light. Liber DLV Had (from Liber CCXX.).
	Three below I.	2. ג The Supreme Ecstasy of Purity. Liber LXXIII.
		1. ב The Universal Affirmations and Denials. Liber B (I.).
		0. א The transcending of all these; yea, the transcending of all these.

Seven Inferiors: Seven Superiors: Seven above All:
and Seven Interpretations of every Word.

LIBER תישארב

VIÆ MEMORIÆ

SVB FIGVRÂ

CMXIII

A∴A∴

Publication in Class B.

Imprimatur:

N. Fra A∴A∴

LIBER תישארב

VIÆ MEMORIÆ

SVB FIGVRÂ CMXIII

ooo. May be.

[oo. It has not been possible to construct this book on a basis of pure Scepticism. This matters less, as the practice leads to Scepticism, and it may be through it.]

o. This book is not intended to lead to the supreme attainment. On the contrary, its results define the separate being of the Exempt Adept from the rest of the Universe, and discover his relation to that Universe.

1. It is of such importance to the Exempt Adept that We cannot overrate it. Let him in no wise adventure the plunge into the Abyss until he have accomplished this to his most perfectest satisfaction.

2. For in the Abyss no effort is anywise possible. The Abyss is passed by virtue of the mass of the Adept and his Karma. Two forces impel him : (1) the attraction of Binah, (2) the impulse of his Karma ; and the ease and even the safety of his passage depend on the strength and direction of the latter.

3. Should one rashly dare the passage, and take the irrevocable Oath of the Abyss, he might be lost therein through Æons of incalculable agony ; he might even be

thrown back upon Chesed, with the terrible Karma of failure added to his original imperfection.

4. It is even said that in certain circumstances it is possible to fall altogether from the Tree of Life, and to attain the Towers of the Black Brothers. But We hold that this is not possible for any adept who has truly attained his grade, or even for any man who has really sought to help humanity even for a single second,[1] and that although his aspiration have been impure through vanity or any similar imperfection.

5. Let then the Adept who finds the result of these meditations unsatisfactory refuse the Oath of the Abyss, and live so that his Karma gains strength and direction suitable to the task at some future period.

6. Memory is essential to the individual consciousness; otherwise the mind were but a blank sheet on which shadows are cast. But we see that not only does the mind retain impressions, but that it is so constituted that its tendency is to retain some more excellently than others. Thus the great classical scholar, Sir Richard Jebb, was unable to learn even the schoolboy mathematics required for the preliminary examination at Cambridge University, and a special act of the authorities was required in order to admit him.

7. The first method to be described has been detailed in Bhikkhu Ananda Metteya's "Training of the Mind" (EQUINOX, I. 5, pp. 28-59, and especially pp. 48-56). We have little to alter or to add. Its most important result, as regards the Oath of the Abyss, is the freedom from all desire or clinging to anything which it gives. Its second result is to

---

[1] Those in possession of Liber CLXXXV. will note that in every grade but one the aspirant is pledged to serve his inferiors in the Order.

aid the adept in the second method, by supplying him with further data for his investigation.

8. The stimulation of memory useful in both practices is also achieved by simple meditation (Liber E), in a certain stage of which old memories arise unbidden. The adept may then practise this, stopping at that stage, and encouraging instead of suppressing the flashes of memory.

9. Zoroaster has said, "Explore the River of the Soul, whence or in what order you have come; so that although you have become a servant to the body, you may again rise to that Order (the A∴ A∴) from which you descended, joining Works (Kamma) to Sacred Reason (the Tao)."

10. The Result of the Second Method is to show the Adept to what end his powers are destined. When he has passed the Abyss and become NEMO, the return of the current causes him "to appear in the Heaven of Jupiter as a morning star or as an evening star."[1] In other words, he should discover what may be the nature of his work. Thus Mohammed was a Brother reflected into Netzach, Buddha a Brother reflected into Hod, or, as some say, Daath. The present manifestation of Frater P. to the outer is in Tiphereth, to the inner in the path of Leo.

11. First Method. Let the Exempt Adept first train himself to think backwards by external means, as set forth here following.

(a) Let him learn to write backwards, with either hand.

(b) Let him learn to walk backwards.

---

[1] The formula of the Great Work "Solve et Coagula," may be thus interpreted. Solve, the dissolution of the Self in the Infinite; Coagula, the presentation of the Infinite in a concrete form to the outer. Both are necessary to the Task of a Master of the Temple.

(c) Let him constantly watch, if convenient, cinemato-graph films, and listen to phonograph records, reversed, and let him so accustom himself to these that they appear natural, and appreciable as a whole.

(d) Let him practise speaking backwards; thus, for "I am He" let him say, "Eh ma I."

(e) Let him learn to read backwards. In this it is difficult to avoid cheating one's self, as an expert reader sees a sentence at a glance. Let his disciple read aloud to him backwards, slowly at first, then more quickly.

(f) Of his own ingenium let him devise other methods.

12. In this his brain will at first be overwhelmed by a sense of utter confusion; secondly, it will endeavour to evade the difficulty by a trick. The brain will pretend to be working backwards when it is really normal. It is difficult to describe the nature of the trick, but it will be quite obvious to anyone who has done practices (a) and (b) for a day or two. They become quite easy, and he will think that he is making progress, an illusion which close analysis will dispel.

13. Having begun to train his brain in this manner, and obtained some little success, let the Exempt Adept, seated in his Asana, think first of his present attitude, next of the act of being seated, next of his entering the room, next of his robing, et cetera, exactly as it happened. And let him most strenu-ously endeavour to think each act as happening backwards. It is not enough to think : " I am seated here, and before that I was standing, and before that I entered the room," etc. That series is the trick detected in the preliminary practices.

LIBER תישארב

The series must not run "ghi-def-abc," but "ihgfedcba": not "horse a is this" but "esroh a si siht." To obtain this thoroughly well, practice (c) is very useful. The brain will be found to struggle constantly to right itself, soon accustoming itself to accept "esroh" as merely another glyph for "horse." This tendency must be constantly combated.

14. In the early stages of this practice the endeavour should be to meticulous minuteness of detail in remembering actions ; for the brain's habit of thinking forwards will at first be insuperable. Thinking of large and complex actions, then, will give a series which we may symbolically write "opqrstu-hijklmn-abcdefg." If these be split into detail, we shall have "stu-pqr-o—mn-kl-hij—fg-cde-ab," which is much nearer to the ideal "utsrqponmlkjihgfedcba."

15. Capacities differ widely, but the Exempt Adept need have no reason to be discouraged if after a month's continuous labour he find that now and again for a few seconds his brain really works backwards.

16. The Exempt Adept should concentrate his efforts upon obtaining a perfect picture of five minutes backwards rather than upon extending the time covered by his meditation. For this preliminary training of the brain is the Pons Asinorum of the whole process.

17. This five minutes' exercise being satisfactory, the Exempt Adept may extend the same at his discretion to cover an hour, a day, a week, and so on. Difficulties vanish before him as he advances ; the extension from a day to the course of his whole life will not prove so difficult as the perfecting of the five minutes.

18. This practice should be repeated at least four times

daily, and progress is shown firstly by the ever easier running of the brain, secondly by the added memories which arise.

19. It is useful to reflect during this practice, which in time becomes almost mechanical, upon the way in which effects spring from causes. This aids the mind to link its memories, and prepares the adept for the preliminary practice of the Second Method.

20. Having allowed the mind to return for some hundred times to the hour of birth, it should be encouraged to endeavour to penetrate beyond that period. If it be properly trained to run backwards, there will be little difficulty in doing this, although it is one of the distinct steps in the practice.

21. It may be then that the memory will persuade the adept of some previous existence. Where this is possible, let it be checked by an appeal to facts, as follows.

22. It often occurs to men that on visiting a place to which they have never been, it appears familiar. This may arise from a confusion of thought or a slipping of the memory, but it is conceivably a fact.

If, then, the adept "remember" that he was in a previous life in some city, say Cracow, which he has in this life never visited, let him describe from memory the appearance of Cracow, and of its inhabitants, setting down their names. Let him further enter into details of the city and its customs. And having done this with great minuteness, let him confirm the same by consultation with historians and geographers, or by a personal visit, remembering (both to the credit of his memory and its discredit) that historians, geographers, and himself are alike fallible. But let him not trust his memory to assert its conclusions as fact, and act thereupon, without most adequate confirmation.

23. This process of checking his memory should be practised with the earlier memories of childhood and youth by reference to the memories and records of others, always reflecting upon the fallibility even of such safeguards.

24. All this being perfected, so that the memory reaches back into æons incalculably distant, let the Exempt Adept meditate upon the fruitlessness of all those years, and upon the fruit thereof, severing that which is transitory and worthless from that which is eternal. And it may be that he being but an Exempt Adept may hold all to be savourless and full of sorrow.

25. This being so, without reluctance will he swear the Oath of the Abyss.

26. Second Method. Let the Exempt Adept, fortified by the practice of the First Method, enter the preliminary practice of the Second Method.

27. Second Method. Preliminary Practices. Let him, seated in his Asana, consider any event, and trace it to its immediate causes. And let this be done very fully and minutely. Here, for example, is a body erect and motionless. Let the adept consider the many forces which maintain it; firstly, the attraction of the earth, of the sun, of the planets, of the farthest stars, nay, of every mote of dust in the room, one of which (could it be annihilated) would cause that body to move, although so imperceptibly. Also, the resistance of the floor, the pressure of the air, and all other external conditions. Secondly, the internal forces which sustain it, the vast and complex machinery of the skeleton, the muscles,

the blood, the lymph, the marrow, all that makes up a man. Thirdly, the moral and intellectual forces involved, the mind, the will, the consciousness. Let him continue this with unremitting ardour, searching Nature, leaving nothing out.

28. Next let him take one of the immediate causes of his position, and trace out its equilibrium. For example, the will. What determines the will to aid in holding the body erect and motionless?

29. This being determined, let him choose one of the forces which determined his will, and trace out that in similar fashion; and let this process be continued for many days until the interdependence of all things is a truth assimilated in his inmost being.

30. This being accomplished, let him trace his own history with special reference to the causes of each event. And in this practice he may neglect to some extent the universal forces which at all times act on all, as for example the attraction of masses, and let him concentrate his attention upon the principal and determining or effective causes.

For instance, he is seated, perhaps, in a country place in Spain. Why? Because Spain is warm and suitable for meditation, and because cities are noisy and crowded. Why is Spain warm? and why does he wish to meditate? Why choose warm Spain rather than warm India? To the last question: Because Spain is nearer to his home. Then why is his home near Spain? Because his parents were Germans. And why did they go to Germany? And so during the whole meditation.

31. On another day, let him begin with a question of another kind, and every day devise new questions, not only concerning his present situation, but also abstract questions.

LIBER תישארב

Thus let him connect the prevalence of water upon the surface of the globe with its necessity to such life as we know, with the specific gravity and other physical properties of water, and let him perceive ultimately through all this the necessity and concord of things, not concord as the schoolmen of old believed, making all things for man's benefit or convenience, but the essential mechanical concord whose final law is *inertia*. And in these meditations let him avoid as if it were the plague any speculation sentimental or fantastic.

32. Second Method. The Practice Proper. Having then perfected in his mind these conceptions, let him apply them to his own career, forging the links of memory into the chain of necessity.

And let this be his final question : To what purpose am I fitted? Of what service can my being prove to the Brothers of the A∴ A∴ if I cross the Abyss, and am admitted to the City of the Pyramids?

33. Now that he may clearly understand the nature of this question, and the method of solution, let him study the reasoning of the anatomist who reconstructs an animal from a single bone. To take a simple example.

34. Suppose, having lived all my life among savages, a ship is cast upon the shore and wrecked. Undamaged among the cargo is a "Victoria." What is its use? The wheels speak of roads, their slimness of smooth roads, the brake of hilly roads. The shafts show that it was meant to be drawn by an animal, their height and length suggest an animal of the size of a horse. That the carriage is open suggests a climate tolerable at any rate for part of the year. The height of the box suggests crowded streets, or the spirited character of the

animal employed to draw it. The cushions indicate its use to convey men rather than merchandise; its hood that rain sometimes falls, or that the sun is at times powerful. The springs would imply considerable skill in metals; the varnish much attainment in that craft.

35. Similarly, let the adept consider of his own case. Now that he is on the point of plunging into the Abyss, a giant Why? confronts him with uplifted club.

36. There is no minutest atom of his composition which can be withdrawn without making him some other than he is, no useless moment in his past. Then what is his future? The " Victoria " is not a waggon; it is not intended for carting hay. It is not a sulky; it is useless in trotting races.

37. So the adept has military genius, or much knowledge of Greek: how do these attainments help his purpose, or the purpose of the Brothers? He was put to death by Calvin, or stoned by Hezekiah; as a snake he was killed by a villager, or as an elephant slain in battle under Hamilcar. How do such memories help him? Until he have thoroughly mastered the reason for every incident in his past, and found a purpose for every item of his present equipment,[1] he cannot truly answer even those Three Questions that were first put to him, even the Three Questions of the Ritual of the Pyramid; he is not ready to swear the Oath of the Abyss.

38. But being thus enlightened, let him swear the Oath of the Abyss; yea, let him swear the Oath of the Abyss.

[1] A Brother known to me was repeatedly baffled in this meditation. But one day being thrown with his horse over a sheer cliff of forty feet, and escaping without a scratch or a bruise, he was reminded of his many narrow escapes from death. These proved to be the last factors in his problem, which, thus completed, solved itself in a moment.   O. M.

ADONIS
AN ALLEGORY
BY

ALEISTER CROWLEY

Inscribed to Adonis.

PERSONS OF THE ALLEGORY

THE KING OF BABYLON, *tributary to the King of Greece*
HERMES, *a Greek Physician*
THE LADY PSYCHE
THE COUNT ADONIS, *at first known as the Lord Esarhaddon*
THE LADY ASTARTE
The Warriors of the King of Babylon
HANUMAN, *Servant to Hermes*
CHARIS,
ELPIS, } *Attendants on Psyche*
PISTIS,
Three Aged Women
Handmaidens and Slaves of Astarte

ADONIS

ACT I

SCENE 1: *The hanging gardens of Babylon. R., the House of the Lady Astarte; L., a gateway; C., a broad lawn enriched with clustered flowers and sculptures. The sun is nigh his setting. On a couch under the wall of the city reposes the Lord Esarhaddon, fanned by two slaves, a negro boy and a fair Kabyle girl, clad in yellow and blue, the boy's robes being covered with a veil of silver, the girl's with a veil of gold.*

They are singing to him softly:

THE BOY. All crimson-veined is Tigris' flood;
　The sun has stained his mouth with blood.

THE GIRL. Orange and green his standards sweep.

THE BOY. His minions keen.

THE GIRL. 　　　　　　　　His maidens weep.

THE BOY. But thou, Lord, thou! The hour is nigh
　When from the prow of luxury
　Shall step the death of all men's hearts,
　She whose live breath, a dagger's darts,
　A viper's vice, an adder's grip,
　A cockatrice 'twixt lip and lip,
　She whose black eyes are suns to shower

119

THE EQUINOX

Love's litanies from hour to hour,
Whose limbs are scythes like Death's, of whom
The body writhes, a lotus-bloom
Swayed by the wind of love, a crime
Too sweetly sinned, the queen of time,
The lady of heaven, to whom the stars,
Seven by seven, from their bars
Lean and do worship—even she
Who hath given all her sweet self to thee,
The Lady Astarte!

THE GIRL.   Peace, O peace!
A swan, she sails through ecstasies
Of air and marble and flowers, she sways
As the full moon through midnight's haze
Of gauze—her body is like a dove
And a snake, and life, and death, and love!

THE BOY. Even as the twilight so is she,
Half seen, half subtly apprehended,
Ethereally and bodily.
The soul incarnate, the body transcended!

THE GIRL. Aching, aching passionately,
Insufferably, utterly splendid!

THE BOY. Her lips make pale the setting sun!

THE GIRL. Her body blackens Babylon!

THE BOY. Her eyes turn midnight's murk to grey!

THE GIRL. Her breasts make midnight of the day!

THE BOY. About her, suave and subtle, swims
The musk and madness of her limbs!

THE GIRL. Her mouth is magic like the moon's.

THE BOY. Her breath is bliss!

ADONIS

THE GIRL.   Her steps are swoons!
                  [ENTER ASTARTE, *with her five handmaidens.*

THE BOY. Away, away!

THE GIRL.   With heart's accord,
   To leave his lady to our lord.   [*They go out.*

THE BOY. Let him forget our service done
   Of palm-leaves waved, that never tires,
   In his enchanted Babylon
   Of infinite desires!

[ASTARTE *kneels at the foot of the couch, and taking
   the feet of Esarhaddon in her hands, covers them with
   kisses.*

ASTARTE. Nay, never wake! unless to catch my neck
   And break me up with kisses—never sleep,
   Unless to dream new pains impossible
   To waking!
               Girls! with more than dream's address,
   Wake him with perfume till he smile, with strokes
   Softer than moonbeams till he turn, and sigh,
   With five slow drops of wine between his lips
   Until his heart heave, with young thrills of song
   Until his eyelids open, and the first
   And fairest of ye greet him like a flower,
   So that awakened he may break from you
   And turn to me who am all these in one.

1ST MAIDEN.   Here is the wealth
             Of all amber and musk,
             Secreted by stealth
             In the domes of the dusk!

THE EQUINOX

2ND MAIDEN.
    Here the caress
    Of a cheek—let it stir
    The first liens of liesse
    Not to me—but to her!

3RD MAIDEN.
    Here the quintessence
    Of dream and delight,
    Evoking the presence
    Of savour to sight!

4TH MAIDEN.
    List to the trill
    And the ripple and roll
    Of a tune that may thrill
    Thee through sense to the soul!

5TH MAIDEN.
    Look on the fairest,
    The masterless maid!
    Ere thine eye thou unbarest,
    I flicker, I fade.

ALL. Wake! as her garland is tossed in the air
    When the nymph meets Apollo, our forehead is bare.
    We divide, we disperse, we dislimn, we dissever,
    For we are but now, and our lady for ever!

                          [They go out.

ESARHADDON. I dreamed of thee!
    Dreams beyond form and name!
    It was a chain of ages, and a flash
    Of lightning—which thou wilt—since—Oh I see
    Nothing, feel nothing, and am nothing—ash
    Of the universe burnt through!

122

ADONIS

ASTARTE.   And I the flame!

ESARHADDON. Wreathing and roaring for an ageless æon,
    Wrapping the world, spurning the empyrean,
    Drowning with dark despotic imminence
    All life and light, annihilating sense—
    I have been sealed and silent in the womb
    Of nothingness to burst, a babe's bold bloom,
    Into the upper æthyr of thine eyes.
    Oh! one grave glance enkindles Paradise,
    One sparkle sets me on the throne above,
    Mine orb the world.

ASTARTE. Nay, stir not yet.   Let love
    Breathe like the zephyr on the unmoved deep,
    Sigh to awakening from its rosy sleep;
    Let the stars fade, and all the east grow grey
    And tender, ere the first faint rose of day
    Flush it.   Awhile!   Awhile!   There's crimson bars
    Enough to blot the noblest of the stars,
    And bow for adoration ere the rim
    Start like God's spear to ware the world of Him!
    Softly!

ESARHADDON. But kiss me!

ASTARTE.   With an eyelash first!

ESARHADDON. Treasure and torture!

ASTARTE.   Tantalising thirst
    Makes the draught more delicious.   Heaven were worth
    Little without the purgatory, earth!

ESARHADDON. You make earth heaven.

ASTARTE.   And heaven hell.   To choose thee
    Is to interpret misery " To lose thee."

THE EQUINOX

ESARHADDON. Ay! death end all if it must end thy
    kiss!

ASTARTE. And death be all if it confirm life's bliss!

ESARHADDON. And death come soon if death fill life's
    endeavour!

ASTARTE. And if it spill life's vintage, death come never!

ESARHADDON. The sun sets. Bathe me in the rain of
    gold!

ASTARTE. These pearls that decked it shimmering star-cold
  Fall, and my hair falls, wreathes an aureole.
  Even as thy love encompasses my soul!

ESARHADDON. I am blinded; I am bruised; I am stung.
    Each thread
  Hisses.

ASTARTE. There's life there for a thousand dead!

ESARHADDON. And death there for a million!

ASTARTE.   Even so.
  Life, death, new life, a web spun soft and slow
  By love, the spider, in these palaces
  That taketh hold.

ESARHADDON.   Take hold!

ASTARTE.   Keen joyaunces
  Mix with the multitudinous murmurings,
  And all the kisses sharpen into stings.
  Nay! shall my mouth take hold? Beware! Once fain,
  How shall it ever leave thy mouth again?

ESARHADDON. Why should it?

ASTARTE.   Is not sleep our master yet?

ESARHADDON. Why must we think when wisdom would
    forget?

124

ADONIS

ASTARTE. Lest we in turn forget to fill the hour.

ESARHADDON. The pensive bee leaves honey in the flower.

ASTARTE. Now the sun's rim is dipped. And thus I dip
   My gold to the horizon of thy lip.

ESARHADDON. Ah! . . .

ASTARTE.   There's no liquor, none, within the cup.

ESARHADDON. Nay, draw not back; nay, then, but lift
      me up.
   I would the cup were molten too; I'd drain
   Its blasting agony.

ASTARTE.   In vain.

ESARHADDON.   In vain?
   Nay, let the drinker and the draught in one
   Blaze up at last, and burn down Babylon!

ASTARTE. All but the garden, and our bed, and—see!
   The false full moon that comes to rival me.

ESARHADDON. She comes to lamp our love.
                [*A chime of bells without.*

ASTARTE.   I'll tire my hair.
   The banquet waits. Girls, follow me.
           [*They go out, leaving* ESARHADDON.

ESARHADDON.   How fair
   And full she sweeps, the buoyant barge upon
   The gilded curves of Tigris. She's the swan
   That drew the gods to gaze, the fawn that called
   Their passion to his glades of emerald,
   The maid that maddened Mithras, the quick quiver
   Of reeds that drew Oannes from the river! . . .
   She is gone. The garden is a wilderness.
   Oh for the banquet of the lioness,

THE EQUINOX

The rich astounding wines, the kindling meats,
The music and the dancers! Fiery seats
Of empire of the archangels, let your wings
Ramp through the empyrean! Lords and Kings
Of the Gods, descend and serve us, as we spurn
And trample life, fill death's sardonyx urn
With loves immortal—how shall I endure
This moment's patience? Ah, she comes, be sure!
Her foot flits on the marble. . . . Open, gate!

[*The gate, not of the house but of the garden, opens.
The Lady Psyche appears. She is clothed in deep
purple, as mourning, and her hair is bound with
a fillet of cypress and acacia. She is attended by
three maidens and three aged women.*

What tedious guest arrives?

PSYCHE.   White hour of fate!
    I have found him!

ESARHADDON.   Who is this? . . . Fair lady, pardon.
    You seek the mistress of the garden?

PYSCHE. I thought I had found the lord I seek.
    Your pardon, lord. These eyes are weary and weak
    With tears and my vain search.

ESARHADDON.   Whom seek you then?

PSYCHE. My husband—my sole miracle of men,
    The Count Adonis.

                [ESARHADDON *staggers and falls on the couch.*

PSYCHE.   You know of him?

ESARHADDON.   No.
    I cannot tell what struck me so.
    I never heard the name.

ADONIS

PYSCHE.   Indeed, your eyes
    Are liker his than wedded dragon-flies!
    Your brows are his, your mouth is his—
    Yet all's awry!

ESARHADDON.   May be it is!

PYSCHE. Oh, pardon.   Mine is but a mad girl's glance.
    Adonis is this soul's inheritance.
    All else is madness.

ESARHADDON. Mad! Mad! Mad! Mad! Mad!
    Why say you this? Who are you? Sad? Glad?
       Bad!
    Bad! Bad! Speak, speak! Bleak peak of mystery?
    Weak cheek of modesty?

PSYCHE.   Oh, pardon me!
    I did not mean to move you thus.

ESARHADDON.   I am stirred
    Too easily.   You used a shameful word!

PSYCHE. Accept my sorrow.   I am all alone
    In this black night.   My heart is stone,
    My limbs are lead, mine eyes accurst,
    My throat a hell of thirst. . . .
    My husband—they suppose him dead. . . .
    They made me wear these weeds.   Could I
    In my heart credit half they said,
    Not these funereal robes should wrap me round,
    But the white cerements of a corpse, and high
    Upon a pyre of sandal and ebony,
    Should dare through flame the inequitable profound!
    But only these of all mine household come
    In faith and hope and love so far from home,

127

And these three others joined me—why, who knows?
But thou, lord, in whose face his likeness shows—
At the first glance—for now, i' faith, 'tis gone!—
Hast thou dwelt alway here in Babylon?

ESARHADDON. Now must I laugh—forgive me in your
    sorrow!
My life's not yesterday and not to-morrow.
I live; I know no more.

PSYCHE.   How so?

ESARHADDON.   I fear
I know but this, that I'm a stranger here.
They call me the Lord Esarhaddon—name
Borrowed or guessed, I cannot tell! I came
Whence I know not—some malady
Destroyed my memory.

PSYCHE. Oh, were you he! But yet I see you are not.
Had you no tokens from the life forgot?

ESARHADDON. Nay, I came naked into Babylon.
I live the starlight and sleep through the sun.
I am happy in love, I am rich, I eat and drink,
I gather goods, I laugh, I never think.
Know me the prince of perfect pleasure!

PSYCHE.   Yet
Is there not something that you would forget?
Some fear that chills you? While you talk to me
I see you glance behind you fearfully.

ESARHADDON (*with furtive fear amounting to horror*).
You see the Shadow?

PSYCHE.   No: slim shadows stretch
From yonder moon, and woo the world, and etch

128

ADONIS

With their fantastic melancholy grotesques
The earth—man's destiny in arabesques.

ESARHADDON. You are blind! You are mad!   See where
    he stands!

It is the King of Babylon,
Reeking daggers in his hands—
And black blood oozes, oozes, throbs and dips
From his eyes and nostrils to his lips
That he sucks, gnashing his fangs.   Upon
His head is a crown of skulls, and monkeys mew
And gibber and mop about him.   Skew! Spew! Ugh!
Hu! Mow! Mow! Mow! they go—cannot you
    hear them?
What? have you courage to go near them?

PSYCHE. Nothing is there.

ESARHADDON.   Oh, but he has the head
Of a boar, the black boar Night! All dead, dead,
    dead,
The eyes of girls that once were beautiful
Hang round his neck.   Whack! Crack! he slaps a skull
For a drum—Smack! Flack! Thwack! Back, I'll not
    attack.
Quack! Quack! there's ducks and devils on his back.
Keep him away.   You want a man, you say?
Well, there's a king for you to-day.
Go, kiss him! Slobber over him!   His ribs
Should be readily tickled.   Wah! Wah! Wah! she jibs.
Ugh! there he came too close.   I'll bite the dust;
I'll lick the slime of Babylon.   Great lust,
Great god, great devil, gra-gra-gra-gra! Spare me!

Take this wench, though she were the womb that
    bare me!
See! Did I tell you, he's the King, the King,
The King of Terrors. See me grovelling!
Yah! Ha!

PSYCHE.   There's nothing there. Are you a man
To craze at naught?

ESARHADDON.   Immitigable ban!
Immitigable, pitiful, profound—
Ban, can, fan, ran, and pan is underground,
Round, bound, sound—Oh have pity! . . .

                                 Who art thou
Whose coming thus unmans me? Not till now
Saw I, or felt I, or heard I, the King
So mumbling near; black blood's on everything.
Boo! Scow! Be off! Out! Vanish! Fly! Begone!
Out! Off! Out! Off! I'm King of Babylon.
Oh no! Thy pardon. Spare me! 'Tis as a slip
O' th' lip. Now flip! rip! bawdy harlot, skip!
[*He threatens her. She trembles, but holds her ground.*
Strip, yes, I'll strip you naked, strip your flesh
In strips with my lips, gnaw your bones like a dog.
Off, sow! Off, grumpet! Strumpet! Scum-pit! Flails
    to thresh
Your body! Clubs to mash your face in! Knives
To cut away your cat's nine lives!

ASTARTE. (*Entering hastily.*) What's this? Who are
    you? What right have you to come
And make this havoc in the home?
Can you not see what wreck your tempest makes?

ADONIS

Begone!   I have a fiery flight of snakes
To lash you hence!

PSYCHE.   It may be mine's the right.
It may be you are nothing in my sight.
It may be I have found my lord at last;
And you—his concubine?   May be out-cast.

ASTARTE. This is the sure thing, that I chase thee. Slaves!
Hither your whips! that are more black with blood
Of such as this thing than your skins with kisses
Of your sun's frenzy.   [*The slaves run up.*

PSYCHE.   Thou vain woman!   Now
I know him, lost, wrecked, mad, but mine, but mine,
Indissolubly dowered with me, my husband,
The Count Adonis!

ESARHADDON.   Ah!
                    [*He falls, but into the arms of* ASTARTE.

ASTARTE.   Ho! guard us now
And lash this thing from the garden!
[*The slaves form in line between* PSYCHE *and the others.*

PSYCHE.   Adonis!

ESARHADDON.   Ah!
Astarte, there's some sorcery abroad.

ASTARTE. The spell is broken, dear my lord.
There is a wall of ebony and steel
About us.

ESARHADDON. What then do I feel
When that name sounds?

ASTARTE. A trick of mind.
Things broken up and left behind
Keep roots to plague us when we least expect them.

THE EQUINOX

The wise—and thou art wise—let naught affect them.
Let us to feast!

ESARHADDON.   Ah no! I tremble still,
Despite my reason and despite my will.
Let me lie with thee here awhile, and dream
Upon thine eyes beneath the moon,
Whose slanted beam
Lights up thy face, that sends its swoon
Of languor and hunger through
The infinite space that severs two
So long as they cannot rise above
Into the unity of love.
However close lock hands and feet,
Only one moment may they meet;
When in the one pang that runs level
With death and birth, the royal revel,
The lover and the loved adore
The thing that is, when they are not.

ASTARTE.   No more!
Bury thy face between these hills that threat
The heaven, their rosy spears (the gods that fret)
Tipping thine ears, and with my hair I'll hide thee;
And these mine handmaidens shall stand beside thee,
And mix their nightingale with lion
Of the guard that chorus and clash iron,
While as a river laps its banks
My fingertips caress thy flanks!

(*Chorus.*)

MEN. Under the sun there is none, there is none
That hath heard such a word as our lord hath begun.

ADONIS

WOMEN. Under the moon such a tune, such a tune
   As his thought hath half caught in this heaven of June.
MEN. Never hath night such a light, such a rite!
WOMEN. Never had day such a ray, such a sway!
MEN. Never had man, since began the earth's plan,
   Such a bliss, such a kiss, such a woman as this!
WOMEN. Never had maid since God bade be arrayed
   Earth's bowers with his flowers, such a man to her
      powers!
MEN. Mix in the measure,
   Black grape and white cherry!
   A passion, a pleasure,
   A torment, a treasure,
   You to be mournful and we to be merry!
WOMEN. We shall be solemn
   And grave and alluring,
   You be the column
   Upstanding, enduring.
   We be the ivy and vine
   To entwine—
   My mouth on your mouth, and your mouth on
      mine!
MEN. Burnish our blades
   With your veils,
   Merry maids!
WOMEN. Sever their cords
   With the scales
   Of your swords!
MEN. As a whirlwind that licks up a leaf
   Let us bear

THE EQUINOX

You, an aureate sheaf
Adrift in the air !

WOMEN. As a butterfly hovers and flits,
Let us glide
To bewilder your wits
Bewitched by a bride !

MEN. Now, as the stars shall
Encircle the moon,
Our ranks let us marshal
In time and in tune !

WOMEN. Leading our lady and lord
To the feast,
Ere the night be abroad,
The black rose of the east !

MEN AND WOMEN. Arise ! arise ! the feast is spread,
The wine is poured ; the singers wait
Eager to lure and lull ; the dancers tread
Impatient to invoke the lords of Fate.
Arise, arise ! the feast delayed delays
The radiant raptures that must crown its ways.

ASTARTE. Come now. Ah ! still the pallor clings ?
Wine will redeem the roses. Stretch the strings
Of thy slack heart ! Still trembling ? Lean on me !
This shoulder could hold up eternity.

[*They go forth to the banquet.*

134

ADONIS

SCENE II. THE HALL OF THE PALACE OF ASTARTE. *Onyx,
alabaster, porphyry and malachite are the pillars ; and
the floor of mosaic. In the high seat is* ASTARTE, *on her
right* HERMES, *a Greek physician. He is a slight, old
man, with piercing eyes and every mark of agility and
vigour. His dress is that of a Babylonish physician.*

HERMES. And now, polite preliminaries past,
    Tell me, dear lady, what the little trouble is !
ASTARTE. It was quite sudden.
HERMES.   Good ; not like to last.
    It bursts, such malady a brittle bubble is !
    How is the pulse ? Allow me !
ASTARTE.   Not for me
    Your skill. My husband's lost his memory.
HERMES. Yet he remembers you ?
ASTARTE.   O quite, of course !
HERMES. Let it alone ! Don't flog the willing horse !
    Were I to cure him by my magic spells,
    The odds are he'd remember someone else !
ASTARTE. Ah, but—a month ago—a woman came—
HERMES. Cool—warm—hot—now we're getting near the
        flame !
ASTARTE. And what she said or did who knows ?
HERMES.   These men !
ASTARTE. Yes ! But he's never been the same since then !
    I've taken endless trouble not to fret him,
    Done everything I could to please and pet him,
    And now this wretched woman has upset him !

THE EQUINOX

HERMES. Was he distressed much at the time?

ASTARTE.   Distressed?
  Mad as an elephant in spring!

HERMES.   I guessed
  It.   Think he took a fancy to the girl?

ASTARTE. Well, honestly, I don't.   My mind's a whirl
  With worry.   She's a flimsy creature, rags
  Of sentiment, and tears, and worn-out tags
  Of wisdom.

HERMES.   Yes, you've nothing much to fear
  While you appear as . . . what you do appear.

ASTARTE. Well, there they stood, crying like butchered
      swine,
  She and her maids.   It seems she's lost her man,
  Can't get another, wanted to claim mine.
  I put a stopper on the pretty plan.
  But ever since—well, I can't say what's wrong,
  But something's wrong.

HERMES.   Yes; yes.   Now is it long?

ASTARTE. About a month.

HERMES.   What physic have you tried?

ASTARTE. The usual things; young vipers skinned and
      dried
  And chopped with rose-leaves; cow's hoof stewed in
      dung,
  One pilule four times daily, on the tongue;
  Lark's brains in urine after every meal,
  With just a touch of salt and orange-peel.

HERMES. And yet he is no better?

ASTARTE.   Not a whit.

136

ADONIS

Oh yes, though, now I come to think of it,
Snails pounded up and taken after food
Did seem to do some temporary good.
Of course we kept him on a doubled diet.

HERMES. Have you tried change of air, and rest, and
    quiet?

ASTARTE. No ; what a strange idea!

HERMES.   As strange as new.
Yet there seems somehow something in it too!
Still, here's where silence is worth seven speeches—
I might get strangled by my brother leeches.
Now, are you sure you want him cured?

ASTARTE.   Why, yes,
Why should I call you in?

HERMES.   But none the less
It might be awkward his remembering more.

ASTARTE. I simply want him as he was before.

HERMES. And if it should turn out, as I suspect,
He was this woman's husband.

ASTARTE.   Then select
A—you know—something suitable—to put her
Where she won't worry me, or want a suitor.

HERMES. I understand you ; but I'm old ; your beauty
Might fail to make me careless of my duty.

ASTARTE. I'll take the risk.

HERMES.   Then let me see the victim ;
If bound, we'll loosen him ; if loose, constrict him.
There, madam, in one phrase from heart to heart,
Lies the whole mystery of the healer's art!
Where is the pathic?

137

THE EQUINOX

ASTARTE.   Hush! in Babylon
We say " the patient."

HERMES.   Yes?

ASTARTE   It's often one.
For Babylonish is so quaint a tongue
One often goes too right by going wrong!
I'll call him from the garden.   [*Goes out.*

HERMES (*alone*).   Is there need
To see the man?   He's simply off his feed.
A child could see the way to make him hearty:
More exercise, less food—and less Astarte!

                         [*Enter* ESARHADDON.

I greet your lordship.

ESARHADDON. Greeting, sir!

HERMES.   And so
We're not as healthy as a month ago?
The pulse? Allow me! Ah! Tut! Tut! Not bad.
The tongue?   Thanks!   Kindly tell me what you had
For dinner.

ESARHADDON.   Nothing: practically nothing.
I seem to look on food with utter loathing.

HERMES. Just so; but you contrived to peck a bit?

ESARHADDON. Only a dozen quails upon the spit,
A little sturgeon cooked with oysters, wine,
Mushrooms and crayfish. . . .

HERMES.   That is not to dine.

ESARHADDON. Well, after that I toyed with pheasant
    pasty,
Sliced—you know how—with pineapple.

HERMES.   Eat hasty?

138

ESARHADDON. No, not at all.   Well, then a sucking-pig
    Stuffed with grape, olive, cucumber, peach, fig,
    And lemon.   Then I trifled with a curry——
HERMES. You're sure you didn't eat it in a hurry?
ESARHADDON. Quite sure.   The curry was simplicity
    Itself — plain   prawns.   Then   there   was — let   me
        see !—
    A dish of fruit, then a kid roasted whole,
    Some venison fried with goose-liver, a roll
    Of very tender spicy well-cooked veal
    Done up with honey, olive oil, and meal,
    Some sweets, but only three or four, and those
    I hardly touched.
HERMES.   But why now ?
ESARHADDON.   I suppose
    I wasn't hungry.
HERMES.   Diagnosis right ;
    A simple case of loss of appetite !
    Surely they tempted you with something else.
ESARHADDON. A few live lobsters broiled within their
        shells.
    I ate two only.
HERMES.   That explains the tongue.
    Now let me listen !
                  Sound in heart and lung.
    (And I should think so !) 'Twas a sage that sung :
    "Whom   the   Gods   love,   love   lobsters;   they   die
        young."
    And a yet greater sage sublimely said :
    " Look not upon the lobster when it's red ! "

ESARHADDON. A Babylonish bard has said the same
  Of wine.
HERMES.   Ah, wine now? Out with it! Die game!
ESARHADDON. By fin and tail of great Oannes, I
  Am the mere model of sobriety.
HERMES. What did you drink for dinner?
ESARHADDON.   Scarce a drop
  At any time—four flagons, there I stop.
  With just a flask of barley-wine to top.
HERMES. Just so becomes a nobleman of sense
  Whose moderation errs toward abstinence.
ESARHADDON. Abstinence! That's the word I couldn't
    think of!
  I'm an abstainer.   Everything I drink of
  Is consecrated by a melancholic
  Priest.
HERMES.   Which prevents it being alcoholic!
ESARHADDON. Sir, you appear to understand my case
  As no one else has done.   Appalling face
  These quacks have that crowd Babylon.   Your
    fee?
  Though none can pay the service done to me.
HERMES. One moment.   What about your memory?
  Well, never mind, just follow my advice;
  That will come back before you say " knife " twice.
  First, fire your slaves, the rogues that thieve and
    laze:
  A slave's worse than two masters now-a-days.
  Next, live on nothing but boiled beans and tripe,
  With once a week a melon—when they're ripe.

ADONIS

Next, send the Lady Astarte up the river;
She looks to me to have a touch of liver.
And you must teach your muscles how to harden,
So stay at home, and labour in the garden!

ESARHADDON. You damned insulting blackguard! Char-
latan!
Quack! Trickster! Scoundrel! Cheating medicine-
man!
You ordure-tasting privy-sniffing rogue,
You think because your humbug is the vogue
You can beard me?

HERMES.   I'll tell you just one thing.
Disobey me, and—trouble with the King!

ESARHADDON. Ring-a-ling-ting! Ping! Spring!

HERMES.   That's cooked his goose.
I'll tell Astarte, though it's not much use. [*He goes out*.
It's only one more of life's little curses—
The best of women make the worst of nurses!

THE EQUINOX

SCENE III. THE CONSULTING-ROOM OF HERMES. *It has two parts, the first filled with stuffed crocodiles, snakes, astrolabes, skeletons, lamps of strange shape, vast rolls of papyri, vases containing such objects as a fœtus, a mummied child, a six-legged sheep. Hands (obviously those of criminals) have been painted with phosphorus, and give light. Sculptures of winged bulls and bricks inscribed with arrow-head characters are ranged about the walls. A chain of elephant's bones covered with its hide contains the doctor, who is dressed as before in a long black robe covered with mysterious characters. On his head is a high conical cap of black silk dotted with gold stars. In his right hand is a wand of human teeth strung together, in his left a " book" of square palm-leaves bound in silver. At the back of the room is a black curtain completely veiling its second portion. This curtain is covered with cabalistic characters and terrifying images in white.*

[*Enter the servant of* HERMES, *a negro uglier than an ape. He is immensely long and lean; his body hangs forward, so that his arms nearly touch the ground. He is clad in a tightly fitting suit of scarlet, and wears a scarlet skull-cap. He makes deep obeisance.*]

HERMES. Speak, Hanuman!

HANUMAN.   A lady.

    [HERMES *nods gravely.* Exit HANUMAN.

HERMES.   Abaoth!

Abraxas! Pur! Pur! Aeou! Thoth!

    [*Enter the* LADY PSYCHE *with one attendant.*

ADONIS

Ee! Oo! Uu! Iao Sabaoth!
Dogs of Hell!
Mumble spell!
Up! Up! Up!
Sup! Sup! Sup!
U! Aoth!
Abaoth!
Abraoth!
Sabaoth!
Livid, loath,
Obey the oath!
Ah!   [*He shuts the book with a snap.*
You have come to me because you are crossed
In love.
PSYCHE.   Most true, sir!
HERMES.   Ah! you're Greek!
PSYCHE. As you yourself, sir.
HERMES.   Then I've lost
My pains.   I need not fear to speak.
I took you for a fool.   Ho! veil, divide!
         [HANUMAN *appears and lays his hand on a cord.*
Things are much pleasanter the other side.
[*The doctor throws off his cloak and cap, his straggling
    white hair and long pointed beard, appearing as a
    youth dressed fashionably; at the same time the
    curtain pulled back shows a room furnished with
    the luxury of a man of the world. A low balcony
    of marble at the back gives a view of the city, and
    of the Tigris winding far into the distance, where
    dim blue mountains rim the horizon.*]

THE EQUINOX

[*The doctor conducts his client to a lounge, where they sit.*

HERMES. Bring the old Chian, Hanuman!

[*The negro goes to obey.*

                                   This joke
Is the accepted way of scaring folk;
And if they're scared, they may find confidence
Which is half cure.   Most people have no sense.
If only they would sweat, and wash, eat slow,
Drink less, think more, the leech would starve or go.
But they prefer debauchery, disease,
Clysters, drugs, philtres, filth, and paying fees!
Now then, to business!

PSYCHE.   Tell me how you guessed
It was my heart that found itself distressed!

HERMES. I always sing a woman just that song;
In twenty years I've never once been wrong.
Seeing me thus marvellously wise,
Veneration follows on surprise:
Sometimes they will do what I advise!

PSYCHE. I see.   You have real knowledge.

HERMES. Not to be learnt at college!

PSYCHE. Good; you're my man.   I am come from Greece,
Where the Gods live and love us, sorrowing
For my lost husband.   I have found him here,
But with his memory gone, his mind distraught,
Living in luxury with a courtesan
(I could forgive him that if he knew me),
Filled with a blind unreasoning fear of what
Who knows?   He's haunted by a spectre king.

144

ADONIS

HERMES. Physicians must know everything:
   Half the night burn learning's candle,
   Half the day devote to scandal.
   Here's the mischief of the matter
   That I learn most from the latter!
   Yesterday I paid a visit
   To the fair . . . Astarte, is it?
   Saw the kitchen and the closet,
   Deduced diet from deposit,
   Saw where silkworm joined with swan
   To make a bed to sleep upon,
   Saw the crowd of cringing knaves
   That have made their masters slaves,
   Saw Astarte—diagnosed
   What had made him see a ghost!
PSYCHE. Can you cure him?
HERMES.   In my hurry
   (And a not unnatural worry
   At the name of lobster curry)
   I so far forgot my duty
   As to mention to the beauty
   What . . . well! here's the long and short
        of it!
   Just exactly what I thought of it.
   Tempests, by Oannes' fin!
PSYCHE. Sorry that he'd called you in?
HERMES. So much so that I'd a doubt
   If he wouldn't call me out!
PSYCHE. Then he will not hear your counsel?
HERMES. No; I bade him live on groundsel;

THE EQUINOX

But the little social friction
Interfered with the prescription.

PSYCHE. There's no hope, then?

HERMES.   Lend an ear!
We may rule him by his fear!
Somehow we may yet contrive
That he see the King, and live!
Have you influence?

PSYCHE.   At Court?
Plenty, in the last resort.
Letters from his suzerain!

HERMES. You are high in favour then?

PSYCHE. Ay, that needs not to be sworn;
I am his own daughter born.

HERMES. In thy blood the spark divine
Of Olympus?

PSYCHE.   Even in mine!

HERMES. Hark, then! At the Hour of Fears
When the lordly Lion rears
In mid-heaven his bulk of bane
Violently vivid, shakes his mane
Majestical, and Snake and Bull
Lamp the horizon, and the full
Fire of the moon tops heaven, and spurns
The stars, while Mars ruddily burns,
And Venus glows, and Jupiter
Ramps through the sky astride of her,
Then, unattended, let the King
Press on the little secret spring
That guards the garden, and entering

Lay once his hand upon him, even
While in the white arms of his heaven
He swoons to sleep.   That dreadful summons
From the wild witchery his woman's,
That shaft of shattering truth shall splinter
The pine of his soul's winter.
Then do thou following cry once
His name; as from eclipse the sun's
Supernal splendour springs, his sight
Shall leap to light.

PSYCHE.   Shall leap to light!
    Master, this wisdom how repay?

HERMES. I am sworn unto thy father—Nay!
    Weep not and kneel not!   See, mine art
    [*The two other handmaidens are seen standing by their
        fellow.*]
    Hath wrought such wonder in thine heart
    That—look!

PSYCHE.   Ah! Pistis, Elpis! how
    Are you here?   You were not with me now!
    You fled me.   Charis only came
    Through those dark dreams.

HERMES.   Farewell!   Proclaim
    For my reward my art's success.
    More than yourself need happiness.

PSYCHE. Farewell and prosper greatly!
                            [*She goes out with her maidens.*]

HERMES. And thou, live high and stately
    In glory and gree tenfold
    That which thou hadst of old!   [*He draws the curtain.*]

147

THE EQUINOX

SCENE IV: THE ANTECHAMBER OF THE KING'S PALACE. *It is a vast hall of black marble. At the corners four fountains play in basins of coloured marble. At the back a narrow door pillared by vast man-bulls in white marble.*

In mid-stage the LADY PSYCHE, *seated on the ground, her long hair unloosed, her robe of shining silver, mourns.*

With her are the three handmaidens bowed and mourning at front of the stage R., C., *and* L. *The aged women are grouped in front of stage* C., *on the steps which lead to the hall.*

No light comes save through the robes of the LADY PSYCHE *from the jewels that adorn her. Their glimmer is, however, such as to fill the hall with moony radiance, misty dim, and lost in the vastness of the building.*

PSYCHE. Silence grows hateful; hollow is mine heart
    Here in the fateful hall; I wait apart.
    Dimmer, still dimmer darkness veils my sight;
    There is no glimmer heralding the light.
    I, the King's daughter, am but serf and thrall
    Where Time hath wrought her cobweb in the hall.
    This blood avails not; where's the signet ring
    Whose puissance fails not to arouse the King?
    Heir of his heart, I am uncrowned; then, one
    That hath no art or craft in Babylon.
    I left my home and found a vassal's house—
    This lampless dome of death, vertiginous!
    O for the foam of billows that carouse
    About the crag-set columns! for the breeze

ADONIS

That fans their flagging Caryatides!
For the gemmed vestibule, the porch of pearl,
The bowers of rest, the silences that furl
Their wings upon mine amethystine chamber
Whose lions shone with emerald and amber!
O for the throne whereon my father's awe,
Lofty and lone, lets liberty love law!
All justice wrought, its sword the healer's knife!
All mercy, not less logical than life!
Alas! I wait a widowed suppliant
Betrayed to fate, blind trampling elephant.
I wait and mourn. Will not the dust disclose
The Unicorn, the Unicorn that goes
About the gardens of these halls of Spring,
First of the wardens that defend the King?
First flower of Spring, first maiden of the morn,
Wilt thou not bring me to the Unicorn?

[*The Unicorn passes over. He has the swiftness of the horse, the slimness of the deer, the whiteness of the swan, the horn of the narwhal. He couches upon the right side of the* LADY PSYCHE.]

Hail! thou that holdest thine appointed station,
Lordliest and boldest of his habitation,
Silence that foldest over its creation!

[*The Lion passes over. He is redder than the setting sun. He couches upon the left side of the* LADY PSYCHE.]

Hail! thou that art his ward and warrior,
The brazen heart, the iron pulse of war!
Up start, up start! and set thyself to roar!

THE EQUINOX

[*The Peacock passes over. This peacock is so great that his fan, as he spreads it on couching before the face of the* LADY PSYCHE, *fills the whole of the hall.*]

Hail! glory and light his majesty that hideth,
Pride and delight whereon his image rideth,
While in thick night and darkness he abideth!

[*The stage now darkens. Even the light shed by the jewels of the* LADY PSYCHE *is extinguished. Then, from the gate of the Palace between the man-bulls there issueth a golden hawk. In his beak is a jewel which he drops into the lamp that hangs from the height above the head of the* LADY PSYCHE. *This lamp remains dark. During this darkness the Unicorn, the Lion, and the Peacock disappear.*]

Love me and lead me through the blind abysses!
Fill me and feed me on the crowning kisses,
Like flowers that flicker in the garden of glory,
Pools of pure liquor like pale flames and hoary
That lamp the lightless empyrean! Ah! love me!
All space be sightless, and thine eyes above me!
Thrice burnt and branded on this bleeding brow,
Stamp thou the candid stigma—even now!

[*The lamp flashes forth into dazzling but momentary radiance. As it goes out a cone of white light is seen upon the head of* THE LADY PSYCHE, *and before her stands a figure of immense height cloaked and hooded in perfect blackness.*]

THE KING. Come! for the throne is hollow. The eagle hath cried:

Come away! The stars are numbered, and the tide

ADONIS

Turns.   Follow! Follow! Thine Adonis slumbered.
    As a bride
Adorned, come, follow!   Fate alone is fallen and wried.
Follow me, follow!   The unknown is satisfied.
[*The* LADY PSYCHE *is lifted to her feet.   In silence she
    bows, and in silence follows him as he turns and
    advances to the gate while the curtain falls.*]

SCENE V: THE GARDEN OF THE LADY ASTARTE.   THE LORD
    ESARHADDON *is lying on the couch with his mistress.
    Their arms are intertwined.   They and their slaves and
    maidens are all fallen into the abysses of deep sleep.
    It is a cloudless night; and the full moon, approaching
    mid-heaven, casts but the shortest shadows.*

The Murmur of the Breeze

I am the Breeze to bless the bowers,
Sigh through the trees, caress the flowers;
Each folded bud to sway, to swoon,
With its green blood beneath the moon
Stirred softly by my kiss; I bear
The soft reply of amber air
To the exhaled sighs of the heat
That dreams and dies amid the wheat,
From the cool breasts of mountains far—
Their serried crests clasp each a star!
The earth's pulse throbs with mighty rivers;
With her low sobs God's heaven quivers;

THE EQUINOX

The dew stands on her brow ; with love
She aches for all the abyss above,
Her rocks and chasms the lively strife
Of her sharp spasms of lust, of life.
Hark ! to the whisper of my fan,
My sister kiss to maid and man.
Through all earth's wombs, through all sea's waves,
Gigantic glooms, forgotten graves,
I haunt the tombs of kings and slaves.
I hush the babe, I wake the bird,
I wander away beyond stars unstirred,
Soften the ripples of the tide,
Soothe the bruised nipples of the bride,
Help stars and clouds play hide-and-seek,
Wind seamen's shrouds, bid ruins speak,
Bring dreams to slumber, sleep to dream
Whose demons cumber night's extreme.
And softer sped than dream or death
Quiet as the dead, or slain love's breath,
I sigh for loves that swoon upon
The hanging groves of Babylon.
Each terrace adds a shower of scent
Where lass and lad seduce content ;
Each vine that hangs confirms the stress
Of purer pangs of drunkenness ;
Each marble wall and pillar swerves
Majestical my course to curves
Subtle as breasts and limbs and tresses
Of this caressed suave sorceress's
That raves and rests in wildernesses

ADONIS

Whose giant gifts are strength that scars
Her soul and lifts her to the stars,
Savage, and tenderness that tunes
Her spirit's splendour to the moon's,
And music of passion to outrun
The fiery fashion of the sun.
Hush! there's a stir not mine amid the groves,
A foot divine that yet is not like love's.
Hush! let me furl my forehead! I'll be gone
To flicker and curl above great Babylon.

[*The Gate of the Garden opens.* THE LADY PSYCHE
advances and makes way for THE KING OF BABYLON.
*He is attended by many companies of warriors in
armour of burnished silver and gold, with swords,
spears, and shields.*

*These take up position at the back of the stage, in perfect
silence of foot as of throat.*]

[THE LADY PYSCHE *remains standing by the gate;* THE
KING OF BABYLON *advances with infinite stealth,
dignity, slowness, and power, toward the couch.*]

PSYCHE. Life? Is it life? What hour of fate is on the
bell?
Of this supreme ordeal what issue? Heaven or
hell?
I am stripped of all my power now when I need it
most;
I am empty and unreal, a shadow or a ghost.
All the great stake is thrown, even now the dice are
falling.
All deeds are locked in links, one to another calling

Through time: from the dim throne the first rune that
    was ree'd
By God, the supreme Sphinx, determined the last
    deed.

[THE KING OF BABYLON *reaches forth his hand and arm.
It is the hand and arm of a skeleton. He touches
the forehead of the sleeping lord. Instantly, radiant
and naked, a male figure is seen erect.*]

PSYCHE. Adonis!

ADONIS.   Psyche!

           [*They run together and embrace.*

PSYCHE.   Ah! long-lost!

ADONIS.   My wife!

Light, O intolerable! Infinite love! O life
Beyond death!

PSYCHE.   I have found thee!

ADONIS.   I was thine.

PSYCHE.   I thine

From all the ages!

ADONIS.   To the ages!

PSYCHE.   Mine!

          [*The* KING *passes over and departs.*

Chorus of Soldiers

Hail to the Lord!
Without a spear, without a sword
He hath smitten, he hath smitten, one stroke of his
Worth all our weaponed puissances.
There is no helm, no hauberk, no cuirass,
No shield of sevenfold steel and sevenfold brass

ADONIS

Resists his touch; no sword, no spear but shivers
Before his glance.   Eternally life quivers
And reels before him; death itself, the hound of God,
Slinks at his heel, and licks the dust that he hath trod.
                              [*They follow their Lord, singing.*

PSYCHE. I am a dewdrop focussing the sun
    That fires the forest to the horizon.
    I am a cloud on whom the sun begets
    The iris arch, a fountain in whose jets
    Throbs inner fire of the earth's heart, a flower
    Slain by the sweetness of the summer shower.

ADONIS. I am myself, knowing I am thou.
    Forgetfulness forgotten now!
    Truth, truth primeval, truth eternal,
    Unconditioned, sempiternal,
    Sets the God within the shrine
    And my mouth on thine, on thine.

[THE LADY ASTARTE *wakes.   In her arms is the corpse of*
    the LORD ESARHADDON.]

ASTARTE. O fearful dreams! Awake and kiss me! Awake!
    I thought I was crushed and strangled by a snake.
                              [*She rises.   The corpse falls.*

    He is dead!   He is dead!   O lips of burning bloom,
    You are ashen.   [*The jaw falls.*

                The black laughter of the tomb!
    Then let me kill myself!   Bring death distilled
    From nightshade, monkshood.   Let no dawn regild
    This night.   Let me not see the damnèd light
    Of day, but drown in this black-hearted night!
    Ho, slaves!   [ADONIS *and* PSYCHE *advance to her.*

155

ADONIS. Thyself a slave! What curse (unbated
Till patient earth herself is nauseated)
Is worse than this, an handmaiden that creeps
Into her mistress' bed while her lord sleeps,
And robs her?

ASTARTE. And what worse calamity
Than his revenge? But leave me, let me die!
[*She falls prone at their feet.*

PSYCHE. Add robbery to robbery! We need thee
To serve us. Let us raise thee up and feed thee,
Comfort and cherish thee until the end,
Less slave than child, less servitor than friend.

ADONIS. Rise! let the breath flow, let the lips affirm
Fealty and love. To the appointed term
Within thy garden as belovèd guests
Of thine, let us abide. Now lips and breasts
Touching, three bodies and one soul, the triple troth
Confirm.

PSYCHE. The great indissoluble oath!

ASTARTE. Lift me! [*They raise her; all embrace.*
By him that ever reigns upon
The throne, and wears the crown, of Babylon,
I serve, and love.

PSYCHE. This kiss confirm it!

ADONIS. This!

ASTARTE. I have gained all in losing all. Now kiss
Once more with arms linked!

ADONIS. The dawn breaks!

ASTARTE. Behold
Love's blush!

156

ADONIS

PSYCHE.   Light's breaking!

ADONIS.   Life's great globe of gold!

ASTARTE. Come! let us break our fast.

PSYCHE.   My long fast's broken.

ADONIS. Let us talk of love.

PSYCHE.   Love's first-last word is spoken.

ADONIS. Nay! but the tides of trouble are transcended.
   The word's begun, but never shall be ended.
   And though the sun forsake the maiden east,
   Life be for us a never-fading feast.
                    [*They go towards the house, singing.*

ALL. The crown of our life is our love,
   The crown of our love is the light
   That rules all the region above
   The night and the stars of the night;
   That rules all the region aright,
   The abyss to abysses above;
   For the crown of our love is the light,
   And the crown of our light is our love.

THE GHOULS

CROQUIS DE CROQUE-MITAINE

PAR

ALEISTER CROWLEY

To Gwendolen Otter

PERSONS OF THE PLAY

STANISLAS WASKA, *a virtuoso*
FENELLA LOVELL, *his pupil, a gipsy girl*
M'PHERSON, *the doctor at Foyers*
An Undertaker
THE M'ALISTER, *laird of Boleskine and heritor of the burying-ground*
GEORGE FOSTER, *Fenella's lover*

THE GHOULS

SCENE I : *A bedroom in the hotel at Foyers. A large open window gives on Loch Ness and Meallfavournie, ablaze in the sun. In the bed lies Waska, propped with pillows, his face a ghastly ochre. He is absolutely bald and hairless ; all his teeth are gone but the unnaturally long fangs of his canines. By the bed are medicine-bottles on a small table, and on the bed close to his hands, which lie like claws upon the sheets, is his violin-case.*

Over him bends the doctor, a red, burly Scot. By the window stands Fenella, fantastically dressed in red, yellow, and blue, her black hair wreathed with flowers. She is slight, thin, with very short skirts, her spider legs encased in pale blue stockings. Her golden shoes with their exaggerated heels have paste buckles. In her pale face her round black eyes blaze. She is rouged and powdered; her thin lips are painted heavily. Her shoulder-bones stare from her low-necked dress, and a diamond dog-collar clasps her shining throat. She is about seventeen years old. She is standing by a pot of blue china containing a hydrangea, tearing at the blossoms in her nervousness.

THE DOCTOR [*rising and addressing her*]. There is very little likelihood of his regaining consciousness.

FENELLA. He's done for, then?

M'PHERSON. Both lungs gone. I don't know how he's lived this last month.

FENELLA. Oh, he's a tough one. [*Lowering her voice.*] You know, they say he's sold his soul to the devil.

M'PHERSON. If he has, the bill's overdue.

FENELLA. When will he die?

M'PHERSON. One can't say exactly. Maybe an hour, maybe less. Or he might last till morning.

FENELLA. How can I tell?

M'PHERSON. You can't tell. I'll look in again in an hour. I'm off to the laird's; his leddy's near her time. I'll look in as I pass.

FENELLA. All right. I'll wire for the undertaker to come down from Inverness by the afternoon boat.

M'PHERSON. But, Good God! the man isn't dead.

FENELLA. But you say he will be by morning!

M'PHERSON. Anyhow you needn't trouble. He's in the hotel now; he came down this morning for old Mrs Fraser of Stratherrick.

FENELLA. All right. I'll talk to him. [*The doctor goes.*] In an hour's time, then. I hope you'll have something more definite to say—why can't I get into the sunshine? I haven't been out for three days.

M'PHERSON [*at the door*]. Well, you wouldn't have a nurse.

FENELLA. No, I wouldn't. He's my master: I'll never leave him till he's dead. How do I know what she'd do?

M'PHERSON. In an hour then. Good day.

[*He goes out and closes door.*

THE GHOULS

FENELLA [*crying after him*]. Send that undertaker up if you see him! [*Alone, walking up and down the room nervously.*] I wish I dared touch the Strad! But he's not dead yet. I could finish him if I knew how.

FENELLA. [*Goes to window, and whistles. An answering whistle.* FENELLA *leans out.*] It's all right, George, I hope. The doctor says it will be over in an hour, or at latest, by morning. You shall lie in my arms all night. I'll drive you mad. I'll play on the Strad at last. You shall die, dear. Do you love me? . . . Yes, I know. O! I can see it in your eyes. To-night, then. Or to-morrow and for ever! Will you take me to Paris? I should like to live on Montmartre, and set the city on fire while I played, as Nero did. What an orchestra, the roaring flames!

WASKA [*sitting up in bed*]. What the devil are you doing, Fenella? Who are you talking to?

FENELLA. I was talking to myself, master. You haven't been very good company, lately.

WASKA. Ah, you spiteful little beast! If you'd been kind to me I would never have been ill.

FENELLA. I've nursed you.

WASKA. You've stolen my life, damn you, you vampire!

FENELLA. Rubbish!

WASKA. Yes; but I've been with the devil.

FENELLA. What's that?

WASKA. He's given me back my youth and strength.

FENELLA. For what price? What have you to give?

WASKA. Ah yes! I sold my soul for my art. I am to play duets with Paganini in hell. But I've a new trick. I'm to

163

have you for fifty years, and to find new ways to torture your soul for his pleasure.

FENELLA. You devil ! But I'm Christ's ; you can't touch me. I'm a virgin ! I'm a virgin ! He'll save me from you.

WASKA. U ! Hu ! Hu ! you Christ's ! I spit !

FENELLA. Yes ; you shall roast ; I can see your flesh burning and blackening, and smell the stink of it. For ever ! For ever ! Ha ! Ha ! Ha !

WASKA. Ah ! I've my strength back. You shall come to my bed to-night, Fenella.

FENELLA. Faugh !

WASKA. I've the power at last. You ungrateful little wild-cat ! Didn't I pick you out of the gutter, and care for you like my own flesh and blood ? Didn't I dress you fine, and teach you to dance and play ?

FENELLA. You never let me touch the Strad.

WASKA. No ; and you never shall. It's the devil's Strad ; you shan't touch it. Now, dance for me !

FENELLA. I won't.

WASKA. You will. If you don't, I'll put a curse on you ! I'll twist your spider-legs with rheumatism !

FENELLA. All right : I'll dance.

[*She dances lightly and gracefully for him. He claps his hands for the time.*]

WASKA. Bravo ! Bravo ! But put passion into it. You've got to love me now.

FENELLA. Love you ! Love a corpse ! Love a wrinkled, haggard, toothless old wolf. Filth ! Filth ! If you had sense enough to know what your own bed was like—this last month.

164

WASKA. You'll sleep in it to-night.   I'll get a child on you to-night!   An imp!   A monster!   A thing with horns and hoofs!

FENELLA. You'll die to-night!   Your pact's up.   Die, stink, rot, you rag!   And all the sulphur of hell will never fumigate your soul.

WASKA. I'll beat you for this.   Bring me the whip!

FENELLA. Your dog-whip days are done.   [*She finds the whip.*]   Take that!   [*She lashes him across the face.   No blood follows the blow.*]   See!   you've no strength.

[*She gives him a little push.   He falls back on the pillow, gasping.*]

WASKA. Now hear me curse you!   [*A knock at the door.*]

FENELLA [*excitedly*]. Come in!

[*The undertaker, hat in hand, comes cringing in.*]

UNDERTAKER. Good evening, miss.   I heard you were wanting to see me.

FENELLA. Yes, measure this corpse.

UNDERTAKER. Why, miss, the man's not dead.

FENELLA. He will be to-night.

UNDERTAKER. I'll come again, miss, when I hear from the doctor.   [*He turns to go.*]

WASKA [*rising*]. Yes!   it's true, you!   But mark me, you can make no boards tough enough nor clamps of steel to hold me!   There's no grave deep enough to bury me, no earth that will lie on me.   I'm the devil's fiddler, Mr Undertaker! Now am I afraid, or are you?

UNDERTAKER. I see he's not in his right mind, miss. Consumptives is often like that at the last.   [*He goes out.*]

WASKA. It's true, Fenella, I'm dying.   I lied to you.

Now come here! D'ye see, I'm tired of my bargain. I'm afraid of hell. Look you, here's my plan. You'll bury the Strad with me, and maybe, when the trumpet sounds, if I play the "Messiah," Christ'll hear me, and take me up to heaven. There's not many fiddlers like me either in heaven or on earth. Paganini's in hell; you can hear it in his music; he's writhing and roasting in hell, I say. Shouldn't that be enough for Master Satan?

FENELLA. I don't care where you are, so long as you're out of here. The Strad's mine, you promised it to me. You swore it on the holy cross!

WASKA. Only if you slept with me. I'm not to be cheated. I'm not the one to give something for nothing, damn you for a greedy, heartless wench.

FENELLA. Damn you! Before you're cold I'll play your dirge on it; and it shall sound like a wedding march.

WASKA. Oh no! you won't! Come closer! [*She obeys.*] Here, you've never seen this. [*He takes a little wooden cross from under the pillow.*] It's the wood of the True Cross! Now swear, or I'll curse you! Take it in your hand! Say it after me.

[*She takes the cross and repeats the oath after him.*

I, Fenella Lovell, the gipsy, swear by my soul's salvation and by the blessed wood of the holy rood, to bury my master's violin with him—don't falter, damn you!—and if I don't, may Christ spit me out, Christ spit me out, and may I fall into hell and be roasted for ever by devils with pitchforks, Amen! And on earth may my hair fall out, and my eyes rot in my head, and the lupus eat my nose, and the cancer eat my tongue, and my throat be twisted, and my lungs wither away, and my heart be torn out, and my liver be eaten by worms, and my bowels be thrown to the dogs. May my skin be white with the leprosy, and my blood corrupted with the plague, and my bones rotted with the pox; so hear me, blessed Christ, Amen ! [FENELLA *falls fainting.*

She won't dare now !

[*A knock at the door.* M'PHERSON *follows it.*

Now, doctor, I'm your man !

[*He falls back on the pillows. The doctor rushes forward, and makes his examination.*]

M'PHERSON. Dead this time, and no error ! Come, Miss Lovell, bear up ! [*He lifts* FENELLA.

FENELLA. Dead, did you say ?

M'PHERSON. I'm sorry to say so.

FENELLA. O, if it had only come ten minutes earlier ! . . . Go ! Leave me ! Send the people to do what must be done !

M'PHERSON. I'm thinking you'd be the better for a doze of physic yourself.

FENELLA. Do you think the priest can take off dead men's curses ?

M'PHERSON. I'm afraid that's hardly in my line. But I'll send for a priest from Fort Augustus. I suppose he was a Catholic ?

FENELLA. He was a devil from hell. Oh go ! Go ! Leave me to horror and to fear. I could kiss death : it's life I shrink from. Go ! Please go !

M'PHERSON. It's the kindest thing I can do. But I'll look in later. [*He goes out.*

FENELLA. Bury it with him ! Oh, if I dared once touch it,

167

I'd dare steal it. But I can't. It's too horrible. They say there are folk who don't fear curses. If I could sell my soul as he did—but how shall I get the devil to hear me? There's a way. But I don't know it. Bury it with him? And—oh! blessed God! thou hast saved me—I see! I see!

[*She runs to the window.*

George! George! He's dead—come up! I've something to tell you. Quick!

[*She dances to the door and impatiently flings it open.* GEORGE FOSTER *comes running up the stairs. He is a sturdy youth with a fat face, long blonde hair, and dull eyes. She throws her arms round him and covers him with kisses and bites.*]

GEORGE. Don't, Fenella darling! You hurt!

FENELLA. The old devil's done for. I'm yours! And the Strad's mine, if you're brave! Oh! kiss me! kiss me! kiss me!

GEORGE. Ought we to make love when he's lying dead?

FENELLA. Oh, your oughts! Did your nurse never tell you that ought stands for nothing?

GEORGE. Anyhow, I don't like it.

FENELLA. He's dead! Can a dead man see and hear? Look! I spit in the filthy face—does he whip me as he used, and curse me? Ah, but he cursed me! And that's where you must help.

GEORGE. I'll help you in anything.

FENELLA. It's a dreadful thing! But you can win me!

GEORGE. I won you long ago.

FENELLA. Not that much! [*She flicks her fingers.*] But if you'll get the Strad for me, I'm yours for ever!

168

GEORGE. Then we'll take it.

FENELLA. O! but I've sworn to bury it with him.

GEORGE. Get the priest to absolve you. I suppose he forced you to swear.

FENELLA. Oh no! I swore it on the wood of the True Cross. But I didn't swear not to get it afterwards!

GEORGE. Get it afterwards?

FENELLA. Yes; dig him up and take it!

GEORGE. O! I couldn't. It's too horrible. You mustn't ask me to do a thing like that.

FENELLA. Well, then, I'll get someone else.

GEORGE. No! I'll do it.

FENELLA. Swear to me!

GEORGE. By the body of Christ, I'll do it.

FENELLA. Then kiss me! Come, where he can see us!

GEORGE. He can't see us. He's dead.

FENELLA. His soul can see.

GEORGE. Those filthy eyes of his glare like a devil's still.

FENELLA. Kiss me! Then we'll put pennies on them. [*She does so.*] That horrible dropped jaw looks as if he were laughing. He used always to laugh hollow, like curses ringing and echoing in the dome of hell.

GEORGE. Let's tie it up with a handkerchief! [*A knock.*

FENELLA. Come in! [*Enter the* UNDERTAKER *as before.*

UNDERTAKER. Pardon, miss, the doctor told me as how the angel 'ad passed.

FENELLA. Yes: he's dead. Measure him. That violin has to be buried with him. He was always afraid of being buried alive; make a very thin shell, so that it can be opened easily.

UNDERTAKER. Right, miss. I'll finish it with short nails. If he was to struggle, it'd come open easy.

FENELLA. Just what I want.

UNDERTAKER. Pardon, miss, but I hope he died easy.

FENELLA. It's never very difficult, is it? I think there are only three people in history who failed at it.

UNDERTAKER. O, miss, I meant right with his Maker.

FENELLA. He was a good Catholic, and believed in the resurrection of the body. So do I. Now we'll leave you to your work.

[*She takes* GEORGE'S *arm, and runs off with him down stairs.*]

UNDERTAKER. A precious old 'un, and by the looks of him a precious bad 'un.

CURTAIN.

THE GHOULS

SCENE II: *The Burying-ground at Boleskine. It is very ancient; the walls are lined with tombs whose tablets have been scarred by bullets. At the back, in mid-stage, is a little tower with a window, intended for a watcher in the days when body-snatching was common. There are many tombs and stones; bones lie here and there, for the digging of every fresh grave disinters several dead.*

It is entered by a wooden grate between square stone pillars on the left, near front of stage. It being the height of summer in the northern Highlands, it is fairly light, although cloudy and moonless.

Near the centre is the fresh tomb of Stanislas Waska, loose earth piled into a mound. The foot of the mound faces the footlights. The gate is opened by FENELLA, *fearfully advancing, followed by* GEORGE *with a spade.*

They tip-toe in silence to the new grave, then stop and listen.

FENELLA. All right. Get along. Every second increases the danger.

GEORGE. I'll work; you listen.

> [*He sets to work to shovel away the loose earth.*

FENELLA. I can hear half way to Foyers on the road.

GEORGE. Yes; you have perfect ears.

FENELLA. No nonsense now. Don't strike the spade in like that; you'll wake the county.

> [*The howl of a bull-dog, exactly like the crying of a child, is heard far off.*]

GEORGE. All right. It's only that damned dog of M'Alister's. He does it every night.

FENELLA. He sees the ghost of old Lord Lovat.

171

THE EQUINOX

GEORGE. Old Lord Lovat?

FENELLA. Yes; they beheaded him after the '45. He rolls his head up and down the corridors.

GEORGE. Pleasant pastime!

FENELLA. What else is a man to do?

GEORGE. What's that tapping? [*He stops to listen.*

FENELLA. Go on! It's only the old woman.

GEORGE. What old woman?

FENELLA. Her son was a lunatic. They let him out cured, as they thought. His mother came up here with him to lay flowers on his father's grave; and he caught her legs and smashed her brains against the wall.

GEORGE. Oh damn it!

FENELLA. You baby! So ever since she comes from time to time to try and pick her brains off the wall.

GEORGE. I'm damned if I like this job. Here, hang the fiddle; let's get out.

FENELLA. The last you'll see of me if you do. There, you're nearly through with the first bit. Hullo! there's a cart.

GEORGE. By God, yes. It's coming this way.

FENELLA. They're bound to see us. Come along; we'll hide in the lookout.

> [*They go up stage and enter the narrow door of the tower. The noise of the cart increases. By and by one distinguishes two drunken voices singing " We are na fou'." They grow very loud and die away again.*
>
> [*Re-enter* FENELLA *and* GEORGE.

GEORGE. That's better. I don't mind carts and Scotchmen. It's your ghosts I'm afraid of.

FENELLA. Get on, then! [*He sets to work again.*

THE GHOULS

FENELLA [*sings in a low voice*]—
  The ghost is chilly in his shroud :—
   Laugh aloud ! Laugh aloud !
  His bones are rattling in the wind ;
   His teeth are chattering with the cold ;
  For he is dead, and out of mind,
   And oh ! so cold !

  He walks and walks and wraps his shroud
   (Laugh aloud ! Laugh aloud !)
  Around his bones. He shivers and glares,
   For hell is in his heart stone-cold—
  What is the use of spells and prayers
   To one so cold ?

  The dogs howl when they scent his shroud.
   Laugh aloud ! Laugh aloud !
  The village lads and lasses feel
   A breath of bitter wind and cold
  Blow from those bones of ice and steel
   So cold ! So cold !

GEORGE. My God, Fenella, I think you want to drive me mad.

FENELLA. Not here, dear. Come, there's nobody about. You may kiss me, for there's the wood of the coffin.

GEORGE. O don't let us lose time !

FENELLA. No ! I'll keep time.

[*She dances fantastically to the rhythm of his shovelling.*]

THE EQUINOX

GEORGE. Don't. You've got all my nerves on edge. What's that? [*He starts violently.*

FENELLA. A nerve, I suppose. Come now. I'll take this end.

[*They lift out the coffin. She produces a chisel.*
And now to crack the nut! Good old undertaker! He's done his job beautifully.

[*The lid of the coffin comes off; they set it aside.*
GEORGE. And there's the Strad for my darling!

[*He gives her the violin, and kisses her.*
FENELLA. Ah! my beauty, my beauty! Mine at last. Don't kiss me, you fool! It's the Strad that I love, not you. Put the lid back quick! We'll be off!

GEORGE. So that's the thanks I get, curse you, is it? I've a jolly good mind to smash the beastly thing.

FENELLA. You dare! Don't be a fool, George! All my love when we're back safely. Take the lid!

[*A whistle is heard, off.*
. . . Oh, my God! . . .

[*A cry off: " Heel, Shiva, heel!"*
GEORGE. It's the M'Alister with his cursed bloodhounds! What does he want at this time o' night?

FENELLA. Oh, he's as mad as a March Hare!

GEORGE. He's the heritor of the graveyard. If he comes, we're done for! Oh God! Oh God! What shall we do?

FENELLA. Do? Why, tell him the whole story. He's a good chap and an artist. He'll understand that you can't bury the third best Strad in the world! And, besides, I'll make love to him.

GEORGE. You treacherous whore!

174

FENELLA. Always a gentleman! I tell you what, my friend. I'm my own mistress now, and tired of being yours.

GEORGE. I wish I'd cut my hand off rather than helped you.

FENELLA. Cut your stupidity off, and your talk. Here's the laird on the road now.

[THE M'ALISTER *appears leaning on the fence.*

THE M'ALISTER. Hullo! what are you doing in my grave-yard, young lady?

FENELLA. Digging up a corpse. . . . Why, it's the M'Alister!

THE M'ALISTER. Yes. Isn't that Miss Lovell? Fine night, isn't it? I suppose you don't want any help? All right.

GEORGE. O thank you, sir. Thank you, sir.

FENELLA. Never mind my poor friend: he's not used to this sort of thing—shut up, will you, you fool! May I come up to tea to-morrow?

THE M'ALISTER. Oh, come to lunch, and we'll try for a rabbit afterwards. Good night! One o'clock. Er — this ghoul act, you know! I should hurry over the meal; there may be all sorts of asses about.

FENELLA. Thanks so much. Good night. Get on, George.

[THE M'ALISTER *goes off.*

You idiot! You nearly spoilt everything.

GEORGE. It's all right.

FENELLA. Yes, no thanks to you! Get on with the work.

[*Loud laughter, off, distant.*

Lord, there's fools abroad! Workmen from Foyers, I should think. [*Points off,* L.] And, yes, there's folk from

Inverfarigaig, too. [*Points off*, R.] I can hear them talking —religion, of all things!

GEORGE. We're caught like rats in a trap! Let's get into the tower!

FENELLA. And leave the body there? We've no time. Blessed Saints of God! I have it. What a fool you are! They're not fond of the road just here, the best of times. I'll try the first kisses of my beauty [*she reaches for the violin*]. —if that doesn't frighten them, I'm a Dutchman!

GEORGE. Oh how clever you are!

FENELLA. Even if they come and see us, they'll think we're devils.

GEORGE. So you are, Fenella!

[*She has taken the violin from its case and begins to play.
In a few moments two bearded men enter* R. *and look
over the wall.*]

THE MEN. Lord, save us! [*They flee in terror.*

FENELLA. Saved! The only thing now is the Foyers men : they may be too drunk to be afraid!

[*She plays again, a wilder melody. Both she and* GEORGE
lose themselves in the beauty of the music. STANISLAS
WASKA *suddenly sits up in his coffin, and tears off the
wrappings. A horrible grin distorts his face, and
with a choking roar he leaps at* GEORGE, *catching him
by the throat.*]

WASKA. Go on, Fenella! You were worthy of the Strad, after all.

[*She shrieks and drops the fiddle.* GEORGE *goes limp,
strangled.*]

I've killed your lover, my fine virgin. I heard every word

you said, I watched every filthy kiss till you put the pennies on my eyes. The devil told the truth after all.

[FENELLA, *breaking from her stupor, starts to flee,* WASKA *stumbles to his feet, roaring, and chases her among the tombs. She trips and falls. He catches her up and carries her to the tower. They disappear.*]

Stop your shrieking, harlot! You'll only drive the folk away! Ah! we'll have a fine new story of Boleskine graveyard.

Satan! Satan! Satan! I thank thee! Thou hast kept thy word and I'll keep mine!

Satan! Satan! Satan! Oh, the bliss! Fenella, mine, mine! Fenella!

[*He thrusts the corpse of* FENELLA *half through the window, where it hangs limp.*]

Mine she was, by God, though I'm dead this hour!

[*He comes out, staggering, falls over a mound, crawls on hands and knees to his grave.*]

Satan! what a morsel! what a bonne bouche! What a savoury to wind up life's feast!

Well, here's my coffin. There's no place like home. I must play my own dirge.   [*He seats himself in it.*

[*He takes the violin, and plays a dirge.*

This time it's the real thing. No play, no pay. I've had my fun, and here's the price of it.   [*He plays again.*

And now Good night.

[*Clasping the fiddle to his breast, he lies down in the coffin. Silence; then the death-rattle.* WASKA *half rises, and falls dead. A pause.*]

[*Enter* THE M'ALISTER, *at the gate.*

VII   M   177

THE EQUINOX

THE M'ALISTER. Too much shrieking and fiddling from my pretty little ghoul.   I wonder what's happened.

[*He enters the graveyard, and approaches the grave.*
Nobody here!   Who's that?

[*Bends over the corpse of* GEORGE, *and examines it.*
Why, you're dead, my poor, putrid poopstick.   Died of too much brains—I don't think.   [*Goes up stage to tower.*
Good God!   Fenella!   What are you doing there?

[*He takes her hand.*
Dead, too.   Died of too much—temperament, I'm betting.
Well, there's nothing alive here but the fiddle.

I'll follow my usual rule and obey the Scriptural injunction to let the dead bury their dead.   But I'm heritor of this graveyard, and I think I'll inherit this fiddle.

[*He packs it into its case, tucks it under his arm, and goes out.*]

All right, Shiva!   Nothing the matter!   Home, boy!

[*He starts to whistle a jig.*

CURTAIN

178

THE FOUR WINDS

THE South wind said to the palms :
My lovers sing me psalms ;
But are they as warm as those
That Laylah's lover knows ?

The North wind said to the firs :
I have my worshippers ;
But are they as keen as hers ?

The East wind said to the cedars :
My friends are no seceders ;
But is their faith to me
As firm as his faith must be ?

The West wind said to the yews :
My children are pure as dews ;
But what of her lover's muse ?

So to spite the summer weather
The four winds howled together.

But a great Voice from above
Cried : What do you know of love ?

Do you think all Nature worth
The littlest life upon earth ?

THE EQUINOX

I made the germ and the ant,
The tiger and elephant.

In the least of these there is more
Than your elemental war.

And the lovers whom ye slight
Are precious in my sight.

Peace to your mischief-brewing !
I love to watch their wooing.

Of all this Laylah heard
Never a word.

She lay beneath the trees
With her lover at her knees.

He sang of God above
And of love.

She lay at his side
Well satisfied,

And at set of sun
They were one.

Before they slept her pure smile curled ;
" God bless all lovers in the World ! "

And so say I the self-same word ;
Nor doubt God heard.

INDEPENDENCE

Come to my arms—is it eve? is it morn?
Is Apollo awake?   Is Diana reborn?
Are the streams in full song?   Do the woods whisper hush
Is it the nightingale?   Is it the thrush?
Is it the smile of the autumn, the blush
Of the spring?   Is the world full of peace or alarms?
Come to my arms, Laylah, come to my arms!

Come to my arms, though the hurricane blow.
Thunder and summer, or winter and snow,
It is one to us, one, while our spirits are curled
In the crimson caress: we are fond, we are furled
Like lilies away from the war of the world.
Are there spells beyond ours?   Are there alien charms?
Come to my arms, Laylah, come to my arms!

Come to my arms! is it life? is it death?
Is not all immortality born of your breath?
Are not heaven and hell but as handmaids of yours
Who are all that enflames, who are all that allures,
Who are all that destroys, who are all that endures?
I am yours, do I care if it heals me or harms?
Come to my arms, Laylah, come to my arms!

SNOWSTORM

A TRAGEDY

BY

ALEISTER CROWLEY

PERSONS REPRESENTED IN THE PROLOGUE

HERMANN, *an Old Woodcutter*
GRIZEL, *his Wife*
DANIEL, *Groom in the Stables of* ERIK, *Prince of Fiordland*

SNOWSTORM

PROLOGUE

*The scene represents the cottage of the woodcutter. It is
surrounded by an infinity of pine trees, giving an impression of great dreariness and monotony. The cottage,
on the contrary, is extremely cheerful, almost gay.
Loving care has been employed to decorate it and to keep
it excellently tidy. There is only a very small clearing
about the cottage, and a natural path through the wood.*
The daylight is slowly fading throughout the scene.
*Enter by the path the woodcutter and his wife, whose names
are* HERMANN *and* GRIZEL. *They carry heavy loads of
wood.*

HERMANN. Terrible hard times. The days and the ways
get longer, and the wood harder to cut, and harder to sell.

GRIZEL. Ay. But the fowls do well. And they do say
the Prince may come to the lodge again soon.

HERMANN. For a day or two. What's that?

GRIZEL. And then there's always George.

HERMANN. Yes; he's head waiter now.

GRIZEL. I mistrusted the lad's going to the big town.
Terrible dangerous are those cities for an honest boy.

HERMANN. Oh! he's a good lad. He's doing well.

GRIZEL. He will soon have a beer-house of his own.

HERMANN. Ah! that's as may be.

[*They throw down their wood by the door of the cottage.*

GRIZEL. He's our own good lad.

[*She goes in and busies herself with the fire, etc.*

HERMANN. What's for supper to-night, lass?

GRIZEL. Peas and bacon. And some of the beer George sent us.

HERMANN. Good! Good! . . . .

It's a hard life, lass, woodcutting. Do you mind the day we wed?

GRIZEL. Nigh thirty years ago. Ye were going to be the Prince's Forester, I mind.

HERMANN. Ah, youth! Life is harder than our dreams tell us.

GRIZEL. That's you men. You must always be dreaming. Cowards, I call you.

HERMANN. No, lass, I see the hardness of life just as much as you do. There's only one thing good enough to take us through it. And that's love.

GRIZEL. Ay, lad.

HERMANN. We've never fallen out, lass?

GRIZEL. I mind the first day ye laid the shaft of the big axe to my back.

HERMANN. Summer lightning, lass. I gave ye no more than ye deserved.

GRIZEL. Ah!

HERMANN. To dance with a low blacksmith! Damn ye, ye were aye a forward wench.

186

SNOWSTORM

GRIZEL. And what of the fair at Stormwald last month?
[She lights the lamp in the cottage.

HERMANN. Ay, in Stormwald the girls are fine.

GRIZEL. If I did clout ye with the fire-shovel, ye deserved it.

HERMANN. No harm, lass, no harm if the girls of Stormwald know a proper man.

GRIZEL. Bah! ye white-headed old sinner. Do ye think I'm afraid of them? And you no better than (*she comes out of the cottage*) this old bundle of wood. Drybones!

HERMANN. We've been happy, lass.
[She sits on the bundle of wood by his side.

GRIZEL. Ay, lad, love's all in life.

HERMANN. It's something to look back on, now that the twilight gathers.

GRIZEL. With you, lad, I don't fear the dark.

HERMANN. George is a fine boy.

GRIZEL. If only Gretel had not died.

HERMANN. God knows best, dear lass!

GRIZEL. Ay, God knows best. But I wish he wouldn't interfere.

HERMANN. Lass! Lass!

GRIZEL. Ye don't understand. A man's aye ready with his God. A wife cares naught for God or for her man, but only for her bairns.   *[HERMANN is beginning to weep.*

It's good you can weep still. You had a true heart, a woman's heart. Ye old fool!
[She brushes away her own tears.

HERMANN. Always my own goodwife! Hark! There's a horse in the forest.

GRIZEL. Some fool of a forester.

HERMANN. A forester wouldn't come here at this time o' night.

GRIZEL. Here he is, whoever it is.

[*A voice off.* "*Hillo—ho! Goodman woodcutter, do you live underground?*"]

HERMANN (*calling*). Take the path to your left. Tie up your horse at the turning.

GRIZEL. What did I tell you? The prince is coming to the lodge and we shall sell all our wood!

HERMANN. I hope we may. . . . Here he comes. You're right, maybe. It's the prince's livery.   [*Enter* DANIEL.

DANIEL. Tum-ti-um-ti-um-tum! Good day and be damned to you, goodman!

HERMANN. Fine day, sir. What d'ye want?

DANIEL. Logs, wooden-head! Great, fat, roaring pine-logs, oozing with sap! Logs, by God, and ho! for the bonny winter!

HERMANN. Ay! so the Prince is come hunting.

DANIEL. No, you old rascal. Mind your own business! Do you think I am the trusted confidant of His Highness through blabbing his affairs?

HERMANN. Beg pardon, Excellency! I mistook your Excellency for that damned, cheating groom, Daniel.

DANIEL. You old ruffian! Well, shut your head, and bring the logs up.

HERMANN. When?

DANIEL. Now.

HERMANN. All right. (*Calls.*) Wife, shoulder the biggest bundle of logs up to the lodge.

188

SNOWSTORM

GRIZEL (*within*). All right.

HERMANN. And what's the news of the Court?

DANIEL. Nothing beyond the usual, goodman. The Princess is so-so—so-so. The Duke left last week. We've been dull, dull.

HERMANN. And what's the madcap Prince been up to?

DANIEL. Our good Prince is busied as ever with the high cares of the Fatherland.

GRIZEL. Nasty, tricky, little beast, I think I do! Always after the girls.

DANIEL. Insolent woman! His Highness is devoted as ever to the Princess Maud.

GRIZEL. None of your theatre girls, all legs, oh no!

HERMANN. Hold your scolding tongue, woman! Get the gentleman a glass of beer!

[*She puts down the load and goes in.*

DANIEL. Thanks, good man. Well, between ourselves, man and man, I don't mind telling you, there's a fair old how-d'ye-do.

HERMANN. Ah! I thought that now.

DANIEL. A real jamboree! A good old buster!

HERMANN. Ha! Ha!

DANIEL. That's really what we're here for. I'm telling you. Oh yes, I'm telling you! Lord God Almighty! It's a rare old jinkytoodleray!

HERMANN. Ha! Ha! Ha! Ha!

DANIEL. Three weeks ago we were on horseback.

HERMANN. Ay!

DANIEL. Outside the Opera.

HERMANN. Ho!

DANIEL. In a dark little street off the Axelstrade.

HERMANN. Hillo-ho!

DANIEL. Masked.

HERMANN. Whew!

DANIEL. Jee! Armed.

HERMANN. Armed!

DANIEL. To the teeth.

HERMANN. Whew.

DANIEL. With a led horse.

HERMANN. He! He!

DANIEL. And we stopped the carriage of pretty Nerissa Wadlstern, and kidnapped her — What d'ye think o' that?

HERMANN. Ye gay young devils! Well, I've done as much myself in my day.

DANIEL. So we dragged her off screaming, and have been keeping out of the way ever since. Oh! I tell you she was a tigress; but he made her love him, somehow. So we're coming back into society. A month's hunting at the Lodge here, for the first step.

[*Enter* GRIZEL *with the beer. They all drink.*

HERMANN. And what does the Princess say to it?

DANIEL. Haven't heard. But I suppose she's about crazy mad.

GRIZEL. So she might be, with her waster of a husband.

HERMANN. Oh! he's a good Prince. But perhaps his wife's a Tartar like some I know!

DANIEL. Here, none of your insolence to their Highnesses! Thanks, goodman, I'll be off. Hurry up to the lodge with those logs!

[*Goes off.*

HERMANN. Ay! I'll load the mule now!

GRIZEL. What mule d'ye mean?

HERMANN. The cross-tempered, two-legged beast!

[*He picks up bundle and puts it on her back. She drops it, and, catching up a faggot, belabours him. He ultimately gets it from her, and returns her blows. During the fight they interchange compliments.*]

HERMANN. Old scarecrow!

GRIZEL. Cross-eyed old satyr!

HERMANN. Wizened witch!

GRIZEL. Pig–dog!

HERMANN. Humped old sow!

GRIZEL. I'll make ye grin the other side of your face, ye monkey!

HERMANN. Black-faced old scavenger!

GRIZEL. Pot–bellied beerswiller!

HERMANN. Ye blasted lying old whore! Take that!

GRIZEL. Dirty bastard! White-headed old crocodile!

[*Both being out of breath, they sit down and begin to cry.*]

HERMANN. I meant no harm, wife, but you angered me.

GRIZEL. Ay! it's always my fault.

HERMANN. No, lass. It was that filthy fellow from the lodge that came between us.

GRIZEL. The breath of a Court is ruin to simple happiness.

HERMANN. Well, kiss, lass!

THE EQUINOX

GRIZEL. There, lad!   [*They kiss.*

And now, we'd better get the wood up to the lodge.

[*They each shoulder a bundle and move amicably off.*

And now, what was he telling you about the Prince?

HERMANN. Ah! that's a State secret!

[*At corner of path.*

GRIZEL. Well, you'll have to tell me!   [*Exeunt.*

PERSONS REPRESENTED IN ACT I

ERIK, *Prince of Fiordland*
MAUD, *his Wife*
NERISSA, *a Violinist*
HEINDRIK, *a Captain of Infantry, attached to the person of the Princess*
FOUR OFFICERS, *junior to Heindrik*
GUSTAVE, *Confidential Servant to Erik*
DANIEL, *a Groom to Erik*

ACT I

WINTER

A northern country. A lodge in the forest. There is a glass outbuilding, luxuriously furnished and decorated. A dining-table with two chairs. Two lounge chairs and a smaller table.

PRINCE ERIC *and* NERISSA *have just finished dinner, and are chatting inaudibly, leaning across the table. He kisses her.*

The Steward GUSTAVE *enters with coffee and liqueurs which he places on the small table. He goes out.*

The PRINCE *takes* NERISSA *under his arm to the lounge chairs. On the way they pass the door, go into the garden, look up at the sky, and shiver.*

ERIK. Snow to-night, snow-maiden!
NERISSA. Yes.

THE EQUINOX

ERIK. But . . .   [*He points to the house.*

NERISSA. Yes.   [*She laughs.*

ERIK. Let us go in.

[*He takes her to chairs, where they sit and drink coffee, etc.*

Enter L., *an officer in furs,* HEINDRIK. *He watches them for a while in silence, makes a sign of warning to some one in the background, and retires discreetly.*]

                [ERIK *touches a bell. Enter* GUSTAVE.

ERIK. Put out the big lights.

GUSTAVE. Yes, Highness.

[*He goes out and does so. In the balcony is only the rosy glow of shaded lamps in the roof.*]

[*Enter* HEINDRIK, L. *This time he beckons to his companions.*

[*Enter* PRINCESS MAUD. *She is muffled in dark furs. Four officers follow. They are among the pines.*]

HEINDRIK. Your Highness was perfectly right.

MAUD. I cannot see properly. I must see with my own eyes.

HEINDRIK. Your Highness should not venture nearer.

MAUD. I must see.

HEINDRIK. Then let us creep through the pines and watch from behind the fountain.

MAUD [*with a gesture of haughty disgust*]. Ah—h! . . . Lead on.   [*They go through the pines and stand watching.*

MAUD. I cannot see yet. Let us go to the doorway.

HEINDRIK. It is dangerous, Highness.

MAUD. I am dangerous. [*She goes stealthily forward and kneels at the door, looking through.* HEINDRIK *follows her. He has drawn his sword.* ERIK *and* NERISSA *are now in each*

194

other's arms. MAUD *nods and rises; they retire to the fountain.*]

MAUD. So! I have seen. Is everything prepared?

HEINDRIK. Your Highness will find everything in order.

[*A baying of great hounds.*

HEINDRIK. Back, Highness!

[*They disappear among the pines, and go off* L.

ERIK. The dogs are uneasy to-night. I am uneasy. I am going to finish my cigar in the forest. No; you must not come. My snow-maiden will take cold.

[*He kisses her and goes into the house, presently reappear-*
ing C. *with three immense grey boarhounds on leash.*
He looses them; they scamper about and return at
his whistle.]

ERIK. Gustave!

[*Enter* GUSTAVE C. ERIK *throws the leash to him.*
GUSTAVE *leashes them and goes off* C. ERIK *goes to*
window, and watches NERISSA, *who is lying back half*
asleep. Then he opens door, and calls.]

ERIK. Nerissa! [*She jumps up.*

NERISSA. Erik!

ERIK. Get your fiddle, dewdrop! I want you to play me the "Abendlied." [*She runs into house.*

ERIK [*sings*]:

.'Twas I that found the icicle on the lip of the crevasse:
'Twas I that found the gentian on the mountain pass:
'Twas I that found the fire to melt the maiden of the
snow:
'Twas I that plucked the flower—and I wear it, so!

[*Placing his hand on his heart.*

195

THE EQUINOX

Nerissa drew the crystal spring from the music wells that
    slumbered;
Nerissa drew my tears till the angels were outnumbered;
And I with trapper's forest-lore, and fisher's craft and wiles,
Hunted the shy bird of her soul, a secret spring of smiles.

                [*Snow begins to fall slowly in the garden.*

The April dawn of love awoke Nerissa's snowy mountain;
The sun of passion thawed at last the frozen fountain;
And I, who shared a sterile throne, share now a blissful bower—
Nerissa, oh Nerissa!   God preserve this hour!

    [*He sees* NERISSA *has returned and is standing at the
       door.*]

ERIK. Go in, child! It is cold. See, the snow is beginning to fall.

    [*He joins her. They enter. He locks and bolts the door.*
      ERIK *throws himself into a chair.*]

ERIK. Now, sweetheart, the "Abendlied."

[NERISSA *plays. During her performance* HEINDRIK *has
    again entered stealthily, and watches.*]

ERIK. And now!

[*He takes* NERISSA *into house, and switches off light.*
    HEINDRIK *gives a warning sign to his companions.
    The light goes up in the room above. Enter* C.,
    GUSTAVE, *advances quietly to fountain, and stands
    waiting.* HEINDRIK *whistles softly.*]

GUSTAVE. Advance. All is safe.

[HEINDRIK *advances. They greet each other, but without
    shaking hands.*]

GUSTAVE. Have you the money?

HEINDRIK. Here.

196

GUSTAVE. Let me count it.

[*He presses the spring of an electric torch, and examines the bag which* HEINDRIK *hands to him.*]

GUSTAVE. A thousand, two, three, four—no, five, six, seven. Don't be so suspicious, Captain, I shall not run away. Ten. Right. And the gold? Ah, the jolly rouleaux. It is in order.

HEINDRIK. The key.

GUSTAVE. Here it is. [*Gives it.*] And the stuff for the dogs?

HEINDRIK. Poor Tiger, and Baresark, and Odin!

[*Gives a packet.*

GUSTAVE. One doesn't make omelettes without breaking eggs. I will be ready for you in ten minutes.

HEINDRIK. There are two cars on the road. Yours is the small one. Your passage is taken. That and your passports are with the driver.

GUSTAVE. Right. I will see to Daniel and the dogs. Keep out of sight.

HEINDRIK. I will wait among the pines.

[*He retires.* GUSTAVE *returns to house.*

[*Enter* NERISSA *in her nightdress at window above, with her violin.*]

ERIK. Well, snow-maiden, are you still angry with me for stealing you?

NERISSA. I loved myself. But now I love you.

ERIK [*sings*]:

> O who on the mountain
> Would tremble and shiver?
> The spray's on the fountain;
> The sun's on the river.

THE EQUINOX

The fields are ablush,
And the valley's alight.
Come! let us crush
Out the wine of delight!

The thaw sends the torrent
Its Bacchanal dance;
The snows that the thaw rent
Glitter and glance.
The garden's a wonder
Of colour impearled;
The spring draws asunder
Its woe from the world.

Come, O my maiden,
Into the woods!
The flowers, dew-laden,
Shake light from their hoods.
Dance to the measure
Of Bacchus and Pan
Primæval, the pleasure
Of maiden and man!

[NERISSA *plays a love-song on her violin, then turns from
the window. The light goes out.*]

ERIK. Nerissa!]

[*Enter* GUSTAVE C. *with* DANIEL, *who is leading a horse,
saddled.*]

GUSTAVE. Take this order to the merchant at Stormwald.
If you ride back at dawn you will be in plenty of time for
your work.

198

DANIEL. Ha! Ha! Ha! Ha! Ha!

GUSTAVE. Ride fast, Daniel.

DANIEL. Oh! I shall have to pull the old fellow out of bed.

GUSTAVE. Pull his house down, if you like, as long as we have the champagne in time for breakfast.

[DANIEL *leaps on the horse and rides off* R. GUSTAVE *waits a minute, then advances to pines* L. HEINDRIK *meets him.*]

GUSTAVE. All well.

HEINDRIK. Be off with you, then. And don't make too much of a splash in Paris with all that money.

GUSTAVE. I am not such a fool. And don't you be such a fool as to get slack with that little monthly cheque, you know.

HEINDRIK. Don't you be frightened about money.

GUSTAVE. You're a bit white. What are *you* frightened of?

HEINDRIK. Only ghosts.

GUSTAVE. Ah, they walk in your forests.

HEINDRIK. We are doing a vile thing. Necessary, as I suppose most vile things are.

GUSTAVE. Oh, you have a conscience! Consciences walk in your forests.

HEINDRIK. I've a heart as well as a sense of duty.

GUSTAVE. Yes, she's a pretty girl.

HEINDRIK. And it was never her fault.

GUSTAVE. It's never the woman's fault in your forests. O race of sentimentalists!

HEINDRIK. He took her as a hound catches a hare.

GUSTAVE. In France "Jugged Hare" is a concoction of cat.

HEINDRIK. Well, this is not France. France is where you belong, you.

199

GUSTAVE. Good luck to your hunting!

HEINDRIK. Good luck!

GUSTAVE. I have it quite safe in your little bag. Good-bye, Heindrik. I suppose you despise me. [HEINDRIK *is silent.*] Well, you know, you too must wait for histories to be written before you get much praise.

HEINDRIK. My duty is clear. I am not asking for praise.

GUSTAVE. All my little need is money.

HEINDRIK. You have earned thirty pieces of silver. Be off! It is time to act.

[*Exit* GUSTAVE, L. *In a moment* HEINDRIK *gives a sign, and* MAUD *and the four officers re-enter from among the pines.*]

MAUD. Now!

HEINDRIK. Highness, your waiting is over.

MAUD. At last. This snow!

HEINDRIK. It hides our footsteps, Highness. May God's mercy cover our deeds.

MAUD. Insolent! This is the second time you have reproached me. A third, and I break you.

HEINDRIK. Pardon, Highness! I know my duty, and I shall do it.

MAUD. It is I who am wronged, is it not?

HEINDRIK. Ah, Highness, forgive me! I am your Highness's faithful servant. But—do we wipe out one wrong by doing another?

MAUD. It is right, what we do, by the law of God and man.

HEINDRIK. Then why do I feel it to be wrong?

MAUD. You are a weak fool. Do your duty!

HEINDRIK. I obey, Highness.

200

MAUD. Without another word.

HEINDRIK. I obey, Highness.   To the death.

[HEINDRIK *and other officers go out* C.   MAUD *paces the
    ground impatiently.   The lights go up, above; there
    is a sound of oaths and scuffling, and a scream.*]

MAUD. Ah! Ah! [*raising her voice*].   Is it done?

HEINDRIK [*opens window wide*].   We have the prisoners,
Highness.

MAUD. Bring the girl here to me.

HEINDRIK. Yes, Highness.

[*He reappears* C. *with* NERISSA, *who wears a cloak.*

MAUD. Did I tell you to cloak her?

HEINDRIK [*represses his speech*].   No, Highness.

MAUD. Take it off.

[HEINDRIK *hesitates.*   NERISSA *advances, and flings her
    cloak upon the ground at* MAUD'S *feet.   She is again in
    her nightdress.*]

MAUD. You wretched vagabond!   You gutter creature!
Off to the woods with you!   Off, baggage.

[NERISSA *stands trembling.*

There are plenty of street-corners in Stormwald.   Off,
you harlot!   [*She raises her hand to strike her.*

[HEINDRIK *interposes between them, draws himself up, and
    salutes* MAUD *stiffly.*]

HEINDRIK. My duty to you, Madam!

[*He draws his revolver, and shoots himself, tumbling at
    her feet upon* NERISSA'S *cloak.*   NERISSA, *terribly
    frightened, screams and runs off into the forest.*   MAUD
    spurns the body of HEINDRIK *with her foot.   The
    lights above go out.   A pause,* MAUD *waiting in stern*

201

THE EQUINOX

silence. Enter the four officers with PRINCE ERIK *bound and gagged.*]

MAUD. Take that gag out! [*They obey.*] Now, Erik, you are coming back to the Palace.

ERIK. What have you done with Nerissa?

MAUD. Pah! The wench ran into the woods—to look for men, I suppose. There were none in the garden.

ERIK. You she-devil! Oh God! God, help me to avenge this night on you!

MAUD. Vengeance! You paltry creature; one new pretty face is enough. Next week you'll have forgotten all about your—fiddle-prostitute.

ERIK. God help me to avenge this night on you!

MAUD [*to the officers*]. Take him to the car! You can come back here and hide this fool's folly.

[*She turns* HEINDRIK *over with her foot.*

THE OFFICER. Yes, Highness!

[*They go out. The four officers return, and lift the corpse
of* HEINDRIK, *which they cover with* NERISSA'S *cloak.
They go out. A pause. The snow ceases to fall.
The moon rises* C. *through the pines. In the distance
is heard the howling of a lonely wolf.*]

CURTAIN.

202

ACT II

SCENE I: *The Capital of Fiordland.   Two years and six
months later.*

PRINCE ERIK
OLAF AND KARL, *two Nobles*
Officers of his Suite
THE PRINCESS MAUD.   HELENA, *her companion*
Promenaders, Beer-drinkers.   A Flower Girl
NERISSA

*A number of people are enjoying the afternoon sunshine.
Some walk and chat, others sit and drink.*

A DRINKER. [*Sings.*] The North has a thousand beauties, and
    the South has only one.
  But we have borrowed a splinter from the spear of
    Captain Sun.
  We have trees as green as their trees;
  We have apple trees and pear trees!
  We have girls as sweet as their girls;
  We have flaxen girls and fair girls—
  And chestnut girls and auburn girls—
  And darker girls with raven curls!
  We do not envy their monotony
  Of a nigger for love and a palm-tree for botany!
  [*The guests of the beer-house stamp and beat the tables.*

203

2 DRINKER. Bravo! Bravo!

4 DRINKER. Hullo! Here comes Prince Erik.

3 DRINKER. With Karl and Olaf; I was with them at Heidelberg.

4 DRINKER. Oh! we know you're the dear friend of everybody with a title. But how shortsighted your friends are!

[ERIK, OLAF, *and* KARL *pass over chatting.*

FLOWER GIRL. A pansy for your button-hole, my prince!

ERIK. [*Smiles and accepts it.*] Heart's-ease to you, my child.

[OLAF *hands her a florin.*

FLOWER GIRL [*curtseys*]. Thanks, noble prince. [*To* OLAF.] A thousand thanks, my lord.

[*She runs off, laughing, to other customers.*

2 DRINKER [*slaps* 3 DRINKER *on back*]. But you were really intimate with that Italian Count, Conte Alcesto—or was it Alcestissimo?—Rigo de Righi de Righissimo. Where is he now?

4 DRINKER. " Where are the snows of yester-year ? "

2 DRINKER. " All, all are gone, the old familiar faces."

3 DRINKER. I must be going to the Kurhaus. [*Exit.*

2 DRINKER. Mr Count cost him more florins than he could count !

1 DRINKER [*sings*]. A bumble-bee buzzed in my ear:
  You cannot drink honey ; drink beer !
  Now the wise men of earth
  Cannot measure the girth
  Of the brain of that brilliant bee !
  Bring a bock ! bring a bock !
  Hang sherry and hock !
  Light Lager's the tipple for me !

204

SNOWSTORM

THE WAITER. Hush, sir. The Princess is coming down the street. The second verse won't do.

1 DRINKER. Oh, we'll keep the second verse for after dinner.

THE WAITER. And here's the blind fiddler, coming down yonder to the bridge. [*Point off* L.

2 DRINKER. What, the girl?

THE WAITER. Yes, Snowstorm.

A GUEST [*speaking with a marked foreign accent*]. Why, she is quite a young girl. But her hair is as white as your skies.

THE WAITER. Yes, sir, that's why we call her Snowstorm. But it wasn't always white—it was gold, the pale gold of our Fiordland sun; and her blind eyes were pale and blue and sparkling as our Fiordland seas.

GUEST. And as treacherous, perhaps.

WAITER. No, sir. She was a good girl. These gentlemen will tell you there was never a word against her.

1 DRINKER. Why, who was she? I don't recognise her at all.

2 DRINKER. Nor I.

4 DRINKER. Nor I. I seem to know her walk.

WAITER. Ah, she only came here two days ago. But I know her story. No, sir, I had better not say all I know. But I'll tell you this. A jealous woman threw her into the forest at night in a snowstorm, with only a rag of a nightgown on her back. My father was a woodcutter. He found her in the morning, exhausted in the snow. And when she saw him she got up and ran, screaming. She took him for a wolf.

2 DRINKER. Good God!

WAITER. But he took her to the hut, and my mother tended

her for over a year. I saw her last summer. When Father found her the hair was just as it is now; but it was the long illness that left her blind.

1 DRINKER. Good God! What a chilly story! Can she play the fiddle at all?

WAITER. You shall hear her and judge for yourself, sir.

2 DRINKER. There she comes, over the bridge.

[*Enter* R., *the* PRINCESS MAUD *and* HELENA *with two wait-ing-women and* L., *the* PRINCE *with* KARL, OLAF, *and his officers. They meet and chat amicably.* MAUD *nods, rather furtively, to* HELENA, *who slips away, and presently finds herself in front of stage with* OLAF. *They have their backs to the audience.*]

HELENA. I always love that old house [*pointing*].

OLAF. That one? [*pointing*].

[*Meanwhile she has passed a note from her right hand to his left behind their backs.*]

HELENA. Yes, that one.

OLAF. So do I.

[MAUD *has taken* ERIK'S *arm and walked off with him* L., *They follow.*]

2 DRINKER. Thank God! We can stretch our legs again.

[*They make themselves comfortable.*

1 DRINKER. And here comes your fairy fiddler!

[*Enter* NERISSA, L., *groping her way. Reaching* C., *she takes her fiddle and begins to play a jig. All rise and dance round her, the drinkers with the peasant women and cocottes. The flower girl, in front of stage, does a pas seul.* 2 *and* 4 DRINKERS *join her, and a peasant girl makes the fourth in an eccentric and outrageous quartette. The music stops. All stop, laughing and joking.*

1 DRINKER. Well played, little girl! A ripping dance!

2 DRINKER. Topping, by Jove.

4 DRINKER. Now, gentlemen, here's my hat. Florins for little what's-her-name?—little Snowstorm.

THE WAITER. Make it up to a thousand florins, gentlemen.

1 DRINKER. A thousand florins!

WAITER. She could earn that, once.

1 DRINKER. By Diogenes, you're as drunk as David's sow!

WAITER. Play us something else, Snowstorm. Play us your best.

2 DRINKER. Yes! Play another dance!

NERISSA. Life isn't all dancing, sir.

2 DRINKER. No, by Jove, I suppose your life isn't.

4 DRINKER. Thunder! Nobody's is!

NERISSA. I will play you from Bach.

[*She plays. All are hushed in admiration. At the last few bars re-enter* L., ERIK *with* KARL *and two officers. They stand and listen.* ERIK *grips* KARL'S *shoulder and staggers. She ends. All applaud.*]

KARL. What is it, sir.

ERIK. Nothing. Tell that girl to play again.

KARL [*advancing*]. Mademoiselle, you have the honour to be commanded to play before His Highness.

NERISSA. I will play—I will play for the Prince!

[*She is seized with a storm of emotion. Mastering herself, she begins the "Serenade." But she trembles so violently that the music is marred. As she goes on she recovers herself, when suddenly her E string snaps.*]

207

THE EQUINOX

NERISSA. I am so sorry, your Highness. My E string is broken.

[ERIK *is not very near her, or he might recognise her voice.*

ERIK. Never mind; another time. Give her a gold piece, Karl. [KARL *gives her money.* ERIK *moves off with him.*

ERIK. She can't play at all, Karl! Funny; that first piece sounded so well in the distance. [*They go off* R.

NERISSA [*in a faint voice*]. Erik!

THE WAITER. Look out, gentlemen, she is going to faint.
[*He comes forward, just in time to catch her in his arms.*
  He carries her into the beer-house as the CURTAIN *falls.*]

SCENE II: *The same afternoon.* THE GROUNDS OF THE PALACE.
  It is a formal garden, with box hedges. There are Japanese cypresses, and roses in bloom.
*Behind, a terrace with balustrade, and steps leading to garden.
  A summer-house in one corner. Statuary. In the background, the Palace walls.*

PRINCE ERIK
KARL
OLAF
PRINCESS MAUD
HELENA, *waiting-woman to the Princess*

In the summer-house are MAUD *and* HELENA, *smoking cigarettes.*

HELENA. Is not this dangerous, madam?

MAUD. To see Olaf here? Pshaw! It is nothing. I do things a thousand times more dangerous.

208

HELENA. But why do it at all?

MAUD. It is farewell.   The man bores me.   And he begins to give himself airs.

HELENA. He begins to expect.

MAUD. Which is the psychological moment to disappoint. Oh, Helena! if you knew my heart! It is impossible to understand me.   It is Erik that I love.   Erik is the only man I ever cared for—so much! [*She snaps her fingers.*] These boys!   Damn them all, and their homage and their impudence.   It is only Erik that I love.

HELENA. Yes, Madam.

MAUD. I know you think I am lying.   I know you only understand flirtation.   You do not understand revenge and despair.

HELENA. I have not a Queen's heart, madam.

MAUD. Do you understand?   I never forget that my father is an emperor.   Erik does not love me.   In all his boyish follies I believe he had one love—that fiddling harlot that I threw to the wolves.   Ah! that was my night of perfect passion.

HELENA. I understand love.   I do not understand hate.

MAUD. Then you do not understand love. . . . Why is Olaf late?

HELENA. There is someone on the terrace, now.

[ERIK *and* KARL *enter* L. *on terrace.*

MAUD. Look!

HELENA [*peeps through roof of summer-house, standing on the seat*]. It is the Prince and Count Karl.

MAUD. Hush then!   Let us be smoking!

[*They light fresh cigarettes.*

ERIK. I tell you, Karl, I am sick.   I am sick of life.

THE EQUINOX

KARL. You were merry enough at tennis.

ERIK. And then I saw that blind girl. It was a memory. For half a second her playing reminded me of something—that—that—I have—forgotten. Karl! I am a prince. I have been treated like a dog; and I have never avenged myself—and the woman I loved.

KARL. Avenge yourself now!

ERIK. She is too strong for me. There is no weak point in her armour.

KARL. She?

ERIK. Can you not guess? It is the Princess.

KARL. Highness!

ERIK. I hate her—and I am a doll in her hands.

KARL [*dropping on one knee*]. Highness! I beg you to believe that I am your most devoted servant. . . .

ERIK. Why, yes! I never doubted it. What is it?

KARL. I dare not tell your Highness.

ERIK. Yes, speak! I command you to speak.

KARL. I am not sure—I have thought—things have happened. . . .

ERIK. What things?

KARL. Oh, forgive me! It touches your Highness's honour.

ERIK. The more reason I should know.

KARL. It is . . . some of us think that her Highness forgets her duty. . . .

ERIK. Impossible! She is madly jealous of me.

KARL. I was sure I was wrong, your Highness. But—

ERIK. But!

KARL. The Lady Helena blabs.

210

ERIK. A silly, gossiping fool.

KARL. Not in words, Highness. But she bears herself as if she held great secrets.

ERIK. So do all those in whom princes put their trust. Or—don't put their trust!

KARL. A lover of hers went very suddenly to the Embassy in Madrid.

ERIK. Well? Ah!— . . . Hush! There goes Olaf.

[OLAF *enters* R., *and descends steps, bowing formally to* ERIK *as he passes.*]

I see. And then?

KARL. Watch, Highness. Murder will out.

ERIK. I spy on my wife? I have my honour to consider.

KARL. A two-edged sword.

ERIK. I can confide only in you. . . . If you should see or hear anything . . . tell me. Let me think. The Chancellor is a safe man: we must tell him . . . I will go now to his apartment; do you wait for me in the garden.

KARL. Yes, Highness. . . . I trust your Highness will forgive me.

ERIK. You have given me hope. [*He gives* KARL *his hand.* KARL *falls on one knee and kisses it.* ERIK *goes out*, L. KARL *waits moodily upon the terrace, sunk in thought. Meanwhile* OLAF *has made his way deviously to the summer-house. He bows and kisses the hand of* MAUD.]

MAUD. Keep guard, Helena! [HELENA *goes out and up the path.*] Come, Olaf! [*She draws him to her, and takes him in her arms. They kiss.*]

OLAF. Queen! Queen!

MAUD. This is farewell.

OLAF. I was afraid it was dismissal.

MAUD. Only a holiday. But I love you too much. I am getting reckless. People are beginning to talk.

OLAF. It is my fault. I cannot control myself when I look at you.

MAUD. I have got you the best command in the South. You will come up on leave ; we can meet sometimes.

OLAF. God help me. An hour's absence is torture.

MAUD. A week's absence will cure that.

OLAF. Don't think it. Don't think it !

MAUD. Kiss me ! You must go now. This is dreadfully dangerous. Karl is there on the terrace.

OLAF. Is there no hope for . . .

MAUD. Not till you come back ! Hush. Helena signals. [HELENA *gives a hissing " St !" as* KARL *descends steps.*] Kiss me. Again. Now go. One last kiss. Oh, go ! Farewell, my own Olaf!

OLAF. God preserve your Highness—and keep her love for me.

MAUD. Always. Go now.

OLAF. Good-bye. [HELENA *comes back.* OLAF *steals off.*

HELENA. Danger. Karl is coming down into the garden.

MAUD. Damn ! . . . Oh ! . . . What fun ! Helena, hide yourself. Let him find me here.

HELENA. Oh ! . . . Suppose the Prince comes back ?

MAUD. Go round the summer-house. Knock if he comes out on the terrace.

[HELENA *obeys.* KARL *comes slowly down the garden, deep in thought. He reaches the summer-house.*]

MAUD. Come in, Count!   [KARL *starts violently.*

KARL. I crave your Highness's pardon. I had no idea. . . .

MAUD. Boys never have.

KARL. Have? [*He is still quite confused and embarrassed.*

MAUD. Any ideas. Come in and sit down.

                           [*He obeys, awkwardly enough.*

KARL. I am flattered, Highness, to think that I thought of coming into the summer-house, exactly as your Highness did.

MAUD. Count, you are paying compliments. One day you will be old enough to know that women like to be bullied.

KARL. Your Highness is laughing at me.

MAUD. Of course, but not as you think. That is the meaning of the Woman's Emancipation movement. Men left off beating their wives—and the germs of discontent were sown.

KARL. Your Highness is merry.

MAUD. I am quite serious. The women cannot get their husbands to beat them any more, or cannot get husbands at all. So they force the police to arrest them, and force the doctors to feed them in prison.

KARL. Your Highness is laughing at me.

MAUD. On my honour, I am serious.

KARL. Then your Highness insults my understanding!

MAUD. Exactly. I am trying to get you to slap my face.

KARL. I strike your Highness?

MAUD. Is it not a smooth cheek—and in your heart wouldn't you love to smack it?

KARL. I would kill the scoundrel who offered to lift . . .

MAUD. Quite, quite. But it is I who am offering. Won't you box my ears? Just one little one?

KARL. Highness! Highness! You don't know what you are saying.

MAUD. Just once! . . . You men have no courage.

KARL. I dare do all that a man should; if I dared to do more, I should be less.

MAUD. That is Shakespeare, and quite spoilt. Come! If you daren't touch my cheek with your hand, do you dare with your lips?

KARL. I trust I know my duty too well to insult your Highness.

MAUD. Poor Highness! What is a Queen to do who wants a silly boy to kiss her? You would be forward enough with a pretty flower girl. . . . I know you. I suppose I am not pretty enough.

KARL. Your Highness is God's rose.

MAUD. Then why not pick it? One little kiss—just there —you may.

KARL. Your Highness, I may not.

MAUD. Perhaps you don't care for women at all?

KARL. I will love my lady.

MAUD. But I am not your lady, my lord?

KARL. Before God and within my honour—and your Highness's honour—you are my lady and I your humble servant.

MAUD. You are short-sighted.

KARL. I cannot see beyond my duty.

MAUD. Your lady will find you a most dreadful prig! . . . We pay a heavy price for our crowns. Are you not ashamed of yourself? You entrap me into making love to you!

KARL. Before God, Madam. . . .

MAUD. Hush! Hush! You mustn't swear. So you rob me of all my modesty . . . you make me kiss you. [*With a swift movement she draws his face to hers, and kisses him on the mouth. She lets him go, and laughs distractedly at his confusion.*]

KARL [*sobbing and stammering*]. Madam, it is high treason. [MAUD *continues to laugh.*

[HELENA *gives a series of sharp knocks on the woodwork.*

MAUD. So it is! And here's the Prince coming. Run for it!

KARL. I . . . I . . . [MAUD *pushes him out.*

MAUD. You fool! Do you want to ruin me?

[KARL *sees the danger, and glides away along the path.*
Helena! Come back quick.

[HELENA *darts into the summer-house.*

MAUD. Oh, what a fool! Did you ever see such a fool?

HELENA. I am terrified for your Highness. It is madness.

MAUD. No, it's only Maraschino.

HELENA. People have got drunk on Maraschino.

MAUD. I should love to see him drunk.

HELENA. I think you did.

MAUD. What? Do you really think so? Really?

HELENA. There isn't a man alive who wouldn't go mad— on the wine of your vintage. Only the flattery of it is enough, if he were an icicle.

MAUD. Yes, but if you melt an icicle, it only drips away. He's only a prig.

HELENA. And if you take away all his ideas of faith and honour—if you shatter his belief in the goodness of woman . . .

215

THE EQUINOX

MAUD. There's nothing left. You're wrong. He loves me no more than—than—than I love him!

HELENA. Oh, it's impossible. There aren't such men.

MAUD. We shall see. . . Are they gone?

HELENA. No. They've just met. They're going up the steps together. I think the Prince notices something.

MAUD. Keep still, then. I wish they'd go. It's cold here.

HELENA. As the mooncalf observed, your Highness is pleased to jest.

MAUD. How dare you? Hush!

[ERIK, *on terrace, turns and holds* KARL *by the shoulder and looks sharply in his face.*]

ERIK. What's the matter?

KARL. I daren't say. Oh. . . .

ERIK. Who is in the garden? Answer me.

KARL. Her Highness is in the garden.

ERIK. Yes? What has happened?

KARL. Oh, sir, she has made a jest of me!

ERIK. Tell me all. What did she do?

KARL. She pretended, your Highness. . . .

ERIK. Answer me, sir! Pretended what?

KARL. She pretended to be . . .

ERIK. To be what?

KARL. To be in l . . . To be fond of me, Highness.

ERIK. Truth? What did she say?

KARL. Oh, just laughing at me. I do not understand what it all meant.

ERIK. Did she do anything?

KARL. Yes—oh!

216

SNOWSTORM

ERIK. What?

KARL. She kissed me.

ERIK. And you?

KARL. I told her it was high treason.

ERIK. She meant it! She meant it every word! You were right with your gossip. Please God, we'll have her. Look here, boy, run back. Tell her you thought she was testing you; tell her you're madly in love, and if you die for it, you must have another kiss. I'll be near—No! She'd hear me or see me. Test her. Get her to make an assignation. Then we'll trap her.

KARL. Oh, sir, my honour!

ERIK. Your honour is in my keeping—and by God! mine is in yours!

KARL. Sir.

ERIC. Go! I am your officer. It is an order. Carry it out as I would have you. It is the honour of Fiordland that is at stake!

KARL. I obey, Highness.   [*He moves off.*

ERIK. Nerissa! If your spirit still haunts this earth, come! Hover! Witness that your lover strikes at last. Revenge—revenge upon that tigress, that barren she-wolf . . . devil! devil! devil! Nerissa! angel . . . angel whom I dragged from the empyrean, saint whom I tore from your niche, white dove whose wings I soiled . . . be near me! aid me! aid me to my vengeance!

[*Exit* L. KARL *has reached the summer-house. He falls on his knees.* MAUD *and* HELENA *exchange smiles.*]

KARL. Pardon, Highness.

217

THE EQUINOX

MAUD. This gentleman may have some private communication for me. Leave us, Helena!

[HELENA *goes out and keeps guard as before.*

KARL. Oh, your Highness, how can you pardon me? I thought you were testing me—perhaps you are testing me—but if I perish, I love you. I am mad. I love you madly, madly. Now kill me! Call the guards. I love you. Let me once touch the tips of your fingers and then. . . .

MAUD. Karl! my Karl! my own dove. I meant it. I love you. Come to me! Kiss me! I want to feel your strong arms round me.

[*She embraces him. They kiss. He almost faints, for he must allow and return the caress.*]

I cannot bear it! You are killing me. Be quiet; Helena will hear. Go now; leave me; I am faint.

KARL. And when shall I . . .

MAUD. At midnight, at the vestry door of St Hildebrand's.

KARL. I will be there. My Princess!

MAUD. Karl! Karl! Go quickly. The last kiss—till midnight. Send Helena to me. [*He kisses her, and goes up terrace and off* L. [HELENA *returns.*

MAUD. Well?

HELENA. Tara-diddle-iddle-doodle-oodle-ay!

MAUD. I smell a rat; I see him brewing in the air; come, let us nip him in the bud. Just the sort of foolish trick Erik would try on me—to send a boy like that who can no more lie than fly. I soiled him, though!

HELENA. So your Highness will not patronise St Hildebrand!

MAUD. Indeed, we shall be two pilgrims. The fool will

218

hatch some foolish plot—and I shall vindicate my innocence.
And I think I can go one better than that ! Come ; we must
dress for dinner.

HELENA. Our appetites are whetted.

MAUD. Yours, I suppose, for love ; mine, for some
sharper sweetmeat !

[*They go out, through garden, and up steps, and off* R. *A
pause. Re-enter* KARL *and* ERIC., L., *arm in arm, and
walk up and down.*]

ERIK. Very good, boy. Excellent. And now just one
touch to the masterpiece ! We are much of a size . . . I think
I will see how I look in a lieutenant's uniform.

KARL. Oh yes, Highness, that will be much better.

ERIK. So I shall be master of the situation, however things
turn out.

KARL. Your Highness is a Bismarck ! Always master of
the situation !

[*They go off* L., *laughing, as the* CURTAIN *falls.*

PERSONS REPRESENTED

PRINCE ERIK
KARL
PRINCESS MAUD
HELENA
THE FOUR DRINKERS, *with Women, Elsie, Carlotta, and two others*
An old gigantic Priest
THE CHANCELLOR
A Corporal's File
NERISSA
A *Neighbour to* NERISSA

ACT III

*The same day—*11.30 *p.m.*

At the back of the Stage is the Palace. The Prince's apartment is in brilliant light. The other windows are dark. R. is the church of St Hildebrand, the vestry door being well up stage; parallel with the wall runs an avenue of yews. L. a row of houses, and a similar avenue. The whole character of the scene is one of Gothic Gloom.

Enter the Priest L. with two acolytes and enters church. Various townspeople, going home, cross stage. Hymn from within church.

> All ye tottering crags that thrust
> Tortured foreheads from the dust,
> Palaces of fear wherein
> Lurk the sacraments of sin,

220

SNOWSTORM

Be abased before the nod
Of our one Almighty God!
    Crag and pinnacle and spire
    Hear our hymn!
    Disrupt, dislimn!
    God is a consuming fire.

Dwellers of the darkness, flee!
Leave the night to grace and gree!
Whether sleep dissolves the soul
Or vigil gains the godly goal,
Be the Lord a puissant aid
To his children undismayed!
    Crag and pinnacle, etc.

[*Enter* NERISSA *and a neighbour* R.

NEIGHBOUR. That's the Palace, on the right, dearie. There's a light in Prince Erik's room. He's just going to bed, I suppose. Now you're coming along to have a bit of supper with me, lamb, and then you shall go to bed, too.

NERISSA. I don't think I shall sleep much to-night. I think I shall wander about a little, and play tunes to the breezes and the nightingales.

NEIGHBOUR. The owls are the only birds abroad. And there are burglars, lamb. It's very late now.

[*Enter* 1st *and* 3rd DRINKERS L., *with three companions, and a group of women of the town, noisily.*]

1 DRINKER. Hullo! Here's our little blind fiddler girl. Come along, dear. I'll mend your fiddle for you.

NEIGHBOUR. Go away; you're drunk.

THE EQUINOX

ELSIE. So sorry, dear, we won't interfere with you. We're only going home. [NERISSA *and neighbour go off* L.

I DRINKER. We're not going home. I swear it. I call to witness yon bright star. [*Apostrophizes Castle window.*

3 DRINKER. You fool, it isn't a star. It's the moon. It's the beautiful moon.

ELSIE. It's the window of the Castle.

I DRINKER. I tell you it's a star. It isn't the right colour for the moon.

3 DRINKER. It's too big to be a star.

A COMPANION. Boys, it's the sun. The rising sun. It's not the right shape for a window.

I DRINKER. So it is. Well, didn't I say so? The rising sun—the star of day!

CARLOTTA. Oh come along and sleep it off!

I DRINKER. Sleep in the beautiful sunshine? Oh, Carlotta, how wicked you must be! This is the time when respectable people get up, and enjoy the cool air of the morning. Let us go into the fields and pick buttercups!

3 DRINKER. Buttercups and daisies!

I DRINKER. Let's sing a hymn of gladness on this bright and beautiful morning!

3 DRINKER. I tell you it's the moon. Elsie, it's the moon, isn't it? You may kiss me. Now that's the moon. What a plump, pretty face you've got. I'm going to be the man in the moon.

[*He kisses her several times. The others are reeling about the square, except one man who is leaning, in despair, against a tree.*]

CARLOTTA. Come along, dear!

222

SNOWSTORM

1 DRINKER. Why should I come along?

CARLOTTA. You're drunk.

1 DRINKER. You're a liar. I'm not too drunk to stand. I'm not too drunk to sing (*sings*):

> There's nothing like beer
> One's courage to cheer,
> A soldier is certain to tell you;
> And the militant one
> With his sword and his gun
> Is always a jolly good fellow!

3 DRINKER. Oh, that's a rotten song. Strike me! I do believe there's the man in the moon!

[PRINCE ERIK *is seen for a moment at the lighted window. He is in the uniform of a lieutenant.*]

1 DRINKER. You're as drunk as it's humanly possible for a gentleman to be. It's the sun, you owl; there never was a man in the sun. There couldn't be; it's against human nature.

3 DRINKER. Well, let's dance, Elsie, turn the band on again!

1 DRINKER. No, it's absurd. Respectable people don't dance at four o'clock in the morning! But I'll sing. I'll wake the birds. I'll make the cock crow, like poor old Peter did. Poor old Peter

3 DRINKER. I leave all that to Elsie. Elsie, my dear, I want a lark. Just make up one for me, will you?

ELSIE. I'm so tired. I want to go home to bed.

1 DRINKER (*sings*):

> Give rum to the sailor!
> It's always a failure;

THE EQUINOX

He tosses about on the breast of the ocean.
　　He is clumsy and stout,
　　And a booby, a lout,
For his life's a perpet—a perpetual motion !
　　　　[All chorus 3 last lines of each verse.

　　The Temperance crank
　　Gets his booze from the tank,
A liquor less fit for a man than a frog.
　　His mind is a fog,
　　And he lives in the bog—
You may bet you can always find him in the bog !
　　　　　　[Chorus.

　　But the soldier's a chap
　　That can laugh at mishap ;
He finds room in Dame Fortune's and Marian's lap.
　　And why, do you think ?
　　It's a question of drink.
He knows what is good when his stomach might sink !
　　　　　　[Chorus.

　　Now this is the reason
　　His foe he can freeze on,
And defend his good monarch from malice or treason.
　　His heart's full of cheer
　　And his belly of beer,
And he never—he never runs off to the rear!

Chorus.
　　It may sound very queer,
　　But the truth is quite clear.
He never—He never runs off to the rear.

SNOWSTORM

[*During this song all are marching about the Square, some arm-in-arm, some embracing. The light in the Palace goes out.*]

2 DRINKER. Oh my goodness! The sun's gone out.

1 DRINKER. It's only an eclipse, you fool.

3 DRINKER. Elsie wants me to come home. Now what I say is. . . .

1 DRINKER. It's very dangerous to be out of doors in an eclipse. I'm going home. Come along, Carlotta ; I want you to teach me cat's cradle.

CARLOTTA. Not at this time of the night, stupid. I'm going to tie your nose to the knocker, and run away!

[*They all reel off*, R. *A short pause. As their voices die away—one breaks out, off, into the last chorus—other voices are heard, off*, L. *They approach. Enter* ERIK *as a Lieutenant, with an old man, the Chancellor.*]

ERIK. Come over here, Chancellor. You will not be seen behind these trees. I need not ask you to watch closely, and report truthfully, what may occur.

CHANCELLOR. I cannot believe that your Highness is justified.

ERIK. Your eyes must be your judge. If I drop this handkerchief, you will come forward and make the arrest. The men will be concealed in these doorways.

[*The organ plays a voluntary.* ERIK *and* CHANCELLOR *uncover and keep silence.*]

CHANCELLOR. It is a dangerous game, your Highness.

ERIK. I have picked devoted men. The succession is at stake.

CHANCELLOR. Highness, I am an old man, and I know much of successions! It is always best to be dumb, and very nearly always best to be blind.

ERIK. You have wandered too much among the tombs.

CHANCELLOR. I wished to see if ghosts walked.

ERIK. And do they?

CHANCELLOR. Only when madmen call them up! Let the dead alone.

ERIK. On every wind one ghost calls to me.

CHANCELLOR. Ah! There is more in this than the honour of Fiordland. I was sure I knew all about successions!

ERIK. Yes, silence serves their turn. But what if the Blood of Abel crieth from the ground?

CHANCELLOR. Sir, the blood of the martyrs is the seed of the Church. But not by vengeance upon the murderers.

ERIK. Chancellor, it is useless to dissuade me. I have not slept well for a long while.

CHANCELLOR. And so your judgment is clouded.

ERIK. My judgment shall be the forked flash of heaven!

CHANCELLOR. Beware whom it may strike!

ERIK. You always bode.

CHANCELLOR. I have lived long enough to fear calamity. My daughter caught the chill that killed her on the fairest day of summer.

ERIK. Yes, it is your age that speaks. Is it not just as true that storm purifies the air? . . . But enough. Here comes Karl with his men.

[*Enter* KARL *with corporal's file.* CHANCELLOR *conceals himself.*]

ERIK. Get your men into the doorways. [*He consults his watch, with great difficulty; for it is now very dark.*] It is nearly time. Enough now. Not a sound.

226

SNOWSTORM

[KARL *has concealed himself and the soldiers in the door-ways of the houses.* ERIK *in centre of stage, listening. After a long pause he seems to catch a sound; for he smiles, raises his finger as a sign, and goes into the shadow of the vestry porch. Another pause. Foot-steps are heard, and low voices. The footsteps stop. Then* HELENA *enters, behind Church, with great discretion. She looks and listens keenly.*]

HELENA. It is all right.

MAUD [*off*]. Then stay under the trees. They are there?

[HELENA *nods, with a little laugh, and goes back among the trees.* MAUD *enters quietly, and slips round by the vestry.*]

ERIK [*imitating the voice of* KARL]. We are alone, my beautiful. Come; the car is at the back of the houses.

[MAUD *and* ERIK *come out into the square.*

ERIK. My darling! [*He puts his arms about her neck.*

MAUD. What does this mean? How dare you insult your Princess? Do you think I should come here, and not know how to defend myself?

[*With a little dagger she strikes him in the throat. He falls dead.*]

CHANCELLOR [*rushing out*]. By God, Madam, you have killed the Prince!

MAUD. The Prince! Erik! I have killed Love itself! Death! What have I done? Madman! Oh then, what is left for me to do? Erik! Why do you look at me like that? Come home to the Palace!

[*She is now up by Exit* R.

HELENA. Madam, I pray you . . .

227

MAUD. Silence, you fool! I will show you how a queen can die. [*She thrusts the dagger into her side, and falls, off.*] Eric!

[*All are now grouped round the corpse of the Prince. The vestry door opens suddenly. A gigantic priest, with a terrible beard, long and snow-white, brandishing a huge cross of rough wood, rushes out.*]

PRIEST. Begone, revellers! Disturb not the sacred night with your cries! Children of the devil, I am at my prayers, my prayers for your lost souls! Accursèd are ye, accursèd of God! Begone!

[*He retires into the vestry, and slams the heavy door.*

A SOLDIER. He is right! We are accursèd. The place is accursèd.

[*Panic seizes them all, and they rush off* R., *spurning the corpse of the Princess, and crying "Accursèd! The curse of God is upon us! We are accursèd!"*]

[*The cries die away. Absolute silence reigns. After a long pause* NERISSA *is seen among the trees,* L. *She feels her way from tree to tree.*]

NERISSA. This is the square. I wonder if his window is still lighted. He will come to me if he is awake.

[*She is now near centre of stage, almost touching the corpse of* PRINCE ERIK.]

[*She takes her violin and plays "Abide with Me" (or, as an alternative, the Serenade). At the end she waits, then gives a sigh.*]

I suppose he has gone to sleep. I will go back. Perhaps to-morrow!   [*She turns back and goes out.*

CURTAIN.

A BRIEF ABSTRACT OF THE

SYMBOLIC REPRESENTATION

OF THE

UNIVERSE

DERIVED BY DOCTOR JOHN DEE
THROUGH THE SKRYING OF

SIR EDWARD KELLY

[PREFATORY NOTE BY THE EDITOR

We omit in this preliminary sketch any account of the Tables of Soyga, the Heptarchia Mystica, the Book of Enoch, or Liber Logaeth. We hope to be able to deal with these adequately in a subsequent article.]

The HOLY TABLE.

PLATE I.

The Skryer obtained from certain Angels a series of seven talismans. These, grouped about the Holy Twelvefold Table, similarly obtained, were part of the furniture of the Holy Table, as shewn in Plate I., opposite.

Other appurtenances of this table will be described hereafter.

II

Other Pantacles were obtained in a similar manner. Here (Plate II.) is the principal one, which, carved in wax, was placed upon the top of the table. On four others stood the feet of the table.

Note first the Holy Sevenfold Table containing seven Names of God which not even the Angels are able to pronounce.

$$SAAI\tfrac{21}{8}EME.$$
$$BTZKASE\overset{30}{\cdot}$$
$$HEIDENE$$
$$DEIMOL\overset{30}{\cdot}A$$
$$I_{26}MEGCBE$$
$$ILAOI\tfrac{21}{8}VN$$
$$IHRLAAL\tfrac{21}{8}$$

These names are seen written without the heptagram within the heptagon.

By reading these obliquely are obtained names of Angels called—

(1) Filiæ Bonitatis or Filiolæ Lucis.

E

Me

Ese

Iana

Akele

Azdobn

Stimcul

(2) Filii Lucis.

I

Ih

Ilr

Dmal

Heeoa

Beigia

Stimcul

[These are given attributions to the Metals of the Planets in this order: Sol, Luna, Venus, Jupiter, Mars, Mercury, Saturn.]

(3) Filiæ Filiarum Lucis.

S

Ab

Ath

Ized

Ekiei

Madimi

Esemeli

SIGILLVM DEI ÆMETH.

PLATE II.

(4) Filii Filiorum Lucis.

L (El)

Aw

Ave

Liba

Iocle

Hagone(l)

Ilemese

See all these names in the heptagram of the great seal.

So also there are Seven Great Angels formed thus : take the corner letter S, then the diagonal next to it AB, then the next diagonal ATH, then the fourth diagonal, where is I with $\frac{21}{8}$ (which indicates EL), and we have the name—

SABATHIEL

Continuing the process, we get

ZEDEKIEL

MADIMIEL

SEMELIEL

NOGAHEL

CORABIEL

LEVANAEL

These names will be found in the Pentagram and about it. These angels are the angels of the Seven Circles of Heaven. These are but a few of the mysteries of this great seal

SIGILLVM DEI ÆMETH

III

The Shew-stone, a crystal which Dee alleged to have been brought to him by angels, was then placed upon this table, and the principal result of the ceremonial skrying of Sir Edward Kelly is the obtaining of the following diagrams, Plates III.–VIII.

He symbolized the Fourth-Dimensional Universe in two dimensions as a square surrounded by 30 concentric circles (the 30 Æthyrs or Aires) whose radii increase in a geometrical proportion.

The sides of the square are the four great watch-towers (Plates IV.–VII.) which are attributed to the elements. There is also a " black cross " (or " central tablet " according to the arrangement shewn—compare the black cross bordering the tablets in Plate III. with Plate VIII.).

Plate III. gives the general view.

[The reversed letters which form the word PARAOAN are written in Enochian for convenience, as our A and O are not distinguishable reverse from forward.]

Plate IV. gives the complete attribution of the tablet of Air.

The 6th file is called Linea Patris.

The 7th file is called Linea Filii.

The 7th line is called Linea Spiritus Sancti.

This great cross divides the Tablet into four lesser (sub-elemental) Tablets, the left-hand top corner being Air of Air, the right-hand top corner Water of Air, the left-hand bottom corner Earth of Air, the remaining corner Fire of Air.

Each of these lesser Tablets contains a Calvary Cross of ten squares, which governs it.

Plates V., VI., and VII. are similar for the other elements.

This is the way in which the names are drawn from the great Tablets. [Examples taken from Water Tablet.]

234

THE FOUR GREAT WATCH-TOWERS AND THE BLACK CROSS WITHIN GENERAL VIEW.

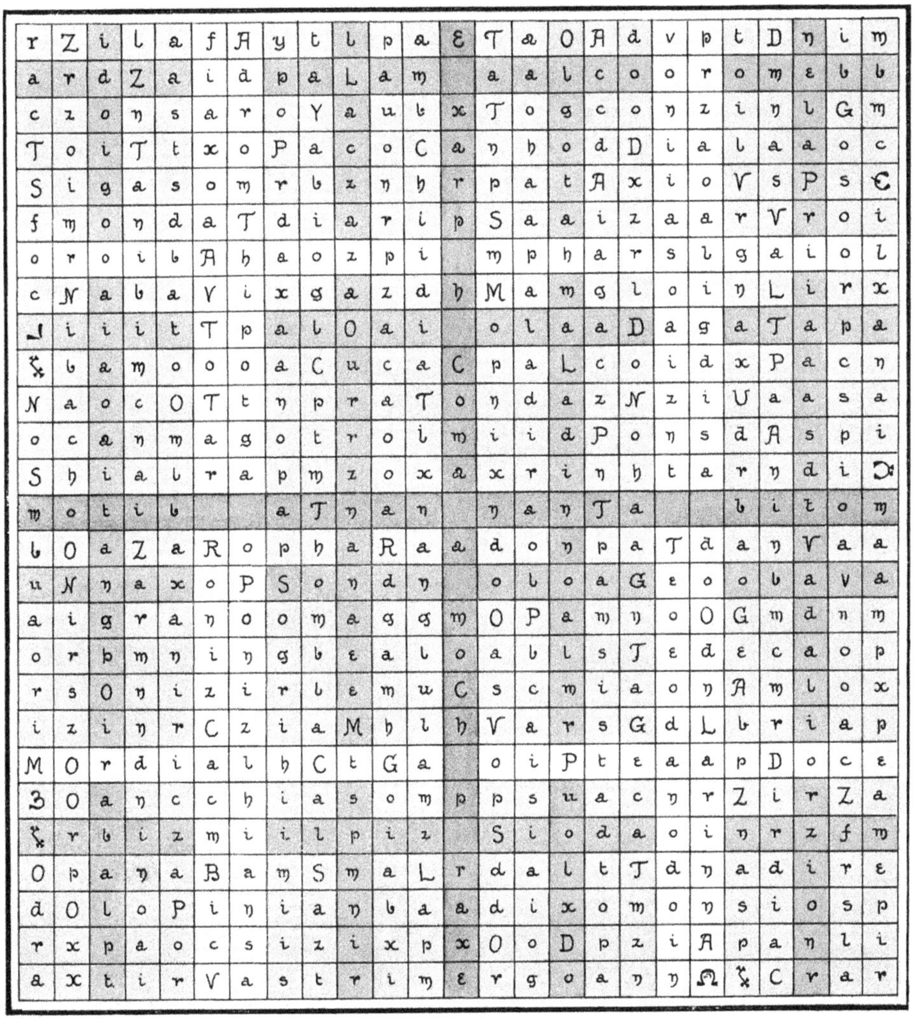

PLATE III.

THE GREAT WATCH-TOWER OF THE EAST, ATTRIBUTED TO AIR.

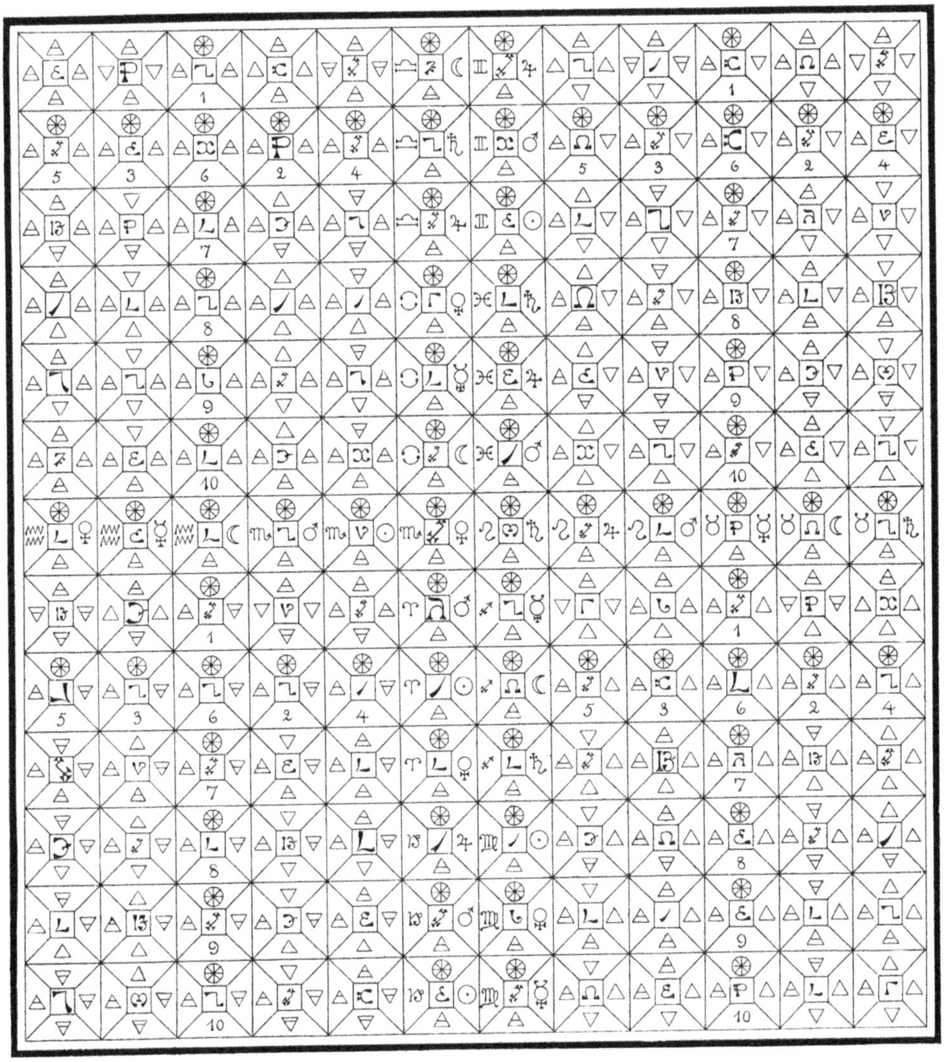

PLATE IV.

PLATE V.

PLATE VI.

THE GREAT WATCH-TOWER OF THE SOUTH, ATTRIBUTED TO FIRE.

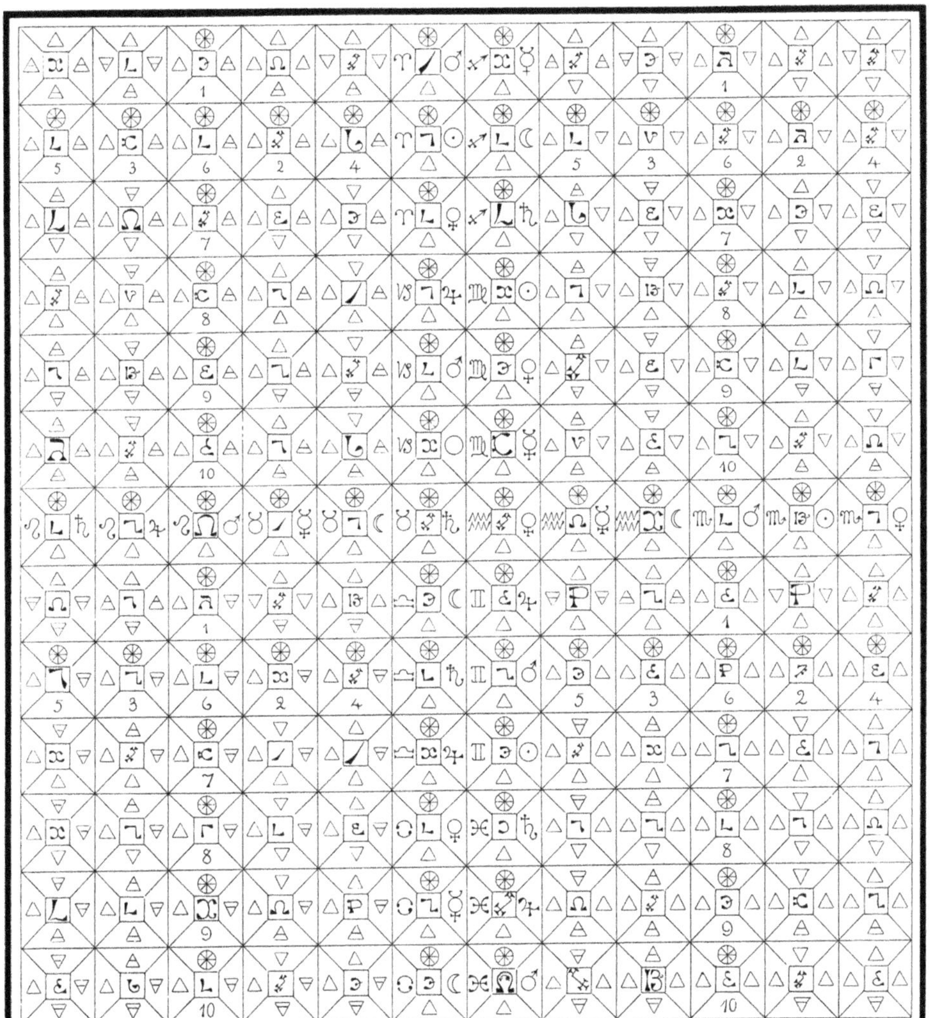

PLATE VII.

THE BLACK CROSS, OR TABLE OF UNION,
ATTRIBUTED TO SPIRIT.

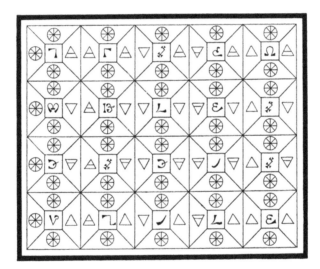

PLATE VIII.

KELLY'S UNIVERSE

1. Linea Spiritus Sancti gives the Three Holy Names of God of 3, 4, and 5 letters respectively.

MPH. ARSL. GAIOL.

2. A whorl around the centre of the Tablet gives the name of the Great Elemental King, RAAGIOSL [similarly for Air BATAIVAH, for Earth ICZHHCAL, for Fire EDLPRNAA].

3. The 3 lines of the central cross of Father, Son, and Holy Ghost give the names of 6 seniors. [Thus the 4 tablets hold 24 "elders," as stated in the Apocalypse.] They are drawn of seven letters, each from the centre to the sides of the tablet.

$$\left.\begin{array}{l} \text{SAIINOV} \\ \text{SOAIZNT} \end{array}\right\} \text{Linea Patris}$$

$$\left.\begin{array}{l} \text{LAOAZRP} \\ \text{LIGDISA} \end{array}\right\} \text{Linea Filii}$$

$$\left.\begin{array}{l} \text{SLGAIOL} \\ \text{LSRAHPM} \end{array}\right\} \text{Linea S.S.}$$

These three sets of names rule the whole tablet, and must be invoked before specializing in the lesser angles of the sub-elements.

4. The Calvary Crosses.

The name upon the cross read vertically is the name which calls forth the powers of the lesser angle.

NELAPR (water of water)
OLGOTA (air of water)
MALADI (earth of water)
IAAASD (fire of water)

235

The name read horizontally on the cross is that which compels the evoked force to obedience.

> OMEBB (water of water)
> AALCO (air of water)
> OCAAD (earth of water)
> ATAPA (fire of water)

5. Above the bar of the Calvary Cross remain in each case four squares. These are allotted to the Kerubim, who must next be invoked.

They are TDIM
> DIMT
> IMTD
> MTDI, being metatheses of these four letters. The initial determines the file governed; *e.g.* TDIM governs the file which reads T(o)ILVR. These angels are most mighty and benevolent. They are ruled by names of God formed by prefixing the appropriate letter from the " black-cross " to their own names.

6. Beneath the bar of the Calvary Cross remain 16 squares not yet accounted for. Here, beneath the presidency of the Kerubim, rule four mighty and benevolent angels—

> INGM
> LAOC
> VSSN
> RVOI

7. Triliteral names of demons or elementals are to be formed from these 16 squares, uniting the two letters on either side of the upright of the cross with a letter chosen

from the Central Tablet or black cross in accordance with rules which will be given in their due place. Thus GM

IN
OC
LA

et cetera, form bases for these triliteral names.

The following rules explain how the sides of the pyramids of which the squares are formed are attributed to the Sephiroth, Planets, Elements, and Zodiacal signs.

1. Great Central Cross. This has 36 squares, for the decanates of the Zodiac.

On the left side of the Pyramid, Linea Patris has the Cardinal signs, the sign of the Element itself at the top, in the order of Tetragrammaton (Fire, Water, Air, Earth) going upwards.

Linea Filii has the Common signs in the same order.

Linea S.S. has the Cherubic signs, that of the element on the left, in the same order, right to left.

But the order of the decans in each sign is reverse, and thus the planets which fill the right-hand side of the Pyramids go in the first two cases downwards, and in the third from left to right.

The upper sides of the Pyramids are all attributed to the Element of Spirit, the lower sides to the Element of the Tablet.

Each square is also referred to the small card of the Tarot which corresponds to the Decan (see 777).

2. Calvary Crosses.

Each has 10 squares.

The upper sides of the Pyramids are uniformly given to

Spirit, the lower sides to the Sephiroth, in the order shewn. The left-hand sides are attributed to the element of the Tablet, the right-hand sides to the sub-element of the lesser angle.

3. Kerubic Squares.

The upper sides pertain to the element of the Tablet, the lower sides to the sub-element. Right- and left-hand sides in this case correspond, according to a somewhat complex rule which it is unnecessary to give here. The attributions to the Court Cards of the Tarot naturally follow.

4. Lesser Squares.

The upper side of each pyramid is governed by the Kerub standing on the pile above it. The lower side is governed by the Kerub also, but in order descending as they are from right to left above. [See angle of Air of Water; the Kerubs go Earth, Fire, Water, Air (from the square marked D, the fifth from the left in the top rank of the Tablet), and downward the lower sides of the squares marked O, D, E, Z go Earth, Fire, Water, Air.]

The left-hand side refers to the element of the Tablet, the right-hand side to the sub-element of the lesser angle.

5. The Black Cross of Central Tablet.

The upper and lower sides are equally attributed to Spirit.

The left-hand sides to the element of the file, in this order from left to right: Spirit, Air, Water, Earth, Fire.

The right-hand sides to the element of the rank in this order: Air, Water, Earth, Fire.

IV

Follows Plate IX., the Alphabet in which all this is written. It is the Alphabet of the Angelic Language. The

PLATE IX.

invocations which we possess in that tongue follow in their due place.

[It is called also Enochian, as these angels claimed to be those which conversed with the "patriarch Enoch" of Jewish fable.]

V.

The Thirty Æthyrs or Aires and their divisions and angels are as follows [We omit for the present consideration of the parts of the earth to which they are stated to correspond, and the question of the attributions to the cardinal points and the Tribes of Israel. These are duly tabulated in Dee's "Liber Scientiæ, Auxilii, et Victoriæ Terrestris."] :—

NAME OF AIRE.	NAMES OF GOVERNORS.				NUMBERS OF SERVITORS.	IN ALL.
1. LIL.	OCCODON	.	.	.	7209	
	PASCOMB	.	.	.	2360	14,931
	VALGARS	.	.	.	5362	
2. ARN.	DOAGNIS	.	.	.	3636	
	PACASNA	.	.	.	2362	15,960
	DIALIVA	.	.	.	8962	
3. ZOM.	SAMAPHA	.	.	.	4400	
	VIROOLI	.	.	.	3660	17,296
	ANDISPI	.	.	.	9236	
4. PAZ.	THOTANF	.	.	.	2360	
	AXZIARG	.	.	.	3000	11,660
	POTHNIR	.	.	.	6300	
5. LIT.	LAZDIXI	.	.	.	8630	
	NOCAMAL	.	.	.	2306	16,736
	TIARPAX	.	.	.	5802	

NAME OF AIRE.	NAMES OF GOVERNORS.	NUMBERS OF SERVITORS.	IN ALL.
6. MAZ.	SAXTOMP . . .	3620	
	VAVAAMP . . .	9200	20,040
	ZIRZIRD . . .	7220	
7. DEO.	OBMACAS . . .	6363	
	GENADOL . . .	7706	20,389
	ASPIAON . . .	6320	
8. ZID.	ZAMFRES . . .	4362	
	TODNAON . . .	7236	13,900
	PRISTAC . . .	2302	
9. ZIP.	ODDIORG . . .	9996	
	CRALPIR . . .	3620	17,846
	DOANZIN . . .	4230	
10. ZAX.	LEXARPH . . .	8880	
	COMANAN . . .	1230	11,727
	TABITOM . . .	1617	

[Note that these 3 names come from the black cross, with the addition of an L. This L is one of the 8 reversed letters in the four watchtowers, the other seven forming the word PARAOAN, *q.v. infra*.]

NAME OF AIRE.	NAMES OF GOVERNORS.	NUMBERS OF SERVITORS.	IN ALL.
11. ICH.	MOLPAND . . .	3472	
	VANARDA . . .	7236	15,942
	PONODOL . . .	5234	
12. LOE.	TAPAMAL . . .	2658	
	GEDOONS . . .	7772	13,821
	AMBRIAL . . .	3391	

SYMBOLIC REPRESENTATION

NAME OF AIRE.	NAMES OF GOVERNORS.				NUMBERS OF SERVITORS.	IN ALL.
13. ZIM.	GECAOND	.	.	.	8111	
	LAPARIN	.	.	.	3360	15,684
	DOCEPAX	.	.	.	4213	
14. VTA.	TEDOOND	.	.	.	2673	
	VIVIPOS	.	.	.	9236	20,139
	OOANAMB	.	.	.	8230	
15. OXO.	TAHANDO	.	.	.	1367	
	NOCIABI	.	.	.	1367	4620
	TASTOXO	.	.	.	1886	
16. LEA.	COCARPT	.	.	.	9920	
	LANACON	.	.	.	9230	28,390
	SOCHIAL	.	.	.	9240	
17. TAN.	SIGMORF	.	.	.	7623	
	AYDROPT	.	.	.	7132	17,389
	TOCARZI	.	.	.	2634	
18. ZEN.	NABAOMI	.	.	.	2346	
	ZAFASAI	.	.	.	7689	19,311
	YALPAMB	.	.	.	9276	
19. POP.	TORZOXI	.	.	.	6236	
	ABAIOND	.	.	.	6732	15,356
	OMAGRAP	.	.	.	2388	
20. KHR.	ZILDRON	.	.	.	3626	
	PARZIBA	.	.	.	7629	14,889
	TOTOCAN	.	.	.	3634	
21. ASP.	CHIRSPA	.	.	.	5536	
	TOANTOM	.	.	.	5635	16,929
	VIXPALG	.	.	.	5658	

NAME OF AIRE.	NAMES OF GOVERNORS.			NUMBERS OF SERVITORS.	IN ALL.
22. LIN.	OZIDAIA	.	. .	2232	
	PARAOAN	.	. .	2326	6925
	CALZIRG	.	. .	2367	
23. TOR.	RONOAMB	.	. .	7320	
	ONIZIMP	.	. .	7262	21,915
	ZAXANIN	.	. .	7333	
24. NIA.	ORCAMIR	.	. .	8200	
	CHIALPS	.	. .	8360	24,796
	SOAGEEL	.	. .	8236	
25. VTI.	MIRZIND	.	. .	5632	
	OBUAORS	.	. .	6333	18,201
	RANGLAM	.	. .	6236	
26. DES.	POPHAND	.	. .	9232	
	NIGRANA	.	. .	3620	18,489
	BAZCHIM	.	. .	5637	
27. ZAA.	SAZIAMI	.	. .	7220	
	MATHVLA	.	. .	7560	22,043
	ORPAMB	.	. .	7263	
28. BAG.	LABNIXP	.	. .	2360	
	FOCISNI	.	. .	7236	18,066
	OXLOPAR	.	. .	8200	
29. RII.	VASTRIM	.	. .	9632	
	ODRAXTI	.	. .	4236	21,503
	GOMZIAM	.	. .	7635	

PLATE X.

SYMBOLIC REPRESENTATION

NAME OF AIRE.	NAMES OF GOVERNORS.	NUMBERS OF SERVITORS.	IN ALL.
30. TEX.	TAONGLA . . .	4632	
	GEMNIMB . . .	9636	27,532
	ADVORPT . . .	7632	
	DOZINAL . . .	5632	

Plate X shows us the names of these governors in the four Watch-Towers. Compare with Plate III.

Note that the sigil of each Governor is unique; the four sigils at the corners of Plate X. without the great square are those of the four great Elemental Kings :—

Air	Tahaoeloj.
Water	Thahebyobeeatan.
Earth	Thahaaotahe.
Fire	Ohooohaatan.

APOLLO BESTOWS THE VIOLIN

A STORY FOR THE STAGE

I

THE pastureland reached from the border of the olives and figs that garlanded the village to the upper slopes of the mountain, whose tumbled rocks, fire-scarred, frowned the menace of eternal sterility, the Universe against struggling man.

It was not often that Daphnis led his goats too far toward the crags, for the plain was green and gracious. Only in one spot was the sward broken. There did mosses and flowers, yellow, blue, and white, cover a mound as soft and firm as a maiden's breast.

Daphnis, true child, loved to make believe that this mound was sacred to some nymph. He would never invade the circle, or allow his goats to wander on it. But he would take his flute and invoke the nymph, or express the faint stirrings of manhood in his boyish breast by some such simple song as this :—

"Goats of mine, give ear, give ear!
Shun this mound for food or frolic!
Heaven is open ; gods are near
To my musings melancholic.
Spring upon the earth begets
Daffodils and violets.

Here it was maybe that Zeus
With his favourite took his pleasure ;
Here maybe the Satyrs use
With the nymphs to tread a measure.
Let no wanton foot distress
This encircled loveliness !

244

APOLLO BESTOWS THE VIOLIN

> Oh, some destined nymph may deign
> Through the lilies to come gliding,
> Snatch from earth the choral swain,
> Hold him in her breast in hiding !
> See, they stir.   It is the wind:
> Of my case they have no mind."

Thus lamenting and complaining the days found him, a monotony pastoral whose cycle was but peace.

But on the day of the summer solstice, as he plainted with the old refrain, the lilies stirred more violently ; and the day was windless.   Also it seemed to him as if a faint mist inhabited their midst.   And he sang :—

> "Mist, is this the fairy veil
> Of the bright one that's for me?
> Too phantastic, false and frail,
> See, it melts to vanity !"

Yet was he eagerly afoot with curiosity, for now the mist rose in fiercer puffs, and little jets of flame spurted and sparkled amid the lilies :—

> "Is it earth herself (he sang) that breathes
> In the bosom of the flowers?
> Is it fatal fire that seethes
> From the heart of hateful powers ? "

And the tumult of the mound increasing ever, he went forward a step toward the circle ; yet again his self-set fear caught him, and he drew back—and yet again his eagerness lured him.   In the end, reality conquered imagination ; he advanced delicately up the knoll.

Like the nipple of a breast, earth protruded, red, puckered, fissured.   This Daphnis saw as he broke through the tall lilies.   From its centre jetted the dusky, rose-red mist.   As he thrust forward his arms to divide the flowers, the beeeze caught a curl of smoke and mixed it with his breath.

His head went back : he half choked.   Then a strangled cry broke from him, turning to wild laughter.   His limbs caught the craze. He leapt and twirled and pirouetted like one stung by a tarantula : and all the while meaningless cries issued from his throat.

The nearer he approached the nipple the more fantastic were his antics, the more strident his laughter.

Now at the foot of the mound appeared a company of merchants and slaves journeying in a caravan. All these, attracted from their path by the unwonted sounds, beheld him thus dancing. The whisper went round: " He is possessed of the spirit of some God," and they all fell upon their faces and worshipped.

Then followed the wonder of all ; for at high noon was the sun wrapped in blackness of eclipse. In the gathering darkness and the strange shadows Daphnis still leapt and laughed ; but as the sun was wholly swallowed by the dragon, he gave one supreme shriek, and fell exhausted.

II

That which had been a mound of flowers was hidden deep beneath a floor of marble, translucent as mother-of-pearl. Along each side four elephants of obsidian, crouching, did homage to the central object of the hall, a slim tripod of silver, and on their backs eight pillars of porphyry were swathed with pythons of gold and black. These supported the dome, which glittered with lapis-lazuli. The shape of the temple was that of a fish or vesica, and nowhere was there any cross or tau to be seen.

Beneath the tripod a circular hole in the marble admitted the dusky vapours which two centuries before had filled Daphnis with enthusiasm.

Beyond and between each elephant stood five priestesses in white robes, their faces wrapped closely even to the eyes, lest the fumes should cause them to fall into trance. Each of these held in her hand a torch filled with oil pressed from the sacred olives that grew in the groves of the temple, and each was blind and deaf from too long continuance in the shrine whose glory was so dazzling and whose music so intense. Each might have been a statue of snow at some antique revelry of a Tsar.

Beyond the last of these, where the temple narrowed, was a shrine hidden, for from the roof hung a veil of purple, on which were written in golden letters the names and titles of Apollo.

It was the hour of worship; with uplifted hands a bearded priest in a voluminous robe of azure and gold cried aloud the invocations. He stood beyond the tripod, his face toward the shrine.

> " Hail to the Lord of the Sun !
> Mystic, magnificent one !
> Who shall contend with him ?   None.
> Hail to the Lord of the Sun !
>
> Hail to the Lord of the Bow !
> He hath chosen an arrow, and lo !
> Shall any avail with him ?   No !
> Hail to the Lord of the Bow !"

And then turning towards the tripod :—

> " Hail to the Lord of the Lyre !
> Diviner of death and desire,
> Prophetic of favour and fire,
> Hail to the Lord of the Lyre !"

With this he turned again and went up to the veil, prostrating himself seven times. Then again he turned and came to the tripod and sang :—

> " Prophetess, pythoness, hear !
> Child of Apollo, descend !
> Smooth from the soul of the sphere
> Of the sun, be upon us, befriend !
> In the soothsaying smoke of the hollow
> Do thou and thine oracle follow
> The word and the will of Apollo !"

So saying, he cast incense upon the opening beneath the tripod, and retired into the shrine. As the smoke cleared, there was found seated upon the tripod a maiden in a close

247

fitting dress of crimson silk broidered with gold. Her masses of black hair, caught at the crown with a fillet of crimson and gold, fell heavily around her. She bore a lyre in her hands. Her eyes were wild and fierce, and she sniffed up the vapours of the cavern with awesome ardour. Feebly at first, afterwards frenetically, she plucked at the strings.

Hardly a minute—a string snapped; the whole music jarred; and the priest ran from the shrine, shrieking "Apollo! Apollo! Veil your faces! Apollo hath descended." Himself he flung upon the marble before the tripod. There was a noise as of thunder; the veil was swept open as by a whirlwind, and Apollo, one flame of gold, entered the temple. As he passed, the priestesses fell dead and their torches were extinct. But a ray of glory from above, a monstrance to the God, followed him. Slowly and majestically he moved to the tripod. In his hands he bore an instrument of wood, of unfamiliar shape. Music of triumph and of glory answered his paces.

To the pythoness he advanced, thus dancing. He took the lyre from her hands and broke it. She stared, entranced. He put the strange instrument into her hands and, drawing down her head, pressed his lips to her forehead. Then he breathed lightly on her hands. Darkness fell, and lightnings rent it; thunders answered them. Apollo was gone. After the thunder the temple was filled with rosy radiance. The old priest, still prone, raised and let fall his hands, in mechanical imitation of the signs of invocation. Obedient, the pythoness began to play upon the instrument given of the God, and the temple shuddered at sounds so ethereal, so soul shaking, so divine. A greater music had been given to the world.

She ended. The old priest rose unsteadily to his feet, crying: "Apollo! Apollo!" staggered, and fell dead before the tripod.

The light went out.

248

DIANA OF THE INLET

BY

KATHARINE SUSANNAH PRICHARD

> Far already thy wild eyes
> Unlock my heart-strings as some crystal shaft
> Reveals by some chance blaze its parent fount
> After long time, so thou reveal'st my soul.
>
> BROWNING.

a

DIANA OF THE INLET

CHAPTER I

It was said that the man who lived alone on the Inlet shore was mad. He lived like a hermit—fished and snared wild-fowl for food, sometimes bartering a wild bees' hive, a platy-pus skin, or a lyre-bird's tail with the islanders or Inlet folk, for a bag of flour or some sail-cloth.

His hut, built of bark and saplings, was on an arm of earth thrown between the Inlet and the roaring Pacific. Wild waters besieged its bold outer shore, but within its embrace the Inlet lay calm as in a basin, sometimes azure, sometimes silver.

Old Mary Mahill knew his story. Moth'r Mary, all the Inlet people called her, for she mothered every ill-used creature, forlorn child or sick cow, in the country-side.

A barque had been blown on the bar in a gale some years before. The Inlet fishermen had rescued one gaunt, white-skinned man from the wreck. He was unconscious, almost lifeless, when they snatched him from the sea. They tended him with kindly sympathy. Moth'r Mary, herself, nursed him through long months of illness—weeks when he lay tossing in high fever, wearying night and day with delirious ravings —the cries of a soul in its agony.

"God! God! If there be a god—. . . Where art Thou —God? . . . There is no god." Always came the same deep, final groan.

Ceaselessly that plaint arose. Its anguish, smiting the starless night, startled the fishermen and the sleeping sea-birds on the midnight sea. It greeted the dawn—a monotonous wailing, vague and clamorous. For long he suffered, and the old woman watched and tended. The feverish energy subsided, deep lethargy seized his exhausted body. Not till the spring, till the awakening merriment of birds and earthly life sent a responsive thrill through sentient nature, did it move. Great-limbed and pallid, with nerveless skeleton body and cavernous eyes, he gazed upon the sunlit young earth and sun-blue sea, uncomprehending.

He grew like a strong animal. In the clear airs, the open life, his limbs filled and became firm. Knowledge of the wild life, the wild creatures of the forest and sea, came to him intuitively. In strength and stature he was before long the finest man on the Inlet shores. But his mind had sustained a shock, and the past was a great blank to him. He went to live alone in an isolated cove of the Inlet. The country-folk thought he was mad, because of the strange and silent life he chose to lead. All that they knew of him was a name; and that was engraved on a ring which had fallen from his finger while he was ill.

Michael Greig!

I recognized it with amazement. I had heard it sounded ın the world of thoughtful men as that of a genius—radiant as the morning star—a man who had leapt into the arena of thought, and stood as it were on a dais, an orator with the flush of youth on his high brows.

His had been an enthusiastic war of words. His argument dredged modern science of the essences of superstition, and yet he used the spiritual hypothesis, the ancient faith, with the reverential simplicity that early association had imbued. The beautiful myth was a halo bound round the brows of his dead mother. The patriarchs of Learning, the magi of knowledge, with incredulity and amaze paid him homage. Wonderment gave place to admiration and applause. The laurels of scholarship were pressed upon him. For awhile the gate to an immortal fame was ajar. "A youthful daring spirit of invention, stimulated by the discoveries of science to take its flight to new and hitherto inaccessible regions," had been written of him.

A recluse, Michael Greig immured himself from the world, that wolfish hunger after knowledge quenching all impulses but one to push beyond. His soul struggled in the solitude of a lonely life, though its wings moved in the serene atmosphere of pure philosophy. Lost in a maze of speculations, in lofty abstractions, his brain grew dizzy. "The consciousness of the limitations of man, that sense of an open Secret—which he cannot penetrate—in which is the essence of religion," probed his faculties, dragging them earthwards. He was impressed with the futility of toiling thought—the inscrutability of the Infinite to the Finite. In a chaos of thought, frenzied with doubt and despair, he cried to the world—that lay with ears a-gape to hear him,

"I know nothing—nothing!"

THE EQUINOX

And the world with resentful censure proclaimed him a charlatan.

Meteor-like, had Michael Greig flashed through the scientific sphere and fallen into obscurity. Abuse engulfed him, and in an overwhelming wave of antagonism the man was lost.

But here I had found him.

He had found a sanctuary in the South, the south beyond the most southerly mountains of Australia; over the ranges of heavily-timbered mountains, which the driving winds shroud in clouds.

There in the Spring is an El Dorado of vegetable gold.

Lavish outspread beauty, wild and rare stretches everywhere, gold, gold, the gold of wattle and gorse. Gold is on the horizon, the dusty road just edging through it. A cloth of gold covers the green-swarded plains. The spirit of tranquility broods over it. Fecund and vernal it is as the "unfooted plains of Arcady," where roamed the herds of Pan.

From the blue spurs of the Hills the plains stretch: long, irriguous, flower-lapped plains, verging on the margent of the sea. On the West the Inlet water creeps into a hollow of the land. The bold outline of the Promontory extends to the outer ocean along its Western side.

The forests are dense. The outskirts of hazelwood make the air redolent of its musky fragrance. The wayside is bright with flowers—heaths, white and scarlet, thrusting speary points through the sombre-tinted bracken. Red fuchsias droop in the bending green; purple sarsaparilla and yellow wild-pea cast vines along the ground encircling the fallen timber. Every variety of acacia makes the shadowy recesses lambent

254

with blossom. Over a stony creek the light woods are laden with a down of creamy flowers. The creek, swollen with plentiful rain, mirrors their drooping shades and the blue patch of sky with its flying scud of clouds. Thin wreaths of smoke curl from smouldering fires in the timber.

CHAPTER II

NEXT day on the Inlet shores I sought and found my fugitive from the world of thought—the man whom the country folk called the madman of the Inlet.

He was a strange being, with splendid barbarian strength of hairy breast and half naked limb. His was the figure of a noble savage, and I realized that he was mad only in that he had gone back several decades in his way of life, and that his memory had suffered an eclipse. He had reverted almost wholly to the being of primitive senses. He was again the sensitized clay, in the place of that electric dust which is our modern composition. His soul gazed through the sightless orbs of reason, on a primitive earth. The great lonely mind, thrown out upon the world, "saw God in clouds, and heard him in the winds."

We fraternized.

One day I tried to stir his memory. We sprawled on a spit of sand. The blue waters of the Inlet spat petulantly on the sea edge.

" Much learning hath made thee mad," I quoted softly.

" I remember an altitude," he answered me, gravely, after some pause, "where my blood froze. Here life glows within me. There is no cold where the sun is."

I drew his memory gently across the path of the past. It

256

was strewn with thorns whose sharp points pricked faint recollection with darting thoughts.

"There was a lark," he said, "that lost his song among the clouds, and broke his wings against the sky. There was a man who strode among the stars. He fell. Maimed, he spent the rest of his days in the fields of idle wandering. He was a madman."

"And now, my Hermit?" I asked quietly. "Would he return?"

"Why should I leave this place?" he demanded impetuously, "leave the wild heavens and the sea, the mountains and the forestry? Their life ebbs and flows with the tide of the soul. I love the wild things, the clouds, the winds, and the sea-birds. In the morning the wild swans rise. You hear them drag the water as they move, see the flash of silver spray. They stretch their long necks as they fly, and the white tips of their outstretched wings shine against the pure morning sky. At night under the shadow of the moon they drift with shrill melancholy piping. All night they wail from their breeding beds on the sheltered shore. The mists creep in from the mainland. The moonlight shines on the water, the waves break in liquid silver. The gulls and gannets with wild unrest startle their mates, and the wind, leaving the sea hushed, sighs up among the landward trees."

His voice fell into silence. The golden sand at our feet was fretted with foam. The tussocky grass about us hissed in the wind.

"Paugh!" spake the Hermit with a strong man's contempt. "Do I want the cities of the world? They are plague spots—filthy and reeking of men's vices. Men and women? Content among the muck-heaps, they are born and die, calling the space between, Life.

"What do I want with men?" he added, fiercely. "They are loathsome. With women? They are emptiness, ephemera of false light. They live and die like gnats in the glare of a day."

The Hermit laughed harshly.

"The whole world is mad! mad! mad!" he continued, "grinding and toiling, seeking and soiling, with its scanty breath, giving birth and dying futilely, because it has lost the way of Life. Here in the solitude is serenity. I live. Leave me this world of sunlight, the sea, the golden sands and clouded skies. The mistress of it all I adore. Her breath it is that sways the sea and the tree-tops, and scatters the stars. Her spirit possesses me. It has murmured to me through space and time."

"Ah, I called the moon Diane," he whispered to me, "and worshipped her. My love for her is like the wind beating along the sea-shore. But it never reaches her. I long the more infinitely."

"Diane!" he called softly, with tenderly love-lit eyes, and outstretched arms. The mellow voice dropped. The throbbing rhythm of it had palpitated with a profound emotion.

"I will tell you!" he said again, with a rush of words. "No one has ever known before. One night she came to me. Clouds were tossed about the moon. Sea-breakers broke with a moaning roar on the Inlet bar. The foam sprang high. Sea-weeds and drift-wood swirled about the edge of the sea. The heavy waves boomed dully along the sands of the Ninety Mile Beach. I heard her cry in the wind. It was fainter and

258

wilder than a wild swan's winging homeward in the twilight. The waves threw her high on the shelly strand. She was cold, almost lifeless. I gathered her into my arms. Her limbs were white, like the gleaming breast of a gull, her hair black as a cloud, dripping with sea-water. Chaste she was in her stillness, and holy. Moaning, I held her body against my breast. All night long, chill and motionless, she lay in my arms. In the dawning her eyelids quivered. She cried. I murmured words of tenderness, that the wind and the sea had taught me to woo her with, in the days when I dreamed and waited her coming.

"'Diane! Diane!' I called her softly, the wild love throbbing in my throat.

"She trembled. Fear shrouded her eyes.

"'Diane!' I prayed. Then sweet contentment filled those beauteous eyes. She was no longer afraid. She clung to me, and slept against my breast.

"We lived here joyously, with laughter, and tears that were the dew of happiness, lived as the birds and flowers do. We chased the rills to their springs in the mountains.

"A creek came down from the hills. We loved him. His life was a merry one in the early year. From a recess in the blue depths of the hills, he sprang. A lucid pool in the green moss-bosom of his mother earth, he lay. The deep shadows of a fern dell sequestered his birth. The latticed roof of his fragrant cradle was myrtle and dog-wood and hazel, tall tree-ferns, blue-tinted sapling gums, and mimosa. Lulled by the low-dropping note of the bell-birds, the whispering winds in the high mountain crags and ravines awakened him. He began to wander. Stray sunlight lit golden upon him. Through bowering trees he caught a glimpse of the blue sky above, and a tossed cloudlet. He began to sing as he wound through the shadows. He murmured against his sides. Radiant and green they were, with meadow fringes of tasselled grass, and yellow-eyed daisies. He mirrored mid-heaven, azure blue. The witchery of wattles encompassed him. Golden-haired like naiads, in the cool recesses, they flung seductive arms about him. Their fragrant presence perfumed the breeze that fanned him. Laughing sleepily, he lay in their caress, wrapt in golden sunshine. The birds in the cool of the bank whistled and warbled, merrily love-making. Silver-bellied minnows, darting on sandy shallows, blew strings of airy pearls. A platypus moved his solitary way in the shadow.

" For miles the creek ran through arcades of waving wood-land, with lulling charm of soft, low singing, and she and I went with him. At night-fall we all three came to the sea. The ascending star radiantly lit the sky. The great hungry heart of the sea yearned for the river. And I—I yearned for the lips of my love." The voice went out of him throbbed with a great emotion.

"So passed a time of perfect happiness—so we lived in Eden. But one day she ran to me with sobbing cries.

"'I must leave you, Tenderness!' she cried piteously; 'must leave you. Remembrance has come, and with it a voice of duty. I thought I had passed the portal of life when the gods sent me to you, but it is not so. I live—and must go to my people.'

"'I held her fast in my arms, and vowed that the gods should not part us.'

"'My gods will part us,' she told me with pitiful eyes.

'They would make thee kempt and shaven, Tenderness,' she cried.

.   .   .   .

"She is gone! she is gone!" moaned the Hermit.

"Sh!" He started. A wild swan wailed from a distant cove.

"Is she calling me, or is it only memory repeating her tones, 'Tenderness! Tenderness!' Diane—my soul!"

He stretched his arms to the silver moon, as she swam over the hummocks into the pale sky.

CHAPTER III

I idled the long summer away with my Hermit.

There was love of men between us. He held my heart with the philosophy and poetry of his madness. Our communion of soul and mind was thought itself speaking.

"There was a fire at the end of the summer," he told me. "The blue haze of smoke touched the far-out sea. The heart of the forest was still when we, she and I, walked there in the heat of the day. The blue breath had crept to its inmost recesses. The air was sultry with fire. The life of the forest was under its spell—the leaves listless, insects sleepily chirring, the birds unheard. In the silence the presaging moan of the fire, hungry for the green world that lay before it, came. It had ravished the ridges. The billowing black smoke swept over the forest. Wreaths of flame leapt higher than the tree-tops. A terrible heat beat against our bodies. She caught at my hand.

"'Let us go to the boat, Tenderness,' she cried. Her beautiful wide eyes were filled with apprehension. She clung to me in fear."

The man's throat throbbed with the slow music of his voice, for remembrance had with it a troubled sweetness.

"'Come! Come!' she urged. I could not move, for the passion of love in me, as I held her, swallowed up fear. She

262

drew me with gentle hands. The flames were breaking into our thicket of ferns and mimosa. We came to the beach. Our boat was heavy and flat-bottomed—an old fisherman's craft. Diane drove the white goats into it, at one end. The wind filled its brown sail, and we moved out into the silver breast of the Inlet. There we watched the fire—billows of flame that leapt in a glory from the leafage—fire clinging and swaying—loose fragments that flashed and melted mysteriously, in the heavy dusk of smoke, with showering sparks. I was Parsee and worshipping. She was afraid.

"'Is it that the Gods are angry with us? Is it a messenger they send to take me away from you?' she cried. Her beautiful wondering eyes kept my face prayerfully.

"'No!' I told her. 'Fire is the All-mighty, the men of old called it life. Does it not speak to you of power infinite and god-like, Beloved?'"

The massive frame trembled with the intensity of his mood.

"Like children, close breathing together with worship and wonder, we watched. The smoke crept out to us, bearing its harsh smell of burning leaves.

"Birds dropped in the boat. Diane loved the birds. They were her musicians of the woodland. Burnt and bruised, with tremulous beating wings, they died in her hands. She smoothed their ruffled wings, holding them to her face with sorrowing love-words. I had been looking towards the shore, and found her with her lap filled with soft dead bodies. Her tears were falling over them.

"'They sang and were happy!' she said. She was aching with the cruel horror of the fire to her beautiful innocents of earth.

263

THE EQUINOX

"'Who told me a God careth for his creatures?' she lamented. 'See, they are panting and hurt, Tenderness!'

"I comforted her.

"'Look at its beauty! Watch with me!' I said, pointing to the fire. She pressed the feathered bodies to her breast in love and grief.

"The fire displayed itself against a pall of smoke, excrescent green leaves of the young gums, burning silver and phosphorescent. Javelins of flame quivered and chased. The incense of burning filled the air. Ah! the majesty and mystery of Fire. All night we watched, making no sound. Only the waves lapping under the boat, and the drift of the wind in the sails, spake. Once Diane whispered low, and quick, and soft, that our hut would burn. Our eyes searched the distant shore. The glare of the fire enwrapped us. We could discern nothing in it. High up, the ranges dark with smoke, the red columns of smouldering trees, struck against the sky. The sea smell, and the cool of the Inlet tides moving gently, refreshed us. Towards dawn she slept, with her head on her arms at my feet."

"Diane!"

The word went out of the man with a deep unfathomable intonation.

"My soul dreaming," he continued, "I kept hand to the helm, and day came. Distant and hazy shores hung on the sea. Smoke, shiftless and blue, drifted along the horizon of the sea and sky. Dim and still the mystic line, like a pencilled veto, stretched. In its desolation the forest faced us, charred and smouldering, all the slender-limbed youth of the greenwood. The giants and patriarchs of yesterday were

264

blackened and fallen. Here and there a warrior scathed but alive outstood, his embattling arms stripped of greenery, of tangled ferns and sweet-scented bushes that had clung about his trunk. Not a flower, not a sound of a living creature. In its clearing our hut remained, the sentinel trees dead about it. It seemed to have won through much suffering, and stood with an air of mute homeness for us. Our hearts went out to it, the bark dwelling of our love. She saw, and the joy of her learning lit my soul. I caught her to my breast.

"'The Gods do love us!' she exclaimed in gladness.

"The creek was crying plaintively. At noon the wind dropped. Afterwards, the noise of thunder rattled and echoed among the hills. It wailed away, with a moaning sob; then awoke again in shattering crashes—a wild beast's angry fury, sounding long, and dull, and dead, as it sank muttering among the valleys. Far over the plains the storm swept. The thunderbolts, snapping, shook the foundations of the hills. The earth trembled. The voices of earth were mute. The thunder broke again and again from its remote rest, muttering, then breaking in impotent clashing, making forests and hills and valleys quake.

"The rain came, shrouding the purple and heavy blue of the hills in mist. At evening the mists lifted. Sunshine gleamed on the rain-wet world. A cloud curled and gathered and hung in the western sky, a white radiant cumulus, with long shaded lines and drifting gulfs of shadow, corrymbi, and fields of snow. The sun lit golden on its spotless edges. In the night-darkness, heavy and thunderous still, in huge shapeless masses this cloud lay. The lightning played against it, revealing mountainous shadows. Spasms of brilliance lit the dark hills, limning each tree and leaflet. The flashes circled the plains and lay out on the cold still sea. Gaps of glory they made among the silent trees, splashes of radiance in the barren blackness. Daggers of light touched forest and sea in a flash. Through the shallow pools of fresh rain-water, mirroring scattered stars, they darted. Then all was ended, of storm and fire. The globe of a silver moon swung serene in a cloudless sky."

There is a marsh near the Inlet where the stillness of death reigns. A stream winds somnolently into it, and drifts to sleep among the water-weeds. The reflection of the blue sky lies in it. We went there together, the Hermit and I. He was in rough, sombre mood.

"She said a nymph slept down there," he told me, his voice vibrant. "A nymph asleep, as women are without love. She used to stoop over those damp edges, staining her white skin with the stagnant waters, to sing and whisper mysterious things of the man-god who would come and catch up the dreamer from her trance, and bear her away. In the summer, at the end of the year, the marsh was dry, the nymph gone. Diane said that she had gone away with her lover. The nymph returns with Autumn. She sleeps all the winters, and springs, and in the summer she leaves with her lover again. The seasons return, but my Love comes not back."

His deep melancholy voice ceased; and he strode hurriedly away.

Peering into the green, slimy depths, I saw in fancy the dreaming nymph, the shadow of her eyes, the ripple of her mouth. She lies with white arms up-thrown. Her drifting hair waves with the sleepy river movement. Sun jewels

266

sparkle in it. The edges of her blue garments crinkle over the marsh. Meadow-weeds broider her robes, green and golden, as she sleeps all the autumns and winters and springs. The fringes of it glisten with workmanship of water-flowers. There is a sheen of green-spun foam motionless upon it. Seed-mosses have woven her a light veiling. Yellow marsh-marigolds with their daisy eyes a-stare stretch in a girdle to the water's edge. They have twined in her dusky hair, with the white star-flowers that shine there. Sometimes she sings in her sleep, dreamy lilting murmurs that drop and flow faintly. The sighing weeds echo the tremulous strain. Over the brilliance of the waste sometimes a sea bird wings. Sky and stream are vivid with the glory of the flowers, and the golden sunlight.

CHAPTER IV

FRAGMENTARY threads of gossip were rife about this Diane of the Inlet. No one knew whence she came—-whither she disappeared. Moth'r Mary constantly affirmed that she was a witch! I laughed to think that serious belief in the black arts was not dead, but found that several old people in this beautiful wilderness of the world clung to ancient superstitions and remnants of folk-lore.

Some fishermen, driven by a fresh breeze to a far corner of the Inlet, had seen a shadowy figure beside the man's on the distant beach. They had heard weird laughter, and the notes of a siren-song softly borne on the wind. Their sails had flapped helplessly in the wind as they tried to turn. They had tacked in the treacherous shallows on the further shore. Until night-fall they struggled vainly. Presently the singing ceased, and behold! the wind at once filled the sails and the smacks crept quietly into the broader swell. The fishermen told their story in the township, and the crones decided that witchery had been used.

A settler's boy, driving home his straying cattle through the marshes in mid-summer, had seen the white reflection of a woman's form in a dark pool of water. Voices came through the trees. It was a mangrove and ti-tree scrub, wreathed with the climbing and trailing vines of creepers. Over the reedy,

268

cress-grown, deep-shadowed, still waters, gauzy-winged insects spawned. The air was thick with them. The sun shone in shafted light on their iridescent wings. Only the wind and the sunlight and these light-winged creatures of air had ever pierced its depths of vaporous shadow. But the boy had seen the tall figure of the Inlet madman among the trees, seen also a reflection of whiteness and floating hair, in the dark pool beside him. He had heard flute-like laughter, its echoing melody in the leafy stillness, and a deep-throated answer. On the outskirts of the marsh, by the beaten narrow track, the half-scared youngster lay in ambush. He had heard the tinkling cattle-bells grow faint in the distance. Then, escaping from the hidden lair, he ran away with the tale.

In the evening, old men foregathered on the verandah of the "Ship Inn." Heads nodded. Tongues wagged wisely. Mysterious tales of sorcery and the like went round. They conjectured that the madman had dealings with the Evil One. This was the reason of his misfortunes. The witch-woman was, therefore, an emissary of the Devil, they concluded.

An old wood-cutter told me his version of the mystery, with professed dissent from the popular notion. He and some mates had been marking trees in a distant part of the forest and saw a strange spectacle.

A woman all wreathed in flowers, bare-armed and bare-footed, was enthroned on the stump of a tree. In her tangled dusky hair showery clematis was woven. The Hermit lay at her feet, a trailing garland in his hands, his eyes upraised. In the silence a branch of hazel-wood snapped. Like a startled wild creature the woman fled. With swift, naked feet, her flower draperies trailing, she vanished down the long forest aisle. The man sprang to his feet, face to face with the surprised intruders. He stood, wild, fierce-eyed, like a lion at bay. His powerful limbs were quivering with passionate strength. Mute and sheepish, the wood-cutter and his mates slunk away down the hill-side.

Wandering high up the range, I sought the scene of this idyll. The mountains rose like a wall from the green of the bush tree-tops. There were depths and depths in their blue recesses. The slope of a timbered spur stood on the verge of a great forest. Through dim arcades of the forest I passed. The primeval majesty, the immensity, of the silent tree-world worked within me. There were patriarchal monarchs of the green-wood, giants of strength and lusty leafage, young trees in their slim, vigorous youth. Maenads, with rugged bark flying from glistening naked limbs, tossed their fragrant foliage. Dead trees with up-raised ghostly arms dolorously wailed a miserere to the blue sky.

The hill-path grew steeper, the trees taller. The mountain gums were like columns of living marble, shining white in the green forest depths. Sometimes their whiteness was splashed with ochre, seamed with coral, stained steely blue. Through a track that was an alley of sweet-smelling flowering shrubs I went.

Restless torrents tossed between the hills, cascading silvery in blue depths of mist. I crept through the dewy fern groves—moist and heated, smelling of life in the fertile mould, through damp ferny coverts of flowers. In the long forest aisles tall waving fern-fans shut away the light. I passed like a pilgrim, worshipping each fresh phase of the way, and found the shrine.

DIANA OF THE INLET

Giant Eucalypts ranged about a grassy glade were the columns of this woodland temple. A high vaulted pavilion of leaves lifted and drifted in the winds, showing the blue of mid-heaven. Musks and hazel-woods thronged. Mimosas entirely golden with massy down of blossoms, and acacias in every hue of yellow, hedged about it.

Fern-fans waved against the light. Uncurling fronds of ferny undergrowth, golden-brown and chrysoprase, spread among the grasses. Clematis lay like snow among the trees, drooping in pendulous masses, casting starry trails to weave and twine over the bushes. The vines of the purple sarsa-parilla ran in festoons, and wound about the stately columns of the gums. At their bases delicate shoots sprang in a thicket of pale blue foliage. Near one end of the screening leafage was the natural altar, a gray, hewn tree-stump. Shafted sunlight played over the grassy lawn. Flights of butterflies fluttered from the shrubs.

I flung myself into the deep fragrant grasses and pondered. There is a mysterious spell in the lonely stillness and beauty of the forest hills. The air, with its mingled musky aroma of trees, its wild, heavy fragrance of flowers, is narcotic. One drifts into a hazy dreamland of imagination. The bird-music swells, the singing and sighing of sweet notes, merry roulades, the long, quivering, tender breaths of sound. Throbbing exultant tremolos, warbling, whispering, and lonely sobbing notes, bouts of gusty merriment, rise and fall distantly on the enchanted air. A shrike's rippled call comes gaily from the misty gullies. White wings sail across the tree-spaces. From under a dewy fern the bell-bird's mellow, liquid note drops falteringly.

THE EQUINOX

With half-closed eye I looked up at the gray tree stump, the woodland altar. And I saw, in fancy, a flower-wreathed woman, with shadowy hair, garlanded with starry clematis, serving as priestess before it, and the figure of a strong man who worshipped.

In this wilderness of deep green forest and sapphire Inlet, Spring made sanctuary. What an Eden it was in its exquisite loveliness and solitude! Two renegade souls of our modern time had made Eden of it. He was the Adam, purged of memory, she the Eve, " new-waked " to woman's primitive innocence and purity.

But the day of their happiness was ended.

" Happiness is the mirage of Life's Desert," I told myself.

Twilight was creeping along the vistas of the forest.

Moth'r Mary told me a story as she clattered backwards and forwards from the well in the gloaming. The old woman, with her stooping figure, short rough skirts, folded shawl and sun-bonnet, had an old-world simplicity. The spring water splashed over her pails. The clanking and jarring of her industrious occupation, the clomping of her hob-nailed boots, accompanied the vigorous recitative. Her tongue ever wagged lustily as she worked.

I hardly heeded the story as I watched the workings of the sunset. The great wall of the forest overhung us. Impenetrable, the green depths faced me, and climbed up the range. Slim white trunks stemmed the darkness. The sun had set in an abandon of gold behind the tree-tops. The afterglow gilded the river meads, where great-horned cattle roamed knee-deep in herbage. Beyond were the glinting fields

272

of yellowed summer grass, the sapphire blue of the Inlet on their far edge.

After the old woman had gone, the story emerged from a cell of my sub-conscious brain. Night came. The wall of the hills was dark, lit with the red stars of far-off fires. I mused over this last development of the Inlet Idyll.

The first lambs of spring were crying like children in the chill winds of the morning, Moth'r Mary had said, when the madman of the Inlet strode into the township. The winter shadow of the hills lay on them still. The gorse was gleaming golden by the roadsides. Flocks of snowy geese meandering along the way-side scattered in terror as he passed. He carried something in his arms. The townsfolk—women, bare-legged children, and a few surly men, gathered curiously. He went to Moth'r Mary's humpy at the far end of the road. She crossed herself, and muttered a prayer against witchcraft, when she saw his stalwart, unkempt figure. All the country-side feared him since the rumours of that strange companion of his solitude had spread.

He was gentle and tender as a woman, as he unfolded his arms. Wrapped in the hare-skins, he carried a child—a dark-skinned baby that wailed fretfully. The man's face was agonized at its cry.

" He is sick," he said, giving the child to Moth'r Mary, with piteous eyes.

Half compassionately, half fearfully, the old woman took the infant. He left it with her, but came often again to the township bringing her fish and sea-fowl. She lost fear at the sight of him; scolded him garrulously, ranted, and interrogated.

But to no purpose. He said the child belonged to him and would say no more.

She protested that the Hermit was "soft," not mad. With serious, tender eyes he watched the child grow, always bringing it some bright feathers or sea-shells to play with.

My first impulse was to attribute the man's action to a compassionate instinct for some woodman's sick child. Scattered through the forests were the bark huts of log-men and road-menders. It found no answering sympathy. The solution to the rustic's mind was the witch woman's existence. I found myself agreeing with them, apart from all fanciful interpretation.

He grew up a slight, wild, merry creature, this boy, and became the scourge of his old foster-mother's life, with his mischievous ways. He was always coming back to her, with a will-o'-the-wisp affection. The neighbours called him "The Devil's Brat," with odd superstition that powers of evil had been agents of his birth. He was a lonely child. The man at the Inlet missed him for weeks sometimes. And at night an elfish face peering in at her window would give Moth'r Mary such a shock that she muttered prayers and charms to herself half the night. Then at dawn her maternal heart would melt when she found a bare, brown body asleep on her doorstep, and saw the pathos of the child face in the weariness and peace of sleep. She crooned a rare wealth of love and pity over him. On winter nights she left the door unlatched, and by the dead leaves round the hearth she knew who had sheltered there. Gifts of wild honey, wattle gum, wild cherries, and such like childish things, he lavished upon her.

He kept the good country-folk in a tremor with his antics.

He stole their fruit, and chased their cattle away till they were lost beyond trace in the hills. He loved to dash into their kitchens, like a wild thing out of the night. He would laugh and blink at the fires. The farmers' wives called him "Devil's Brat," and, with superstitious fear of contamination, chased him away from their own sonsy and blithe children.

CHAPTER V

THOUGHT is the music of consciousness. It is the singing voice of the soul. From a world of intense thinking this man had passed. With clouded brain, as from sleep awakened, he went into the morning of a new life; from the darkness of pessimism into the daylight, with eyes dazzled, and the faith of a child. To him the stars were angels' eyes. Earth was a garden—the garden of God. The winds and the sun and the sea had voices, and breathed in his soul. Tutelary nature bred sense anew, with wild untrammelled strength. The poetry of an intense mind throve. A woman's presence had won him from taciturn savagery.

Was he mad, or was that solitary existence a phase of the eccentricity to which great minds are akin? I asked myself.

What of the woman? Was she some vagabond gipsy creature or perhaps the baggage of a distant islander?

Their mutual love had imparadised life. That was all I knew.

We became close companions, this lonely Man of the Inlet and I. And we would lie together for hours on the sands in the sunlight. In my company his strange restlessness was abated, and although there was a frontier over which his memory of personal things could not pass, his mind in the impersonal realm was vigorous and untrammelled.

276

DIANA OF THE INLET

It was one day just after he had left me that I made a discovery. The point of a sapling with which I carelessly disturbed the sand suddenly brought to light a wreath of red berries tied with a woman's dark hair.

Gently and carefully I searched the sand with my hands, and found two shell-strung armlets and a necklace of gray sea-pearls. A woman's ornaments, surely!

Then a piece of newspaper, yellow with sea-water and scarcely legible, hidden among some shells, came to light. But I read on this scrap of paper a paragraph which intimated that a search party was setting out with a view of discovering traces of a young lady who had been lost overboard from a craft called the " Maiai." The vessel had encountered heavy weather rounding the Promontory. A welcome lull occurring after sunset put the passengers and crew off their guard. Suddenly without the slightest warning an immense sea rose. " Big as a mountain," the captain said. It thundered with terrific crash upon the decks, sweeping the vessel from end to end. In a few minutes the sea was again tranquil. Some seamen had observed a woman's figure standing aft before the sea came. The lady, it was feared, had been swept off in the receding swirl of the wave. Some hope was entertained of her being picked up by stray fishermen and being still alive on some desolate Straits Island.

The paper was torn where a name had been written.

With the guilty sensations of a peeping Tom, I peered further into the mystery. According to the ship's reading, the wave had arisen in lat. 38" 5′, and long. 146" 4′ 5′ west. That would therefore be due east of the Promontory about thirty miles—the place where my hermit found his Diane.

THE EQUINOX

The Powers who in the British churl " chancelled the sense misused" here blinded me. I threw my imagination into the balance with that madman's. The poesy of circumstance, the contemplation of a " soul set free," filled me. A very revelry it was, in the upheaval of those " laws by which the flesh bars in the spirit." Love lies above ourselves. It is that pure inspiration of the great spirit which made idyll in Eden.

This, then, was the haven the immaculate woman of my conception had found. I wondered why she had left her Eden solitudes. Was it fear for the man,—fear of his passion and savage strength if force separated her from him? Did she think he was mad? Would they have fettered those splendid limbs, heaped insult and ignominy on the dignity of that great, simple mind? I seemed to hear a voice pleading with me, the echo of a cry.

" They would make thee kempt and shaven, Tenderness!" And again the hopeful " I will come again!"

This scrap of paper must have come in the drift of fishermen's *débris*. She had seen it and fled to stave off discovery.

I thought deeply on the tangled skein of our instincts and conventions. The tide was low. The channels, between the green mud-banks, were blue as the cloudless sky. Sea-birds were feeding on their edge. Gulls and gannets, gathering along the beach and wading in the silver-laved sand, softly whistled among themselves.

The waves rushed murmuringly. Wild swans sailed over the broad bosom of the Inlet. Sea-snipe wheeled with a flash of silvery wings. Great brown gulls hovered over my head. The wing of a white gull cut the blue sky. The wet sands

278

swarmed with crabs. They peered at me, in reverie, inveighing against the artificialities of life. Pertinently, I read them a sermon.

"Dearly beloved Brethren!" said I. "The night is gathering out in the west. The tide is coming. Surely it will creep over you, and sweep your shells of being into the ocean of the Unknown. Put not your trust, your foolish, fish-like confidence, in sea-fowl, little Brothers. Your opal backs, your yellow, freckled legs and golden claws, are vanity. Behold the gull how he sails the ether, touches the mountain clouds of heaven, pierces the veil of the distance, fathoms the green depths of the sea. He lives, inspiring ozone on the limitless horizon, the incense breath of earth, fed from the foams of summer-lapped islands, and lo! is a Solomon king-crab in all his glory like unto him?

"Crabs! O Crabs! ye are dead in the shells of your conventionalities. You emerald-legged fellow sitting athwart a cockle-bed, mud-grubber, solemn and silent, leave worms and other sweetmeats, mistress, thy prying into massy sea-weeds and tawdry gew-gaws. Regard the sun. Hear the wind —the voice of the world, for it is written, ' ye shall lie on the sea-shore, among the calcareous fragments of shell-fish and amphitrite, till the tempests of time annihilate the record of your existence.'

"One thing is certain that life flies. One thing is certain, and the rest is lies!" I chanted, and said "Amen."

The soiled piece of newspaper was crushed in my hand.

"Good-bye," I called softly to the solitary figure of the Hermit, standing alone in the sunlight. He was looking seawards and did not answer me.

THE EQUINOX

"Good-bye, my friend," I called again. "I am going on embassy to the Moon; shall I tell the woman you want her?" For I wanted to find her—Diana of the Inlet.

I had been wandering at dawn one day. Coming back to my humpy, the sun at the zenith, the hunger of man—human and healthy—gnawed at my vitals. Sounds of disturbance greeted me, a clacking of fowls, and barking of dogs—my household gods in anger. A harsh voice and shrill impish laughter mingled.

Through the trees I could see Moth'r Mary chasing a half-naked youngster with a heavy stick. Her short skirts were flying.

The boy was darting among the apple trees, his bronze limbs brushing the greenery, his mocking and teasing laughter vexing the old woman to tempests of rage. He had apples in his hands, red-russet, striped yellow and scarlet beauties that were the pride and joy of her life. She loved to hoard and gaze at them when the south-wester blew up in sleety rain from the sea, and the snow lay heavily on the gray hills.

She stood still when she saw me, shaking her knotted fists at the recreant. Her gray-green eyes were awful. She spluttered and spat in her haste to tell me of the ragged imp.

He was a handsome, fearless child, and chewed his red apples with wicked eyes that were alive with merry mischief and alert for flight if need be.

"Och! Masther!" cried the old woman, "th' Devil's brat is after thievin' yer apples, surre! Th' ceows 'e 've let into the latment 'f turnips. I wus carryin' pim-kins 'nd marrers from the paddicks, 'n I heart un shoutin'. I thogt that I was dune wid un, I do!"

280

She turned in rage upon the boy. He skipped behind the apple tree.

"Och thin! I'll be after yees!" she yelled. But she trundled away into the house to get me something to eat.

"It's him!" she whispered mysteriously to me, preparing the meal, "th' Devil's brat! Shur-re he do be sassy;" she clasped her old hands, the yellow bony hands of toil. Through the dark thin lashes I saw her eyes gleam tenderly. "Poor baby, whisher, whisher, God bliss 'im! I tuk bard in th' winter mesilf, and T'rasa me darter, surre, she cum 'nd say to me, 'ye're dyin', shurre, y'are,' she ses, 'it's no good feedin' yer, 'n' doin' fer yer; ye'll die,' she ses. 'It'd be waste givin' ye what there's many hungering for.'

"But Devil's brat cum 'n' did fer me, he do."

She raised her hands and sighed happily. "Och! thin," she went on, the withered old face bright with its simple gladness. "I didn't die."

The boy leapt out of the sunshine. He flung a heap of blossom on to the flags of Moth'r Mary's kitchen. Instantly the hum of scores of locusts arose. A merry wild thing, he sped off again with peals of impish laughter.

The old woman clattered after him, inveighing and scolding indefatigably.

CHAPTER VI

AUSTRALIA is the happy hunting ground of my wayward Ego. Elsewhere, the wearied limbs are carried in incessant pilgrimage. Here inebriate, with senses beauty-filled, it droops and dreams like a Lotus-eater, deep asleep yet deep awake.

"Oh! rest ye, brother Mariners! Rest ye!" here in the clear air, dewy plains, the blue hills and heavily shaded valleys. Among the trees the shadows lie. Radiant sunlight falls over the fields. The dead grasses glow golden. Shafts of purest light cross the shadows the trees cast.

A symphony of bird-singing, opening with the first flush of dawn in the mellow plains and forest aisles, fills the air with outbursts at first; and then rapturous melodies, flute-like cadenzas of joy, proclaim, "Beloved, it is morn!" Descanting on the joy of life, the purity of Nature, the arisen sun, the bird-world sings.

Pæans of irresistible joyous praise fill the sunny morning hours. The hoarse bass of crows, kah, kah, kah-ing, away on the plains, the wind's leafy murmur in the trees, and the merry derisive cackle of laughing jackasses, mingle. Wandering bands of magpies in wild vain-glorious minstrelsy warble their lays of romance and daring. Some songster, prolonging the theme with fine conceit in his tuning and turns, out-carols his choir. The soft throaty chatter of parroquets, the chuckle of a gray myna in the bole of a tree, and the buoyant communion of her mate, the long piping call of mud-larks across the flats, the laughing echo of jackasses among the blue depths of distant hills, fuse in the intermezzo of gladness.

Small birds lift their faint, sweet roundelay. They chirp and chatter to each other among the thickets, litanies of love and happiness, little thrilling snatches of song, vibrating, irresponsive ecstasies. The soft chirring of the insect-peopled grasses flourishes sweet accompaniment. All the bright hours the soft singing continues. Large amber-winged grasshoppers idly hum about dandelions in the dry, dead grass. Renegade cicadas sing lustily. Butterflies toss in the light air. The efflorescent trees and sweet shrubs breathe wild warm fragrance.

I was revelling in my pure joy of life in this golden south, when I became conscious that I was not there alone.

A woman was there as well as I, a woman of star-like eyes and chill beauty. She flashed past me in the forest, running like a startled hare. The wild scarlet had leapt to her cheeks. In her loosened hair, briars caught. The vines of a gay, wild weed were twined in it. The heath of the dunes was in sight before her feet lagged.

The sand of the hummocks, the golden gleam of the Ninety-mile sands, caught her eye. She climbed the crest of a hillock. It swept steeply down and another sister hillock rose from its base. Her nostrils caught the sea-smell. Silver meshes of the Inlet were just visible between the hills.

She laughed wildly and sweetly. The roseate heath crept like a flush over the hill-side. The purple mists drifted between the trees in the valley. The full gleam of the distant sunlit Inlet revealed itself.

"Tenderness!" she called with ringing voice.

Sometimes falling in the red heath she ran on, calling often again with quick sweet laughter. She struggled for breath, her limbs trembling and flesh torn.

"Man! Tenderness!" she cried.

Once she waited as she called. Far over the fells the wind had seemed to breathe "Diane!" as it touched her. Merry wanton laughter was wafted away with it. She ran calling along the Inlet beach, calling, calling. No windy murmur answered. Only the echoes rang—echoes of a name.

"Tenderness! Tenderness!" drifted over the Inlet, mingling with the whirr of winds and the cries of the startled seabirds.

"Man! Tenderness!" she cried, sobbing now, "Where are you? Where are you?"

The wind on the heaving sea snatched at the sound.

"Where are you? —— are you?" it wailed.

The clear sandy beach was silent. The bark hut in the sheltered cove was empty, its doors ajar. Along the boisterous little creek was no sign of living creature. Only a water-rat splashed out of sight as the woman lifted the green boughs of the trees. She turned seawards again. Her tremulous lips framed soundlessly the yearning cry. Her eyes were grown dark and distended with the agony of that aloneness.

From out a tussocky hole in the banked-up sand, a dark-skinned, scantily clothed thing, with towsled head and bright, shy eyes crept. It was more like some small wild beast than a child.

284

The woman caught at him.

"Where is he? Where is he?" she asked fiercely. The boy whimpered.

"Where is he?" the hoarse whispered voice implored. This strange woman with her torn clothing insisted roughly.

"Him?" queried the child, fearing, and pointed in the direction of the bark hut.

"Yes! Yes!" panted the woman.

The child cried softly.

"We were getting birds' eggs in the tussocks," he said presently.

"Some one was calling. He put up his arms and ran to the sand-bank, calling to it. He walked right out calling. He was mad. I was feart," wailed the child. "I could see him awhile, his head bobbing about among the breakers, out there."

A brown finger pointed to where the ocean breakers tossed white foam on the Inlet bar.

"Then the sea went over him." The child sobbed as the woman hung over him. "The waves came in bigger 'n bigger. I was feart. The calling came nearer'n nearer. I thought it was witches."

Lifting wild, frightened eyes, he continued, "Moth'r Mary tellt me of th' witch of th' Inlet. I hid in th' grass. It must have been your calling," he added. "I heart you meself, but I thought it was witches—or—dead men coming out of the sea to catch me."

The woman laughed harshly. The child broke away from her detaining clasp.

She ran to the outer beach. For ninety miles the sea

thundered, thundered and crashed on its wind-swept sands. With muffled boom and roar, waves broke on the bar. The waves rushed shorewards, dark-shadowed, foaming-lipped, with dripping jaws agape—the hungry pack of the *loups de mer*. With hollow growl of baffled rage, they crashed in foam and seethed back, shrieking their terror and spite to the far-off sea.

The wild, fleet figure of a woman sped over the sands, calling her prayers and a name to the pitiless winds, in an agony that was madness. Overcome at last, she sank on the sand. The spray sprang over her desolate figure. The wind lashed her wet hair, her face, with its deathly pallor. Her eyes were wide with the unearthly light of infinite pain. She lay on the lonely shore, shrieking a frenzied lamentation.

Night was glooming in. A child stole across the sand. Silently he watched beside the solitary figure. The woman's clothing was soaked, the rime of the sea-spray lay in her tangled hair. The child crept against the dank form. His serious eyes, wet with distress, covered her. He pressed a bare brown hand against her face in mute sympathy. The woman pushed him roughly away. He touched her stiff hands with compassionate sorrow. The woman moved. She drew back and looked at him. Her face stern and sunken, deathly pallid, with eyes distended, and vacant, tense lips, she confronted the child.

"Who are you?" she gasped hoarsely, straining her eyes on the wistful small face.

"Don't know," he whispered awefully, "Moth'r Mary said I b'longed to him," glancing over towards where the hut was hidden in the cove.

286

"She had me, when I was a baby, but I b'longed to him," he reiterated plaintively.

The woman's gaze was steady. She devoured the upturned face with eager eyes. It was wan in the twilight, a child's face, tanned with sun and sea, bearing nobility of feature and luminous eyes.

"What is your name?" she demanded softly.

"Moth'r Mary said, he at the Inlet had sold himself to the Devil. She said that no mortal woman was my moth'r like th' children of th' Dara. She said that I came from a fire in th' earth. They called me the Devil's brat. He said, the gods gave me, and my mother was the moon."

The hoarse chuckle of insane laughter gurgled in the woman's throat. She screamed, clutching at her sea-wet hair, with fearful eyes.

The child began to cry softly.

Then a melting tenderness filled those staring eyes. A smile moved her lips. A low sad sobbing welled sweetly in her throat. She turned to the child with tremulous lips and bosom, and tearful eyes. She called softly to him with infinite love and opened arms. Radiant expectancy was in her shining eyes. He crept into her arms. She cried and sang over him, with voice tuned to a lay of passionate soothing love.

On the lonely sea-shore the breaking waves tossed spectral foam. The sea moaned and wept along its length. A solitary star sprang in the twilight sky.

I found them together, the lonely boy and that wild witch-woman of Inlet superstition; her beautiful face, the haunting sorrow of her eyes, are with me still.

THE EQUINOX

She talked to me with a tender calm. There was deep sadness in the note of her voice. A fearless dignity and expression of chill nobility enwrapped her.

"My mind is clouded with the dream of a distant time," she said, "a pungent memory, phantom-like, has haunted me. In my life and the world beyond, my senses swooned on the memory of the Inlet. Then came a thrill of keener recollection."

She spoke on, with dreaming eyes. The pressure of strong feeling assuaged throbbed in her soft, low voice.

"I recognize in myself that primitive Woman who arises to mock at civilization and creeds," she said. "The blood of Mother Eve beats against my brain."

"I want the man! my man—Adam of the Inlet shores!" her arms moved outwards tremulously. "Here is the I, the woman soaring over the immolation of Life, the detestable, heartless hopelessness of existence. I am come back to the Inlet!" she said.

Her words voiced with a throbbing passion fell softly into silence. Then she spoke again, with the slow speech of a mind far away.

"The moon is rising on the Inlet," she said, "a pale, silver moon in a dim sky; can't you see it, breaking on the dim waters. The wailing of the swans, the cries of the gulls, the moan of the struggling sea, don't you hear them?

"It was the moon he loved as did Endymion. And when I came—a mortal woman, self-sent from a barren and desolate life, he loved and called me after her."

"Diane! Diane!" Was it the faint wailing note of a wild swan that beat the still air?

288

DIANA OF THE INLET

"Coming! Coming!" she cried with low harmonious voice of joyful promise.

She lifted the dark-skinned boy and laid him against her breast.

"Our two selves gave thee Soul, Beloved," she murmured passionately, cradling the soft dark head in her arms.

Round all the Inlet islands the dawn came stealing, out-lining the coves and headlands with a silver thread. All the sea-birds awoke in clamorous choir, with whirring wings. Wild swans took their arrowy flight across the shining surface of the Inlet. Speckled snipe, and red-bills, and oyster-catchers were feeding at the silver brim of the sea. A pelican arose from a sandy cove, and with slow flapping flight winged seawards.

On an upland that gave on the Inlet panorama, a woman stood. Her eyes, and the sorrowful thought stirring in their depths, bade farewell to the beautiful scene, the sapphire blue, locked on the west by bold distant mountains. Purple they were, transfused with the pink glow of the morning sky. The broad expanse of the Pacific lay beyond the Inlet. Sea-breakers rose against the sky. Curlews were rising in clouds, with shining wings, and shrilled distantly their soft melancholy calls.

Her tears were falling. They moved slowly from sight of the Inlet shores—the woman and the child, with clinging hands.

A great moon is rising on the Inlet now, as I have often seen it rise, red-gold. The reflection falling, red-gold like a wedding-ring, clasps earth and sky. Under the moon a line of wild swans drifts with shrill melancholy piping. The moon-light touches the coves. The water waves from gold to silver. Sea and earth are still, as in an enthralment.

The vision of the woman floats to my memory—Diane of the Inlet. Her voice clear and thrilling echoes its own fateful story. Beside her comes a man with splendid strength of limb and primitive mind. I hear his deep, tender calling to the rising moon.

" Diane! Diane!"

All the changing scene and colour of the Inlet rises again before me, and the idyll of the madman of the Inlet and the Diane of his imagination.

FINIS

SILENCE

Amid the thunder of the rolling spheres,
Herself unchanged despite the changing years,
    She stands supreme, alone.
With trembling hands tight pressed to rigid ears,
Deaf to all prayers, and hopes, and human tears,
One voiceless Horror—louder than all fears,
    Filling the great Unknown.

ETHEL ARCHER.

MEMORY OF LOVE

O DREAD Desire of Love! O lips and eyes!
O image of the love that never dies,
But, fed by furtive fire, rages most
When Hope and Faith have been for ever lost!
O oft-kissed lips and soul-remembered eyes,
O stricken heart—the old love never dies!

O Passion of dead lips that used to cling
To warm red living ones that breathed no pain!
O Passion of dead hours that daily bring
To life some phantom pale that died in vain! . . .
Some echo tuned to Memory's dying strain,
Some witness of the immemorial spring!

MEREDITH STARR.

ACROSS THE GULF

ACROSS THE GULF

CHAPTER I

At last the matter comes back into my mind.

It is now five years since I discovered my *stelé* at Bulak, but not until I obtained certain initiation in the city of Benares last year did the memory of my life in the Twenty-Sixth Dynasty when I was prince and priest in Thebai begin to return. Even now much is obscure; but I am commanded to write, so that in writing the full memory may be recovered. For without the perfect knowledge and understanding of that strange life by Nilus I cannot fully know and understand this later life, or find that Tomb which I am appointed to find, and do that therein which must be done.

Therefore with faith and confidence do I who was—in a certain mystical sense—the Priest of the Princes, Ankh-f-na-khonsu, child of Ta-nech, the holy and mighty one, and of Bes-na-Maut, priestess of the Starry One, set myself to tell myself the strange things that befell me in that life.

Thus.

At my birth Aphruimis in the sign of the Lion was ascending, and in it that strange hidden planet that presides over darkness and magic and forbidden love. The sun was united with the planet of Amoun, but in the Abyss, as showing that my power and glory should be secret, and in Aterechinis the second decanate of the House of Maat, so that my passion and pleasure should likewise be unprofane. In the House of Travel in the Sign of the Ram was the Moon my sweet lady. And the wise men interpreted this as a token that I should travel afar; it might be to the great temple at the source of mother Nile; it might be . . .

Foolishness! I have scarce stirred from Thebai.

Yet have I explored strange countries that they knew not of: and of this also will I tell in due course.

I remember—as I never could while I lived in Khemi-land—all the minute care of my birth. For my mother was of the oldest house in Thebes, her blood not only royal, but mixed with the divine. Fifty virgins in their silver tissue stood about her shaking their sistrons, as if the laughter of the Gods echoed the cries of the woman. By the bed stood the Priest of Horus with his heavy staff, the Phoenix for its head, the prong for its foot. Watchful he stood lest Sebek should rise from the abyss.

On the roof of the Palace watched the three chief astrologers of Pharaoh with their instruments, and four armed men from the corners of the tower announced each god as it rose. So these three men ached and sweated at their task; for they had become most anxious. All day my birth had been expected; but as Toum drew to His setting their faces grew paler than the sky; for there was one dread moment in the night which all their art had failed to judge. The gods that watched over it were veiled.

But it seemed unlikely that Fate would so decide; yet so they feared that they sent down to the priest of Thoth to say that he must at all costs avoid the threatening moment, even if the lives of mother and child should pay for it; and still the watchmen cried the hour. Now, now! cried the oldest of the astrologers as the moment grew near—now! Below in answer the priest of Thoth summoned all his skill.

When lo! a rumbling of the abyss. The palace reeled and fell; Typhon rose mighty in destruction, striding across the skies. The world rocked with earthquake; every star broke from its fastening and trembled.

And in the midst lo! Bes-na-Maut my mother; and in her arms myself, laughing in the midst of all that ruin. Yet not one living creature took the slightest hurt! But the astrologers rent their robes and beat their faces on the ground; for the dread moment, the Unknown Terror, had gone by; and with it I had come to light.

In their terror, indeed, as I learnt long after, they sent messengers to the oldest and wisest of the priests; the High-priest of Nuit, who lived at the bottom of a very deep well, so that his eyes, even by day, should remain fixed upon the stars.

But he answered them that since they had done all that they could, and Fate had reversed their design, it was evident that the matter was in the hands of Fate, and that the less they meddled the better it would be for them. For he was a brusque old man—how afterwards I met him shall be written in its place.

So then I was to be brought up as befitted one in my station, half-prince, half-priest. I was to follow my father, hold his wand and ankh, assume his throne.

And now I begin to recall some details of my preparation for that high and holy task.

d

THE EQUINOX

Memory is strangely fragmentary and strangely vivid. I remember how, when I had completed my fourth month, the priests took me and wrapped me in a panther's skin, whose flaming gold and jet-black spots were like the sun. They carried me to the river bank where the holy crocodiles were basking; and there they laid me. But when they left me they refrained from the usual enchauntment against the evil spirit of the crocodile; and so for three days I lay without protection. Only at certain hours did my mother descend to feed me; and she too was silent, being dressed as a princess only, without the sacred badges of her office.

Also in the sixth month they exposed me to the Sun in the desert where was no shade or clothing; and in the seventh month they laid me in a bed with a sorceress, that fed on the blood of young children, and, having been in prison for a long time, was bitterly an-hungered; and in the eighth month they gave me the aspic of Nile, and the Royal Uraeus serpent, and the deadly snake of the South country, for playmates; but I passed scatheless through all these trials.

And in the ninth month I was weaned, and my mother bade me farewell, for never again might she look upon my face, save in the secret rites of the Gods, when we should meet otherwise than as babe and mother, in the garment of that Second Birth which we of Khemi knew.

The next six years of my life have utterly faded. All that I can recall is the vision of the greatness of our city of Thebai, and the severity of my life. For I lived on the back of a horse, even eating and drinking as I rode; for so it becometh a prince. Also I was trained to lay about me with a sword, and in the use of the bow and the spear. For it was said that

Horus—or Men Tu, as we called Him in Thebai—was my Father and my God. I shall speak later of that strange story of my begetting.

At the end of seven years, however, so great and strong had I waxen that my father took me to the old astrologer that dwelt in the well to consult him. This I remember as if it were but yesterday. The journey down the great river with its slow days! The creaking benches and the sweat of the slaves are still in my ears and my nostrils. Then swift moments of flying foam in some rapid or cataract. The great temples that we passed; the solitary Ibis of Thoth that meditated on the shore; the crimson flights of birds;—but nothing that we saw upon the journey was like unto the end thereof. For in a desolate place was the Well, with but a small temple beside it, where the servants—they too most holy! of that holy ancient man might dwell.

And my father brought me to the mouth of the well and called thrice upon the name of Nuit. Then came a voice climbing and coiling up the walls like a serpent, "Let this child become priestess of the Veiled One!"

Now my father was wise enough to know that the old man never made a mistake; it was only a question of a right interpretation of the oracle. Yet he was sorely puzzled and distressed, for that I was a boy child. So at the risk of his life—for the old man was brusque!—he called again and said "Behold my son!"

But as he spoke a shaft of sunlight smote him on the nape of the neck as he bent over the well; and his face blackened, and his blood gushed forth from his mouth. And the old man lapped up the blood of my father with his tongue, and cried gleefully to his servants to carry me to a house of the Veiled One, there to be trained in my new life.

So there came forth from the little house an eunuch and a young woman exceeding fair; and the eunuch saddled two horses, and we rode into the desert alone.

Now though I could ride like a man, they suffered me not; but the young priestess bore me in her arms. And though I ate meat like a warrior, they suffered me not, but the young priestess fed me at her breast.

And they took from me the armour of gilded bronze that my father had made for me, scales like a crocodile's sewn upon crocodile skin that cunning men had cured with salt and spices; but they wrapped me in soft green silk.

So strangely we came to a little house in the desert, and that which befell me there is not given me of the gods at this time to tell; but I will sleep; and in the morning by their favour the memory thereof shall arise in me, even in me across these thousands of years of the whirling of the earth in her course.

CHAPTER II

So for many years I grew sleek and subtle in my woman's attire. And the old eunuch (who was very wise) instructed me in the Art of Magic and in the worship of the Veiled One, whose priestess was I destined.

I remember now many things concerning those strange rituals, things too sacred to write. But I will tell of an adventure that I had when I was nine years of age.

In one of the sacred books it is written that the secret of that subtle draught which giveth vision of the star-abodes of Duant, whose sight is life eternal in freedom and pleasure among the living, lieth in the use of a certain little secret bone that is in the Bear of Syria. Yet how should I a child slay such an one? For they had taken all weapons from me.

But in a garden of the city (for we had now returned unto a house in the suburbs of Thebai) was a colony of bears kept by a great lord for his pleasure. And I by my cunning enticed a young bear-cub from its dam, and slew it with a great stone. Then I tore off its skin and hid myself therein, taking also its jaw and sharpening the same upon my stone. Then at last the old she-bear came searching me, and as she put down her nose to smell at me, taking me for her cub, I drove my sharpened bone into her throat.

I struck with great fortune; for she coughed once, and died.

301

THE EQUINOX

Then I took her skin with great labour; and (for it was now night) began to return to my house. But I was utterly weary and I could no longer climb the wall. Yet I stayed awake all that night, sharpening again upon my stone the jaw-bone of that bear-cub; and this time I bound it to a bough that I tore off from a certain tree that grew in the garden.

Now towards the morning I fell asleep, wrapped in the skin of the old she-bear. And the great bear himself, the lord of the garden, saw me, and took me for his mate, and came to take his pleasure of me. Then I being roused out of sleep struck at his heart with all my strength as he rose over me, and quitting my shelter ran among the trees. For I struck not home, or struck aslant. And the old bear, sore wounded, tore up the skin of his mate; and then, discovering the cheat, came after me.

But by good fortune I found and wedged myself into a narrow pylon, too deep for him to reach me, though I could not go through, for the door was closed upon me. And in the angle of the door was an old sword disused. This was too heavy for me to wield with ease; yet I lifted it, and struck feebly at the claws of the bear. So much I wounded him that in his pain he dropped and withdrew and began to lick his paws. Thus he forgot about me; and I, growing bolder, ran out upon him. He opened his mouth; but before he could rise, I thrust the sword down it. He tossed his head; and I, clinging to the sword-hilt, was thrown into the air, and fell heavily upon my shoulder. My head too struck the ground; and I lay stunned.

When I came to myself it was that a party of men and

women had thrown water in my face and uttered the spells that revive from swoon. Beside me, close beside me, lay mine enemy dead; and I, not forgetful of my quest, took the blade of the sword (for it was snapt) and cut off the secret parts of the bear and took the little bone thereof; and would have gone forth with my prize. But the great lord of the house spake with me; and all his friends made as if to mock at me. But the women would not have it; they came round me and petted and caressed me; so that angry words were spoken.

But even as they quarrelled among themselves, my guardian, the old eunuch, appeared among them; for he had traced me to the garden.

And when they beheld the ring of the holy ancient man the astrologer they trembled; and the lord of the house threw a chain of gold around my neck, while his lady gave me her own silken scarf, broidered with the loves of Isis and Nephthys, and of Apis and Hathor. Nor did any dare to take from me the little bone that I had won so dearly; and with it I made the spell of the Elixir, and beheld the starry abodes of Duant, even as it was written in the old wise book.

But my guardians were ashamed and perplexed; for though I was so sleek and subtle, yet my manhood already glowed in such deeds as this—how should I truly become the priestess of the Veiled One?

Therefore they kept me closer and nursed me with luxury and flattery. I had two negro slave-boys that fanned me and that fed me; I had an harp-player from the great city of Memphis, that played languorous tunes. But in my mischief I would constantly excite him to thoughts of war and of love; and his music would grow violent and loud, so that the old eunuch, rushing in, would belabour him with his staff.

How well I recall that room! Large was it and lofty; and there were sculptured pillars of malachite and lapis-lazuli and of porphyry and yellow marble. The floor was of black granite; the roof of white marble. On the Southern side was my couch, a softness of exotic furs. To roll in them was to gasp for pleasure. In the centre was a tiny fountain of pure gold. The sunlight came through the space between the walls and the roof, while on the other sides I could look through and up into the infinite blue.

There was a great python that inhabited the hall; but he was very old, and too wise to stir. But—so I then believed— he watched me and conveyed intelligence to the old magus of the well.

Now then the folly of my guardians appeared in this; that while all day I slept and languished and played idly, at night while they supposed I slept, I slept not. But I rose and gave myself to the most violent exercises. First, I would go into my bathing-pool and hold my breath beneath the water while I invoked the goddess Auramoth one hundred times. Next, I would walk on my hands around the room; I even succeeded in hopping on one hand. Next, I would climb each of the twenty-four smooth pillars. Next, I would practise the seventy-two athletic postures. Also in many other ways I would strive to make my strength exceeding great; and all this I kept most secret from my guardians.

At last on one night I resolved to try my strength; so, pushing aside the curtain, I passed into the corridor. Springing upon the soldier that guarded me, I brought him to the

304

ground; and with my right hand under his chin, my left on his right shoulder, and my knee at the nape of his neck, I tore his head from his body before he could utter a cry.

I was now in my fifteenth year; but the deed was marvellous. None suspected me; it was thought a miracle.

The old eunuch, distressed, went to consult the magus of the well; whose answer was; " Let the vows of the priestess be taken!"

Now I thought this old man most foolish-obstinate; for I myself was obstinate and foolish. Not yet did I at all understand his wisdom or his purpose.

It often happens thus. Of old, men sent their priests to rebuke Nile for rising—until it was known that his rising was the cause of the fertility of their fields.

Now of the vows which I took upon me and of my service as priestess of the Veiled One it shall next be related.

CHAPTER III

It was the Equinox of Spring, and all my life stirred in me. They led me down cool colonnades of mighty stone clad in robes of white broidered with silver, and veiled with a veil of fine gold web fastened with rubies. They gave me not the Uraeus crown, nor any nemyss, nor the Ateph crown, but bound my forehead with a simple fillet of green leaves—vervain and mandrake and certain deadly herbs of which it is not fitting to speak.

Now the priests of the Veiled One were sore perplexed, for that never before had any boy been chosen priestess. For before the vows may be administered, the proofs of virginity are sought; and, as it seemed, this part of the ritual must be suppressed or glossed over. Then said the High Priest: " Let it be that we examine the first woman that he shall touch with his hand, and she shall suffice." Now when I heard this, I thought to test the God; and, spying in the crowd, I beheld in loose robes with flushed face and wanton eyes, a certain courtesan well-known in the city, and I touched her. Then those of the priests that hated me were glad, for they wished to reject me; and taking aside into the hall of trial that woman, made the enquiry.

Then with robes rent they came running forth, crying out against the Veiled One; for they found her perfect in virginity, and so was she even unto her death, as later appeared.

306

But the Veiled One was wroth with them because of this, and appeared in her glittering veil upon the steps of her temple. There she stood, and called them one by one; and she lifted but the eye-piece of her veil and looked into their eyes; and dead they fell before her as if smitten of the lightning.

But those priests who were friendly to me and loyal to the goddess took that virgin courtesan, and led her in triumph through the city, veiled and crowned as is befitting. Now after some days he that guarded the sacred goat of Khem died, and they appointed her in his place. And she was the first woman that was thus honoured since the days of the Evil Queen in the Eighteenth Dynasty, of her that wearied of men at an age when other women have not known them, that gave herself to gods and beasts.

But now they took me to the pool of liquid silver—or so they called it; I suppose it was quicksilver; for I remember that it was very difficult to immerse me—which is beneath the feet of the Veiled One. For this is the secret of the Oracle. Standing far off the priest beholds the reflection of her in the mirror, seeing her lips that move under the veil; and this he interprets to the seeker after truth.

Thus the priest reads wrongly the silence of the Goddess, and the seeker understands ill the speech of the priest. Then come forth fools, saying "The Goddess hath lied"—and in their folly they die.

While, therefore, they held me beneath the surface of the pool, the High Priestess took the vows on my behalf saying:

I swear by the orb of the Moon;

I swear by the circuit of the Stars;

THE EQUINOX

I swear by the Veil, and by the Face behind the Veil;

I swear by the Light Invisible, and by the Visible Darkness; On behalf of this Virgin that is buried in thy water;

To live in purity and service;

To love in beauty and truth;

To guard the Veil from the profane;

To die before the Veil; . . .

—and then came the awful penalty of failure.

I dare not recall half of it; yet in it were these words: Let her be torn by the Phallus of Set, and let her bowels be devoured by Apep; let her be prostituted to the lust of Besz, and let her face be eaten by the god ——.

It is not good to write His name.

Then they loosed me, and I lay smiling in the pool. They lifted me up and brought me to the feet of the goddess, so that I might kiss them. And as I kissed them such a thrill ran through me that I thought myself rapt away into the heaven of Amoun, or even as Asi when Hoor and Hoor-pa-kraat, cleaving her womb, sprang armed to life. Then they stripped me of my robes, and lashed me with fine twigs of virgin hazel, until my blood ran from me into the pool. But the surface of the silver swallowed up the blood by some mysterious energy; and they took this to be a sign of acceptance. So then they clothed me in the right robes of a priestess of the Veiled One; and they put a silver sistron in my hand, and bade me perform the ceremony of adoration. This I did, and the veil of the goddess glittered in the darkness—for night had fallen by this—with a strange starry light.

Thereby it was known that I was indeed chosen aright.

So last of all they took me to the banqueting-house and

set me on the high throne. One by one the priests came by and kissed my lips: one by one the priestesses came by, and gave me the secret clasp of hands that hath hidden virtue. And the banquet waxed merry; for all the food was magically prepared. Every beast that they slew was virgin; every plant that they plucked had been grown and tended by virgins in the gardens of the temple. Also the wine was spring water only, but so consecrated by the holy priestesses that one glass was more intoxicating than a whole skin of common wine. Yet this intoxication was a pure delight, an enthusiasm wholly divine; and it gave strength, and did away with sleep, and left no sorrow.

Last, as the first gray glow of Hormakhu paled the deep indigo of the night, they crowned and clothed me with white lotus flowers, and took me joyously back into the temple, there to celebrate the matin ritual of awakening the Veiled One.

Thus, and not otherwise, I became priestess of that holy goddess, and for a little while my life passed calm as the unruffled mirror itself.

It was from the Veiled One herself that came the Breath of Change.

On this wise.

In the Seventh Equinox after my initiation into her mystery the High Priestess was found to fail; at her invocation the Veil no longer glittered as was its wont. For this they deemed her impure, and resorted to many ceremonies, but without avail. At last in despair she went to the temple of Set, and gave herself as a victim to that dreadful god. Now all men were much disturbed at this, and it was not known at all of them what they should do.

Now it must be remembered that the ceremonies are always performed by a single priestess alone before the goddess, save only at the Initiations.

The others also had found themselves rejected of her; and when they learnt of the terrible end of the High Priestess, they became fearful. Some few, indeed, concealed their failure from the priests; but always within a day and a night they were found torn asunder in the outer courts; so that it seemed the lesser evil to speak truth.

Moreover, the affair had become a public scandal; for the goddess plagued the people with famine and with a terrible and foul disease.

But as for me, I wot not what to do; for to me always the Veil glittered, and that brighter than the ordinary. Yet I said nothing, but went about drooping and sorrowful, as if I were as unfortunate as they. For I would not seem to boast of the favour of the goddess.

Then they sent to the old Magus in the well; and he laughed outright at their beards, and would say no word. Also they sent to the sacred goat of Khem, and his priestess would but answer, "I, and such as I, may be favoured of Her," which they took for ribaldry and mocking. A third time they sent to the temple of Thoth the Ibis god of wisdom. And Thoth answered them by this riddle: "On how many legs doth mine Ibis stand?"

And they understood him not.

But the old High Priest determined to solve the mystery, though he paid forfeit with his life. So concealing himself in the temple, he watched in the pool for the reflection of the glittering of the Veil, while one by one we performed the adorations. And behind him and without stood the priests, watching for him to make a sign. This we knew not; but when it fell to me (the last) to adore that Veiled One, behold! the Veil glittered, and the old Priest threw up his arms to signal that which had occurred. And the flash of the Eye pierced the Veil, and he fell from his place dead upon the priests without.

They buried him with much honour, for that he had given his life for the people and for the temple, to bring back the favour of the Veiled One.

Then came they all very humbly unto me the child, and besought me to interpret the will of the Goddess. And her will was that I alone should serve her day and night.

Then they gave me to drink of the Cup of the Torment; and this is its virtue, that if one should speak falsely, invoking the name of the Goddess, he shall burn in hell visibly before all men for a thousand years; and that flame shall never be put out. There is such an one in her temple in Memphis, for I saw it with these eyes. There he burns and writhes and shrieks on the cold marble floor; and there he shall burn till his time expire, and he sink to that more dreadful hell below the West. But I drank thereof, and the celestial dew stood shining on my skin, and a coolness ineffable thrilled through me; whereat they all rejoiced, and obeyed the voice of the Goddess that I had declared unto them.

Now then was I alway alone with that Veiled One, and I must enter most fully into that secret period of my life. For, despite its ending, which hath put many wise men to shame, it was to me even as an eternity of rapture, of striving and of attainment beyond that which most mortals—and they initiates even!—call divine.

THE EQUINOX

Now first let it be understood what is the ritual of adoration of our Lady the Veiled One.

First, the priestess performs a mystical dance, by which all beings whatsoever, be they gods or demons, are banished, so that the place may be pure. Next, in another dance, even more secret and sublime, the presence of the Goddess is invoked into her Image. Next, the priestess goes a certain journey, passing the shrines of many great and terrible of the Lords of Khem, and saluting them. Last, she assumes the very self of the Goddess; and if this be duly done, the Veil glittereth responsive.

Therefore, if the Veil glittereth not, one may know that in some way the priestess hath failed to identify herself with Her. Thus an impurity in the thought of the priestess must cause her to fail; for the goddess is utterly pure.

Yet the task is alway difficult; for with the other gods one knoweth the appearance of their images; and steadily contemplating these one can easily attain to their imitation, and so to their comprehension, and to unity of consciousness with them. But with Our Veiled One, none who hath seen her face hath lived long enough to say one word, or call one cry.

So then it was of vital urgency to me to keep in perfect sympathy with that pure soul, so calm, so strong. With what terror then did I regard myself when, looking into my own soul, I saw no longer that perfect stillness. Strange was it, even as if one should see a lake stirred by a wind that one did not feel upon the cheeks and brow!

Trembling and ashamed, I went to the vesper adoration. I knew myself troubled, irritated, by I knew not what. And

312

in spite of all my efforts, this persisted even to the supreme moment of my assumption of her godhead.

And then? Oh but the Veil glittered as never yet; yea more! it shot out sparks of scintillant fire, silvery rose, a shower of flame and of perfume.

Then was I exceedingly amazed because of this, and made a Vigil before her all the night, seeking a Word. And that word came not.

Now of what further befell I will write anon.

CHAPTER IV

So it came to pass that I no longer went out at all from the presence of the goddess, save only to eat and to sleep. And the favour of her was restored to the people, so that all men were glad thereof.

For if any man murmured, he was slain incontinent, the people being mindful of the famine and the disease, and being minded to have no more of such, if it could by any means be avoided. They were therefore exceeding punctual with their gifts.

But I was daily more afraid, being in a great sweat of passion, of which I dared to speak to no man. Nor did I dare to speak even privily in mine own heart thereof, lest I should discover its nature. But I sent my favourite, the virgin Istarah (slim, pallid, and trembling as a young lotus in the West Wind), with my ring of office, to enquire of the old Magus of the well.

And he answered her by pointing upward to the sky and then downward to the earth. And I read this Oracle as if it were spoken "As above, so beneath." This came to me as I had flung myself in despair at the feet of my Lady, covering them with my tears; for by a certain manifest token I now knew that I had done a thing that was so dreadful that even now—these many thousand years hence—I dare hardly write it.

I loved the Veiled One.

ACROSS THE GULF

Yea, with the fierce passion of a beast, of a man, of a god, with my whole soul I loved her.

Even as I knew this by the manifest token the Veil burst into a devouring flame; it ate up the robes of my office, lapping them with its tongues of fire like a tigress lapping blood; yet withal it burnt me not, nor singed one hair.

Thus naked I fled away in fear, and in my madness slipped and fell into the pool of liquid silver, splashing it all over the hall; and even as I fled that rosy cataract of flame that wrapt me (from the Veil as it jetted) went out—went out——

The Veil was a dull web of gold, no more.

Then I crept fearfully to the feet of the goddess, and with my tears and kisses sought to wake her into life once more. But the Veil flamed not again; only a mist gathered about it and filled the temple, and hid all things from my eyes.

Now then came Istarah my favourite back with the ring and the message; and thinking that she brought bad news, I slit her lamb's-throat with the magic sickle, and her asp's-tongue I tore out with my hands, and threw it to the dogs and jackals.

Herein I erred sorely, for her news was good. Having reflected thereon, I perceived its import.

For since the Veil flamed always at my assumption, it was sure that I was in sympathy with that holy Veiled One.

If I were troubled, and knew not why; if my long peace were stirred—why then, so She!

"As above, so beneath!" For even as I, being man, sought to grasp godhead and crush it in my arms, so She, the pure essence, sought to manifest in form by love.

Yet I dared not repeat the ceremony at midnight.

Instead I lay prone, my arms outstretched in shame and pain, on the steps at her feet.

And lo! the Veil flamed. Then I knew that She too blamed Herself alike for her ardour and for her abstinence. Thus seven days I lay, never stirring; and all that time the Veil flamed subtly and softly, a steady bluish glow changing to green as my thought changed from melancholy to desire.

Then on the eighth day I rose and left the shrine and clad myself in new robes, in robes of scarlet and gold, with a crown of vine and bay and laurel and cypress. Also I purified myself and proclaimed a banquet. And I made the priests and the citizens, exceeding drunken. Then I called the guard, and purged thoroughly the whole temple of all of them, charging the captain on his life to let no man pass within. So that I should be absolutely alone in the whole precincts of the temple.

Then like an old gray wolf I wandered round the outer court, lifting up my voice in a mournful howl. And an ululation as of one hundred thousand wolves answered me, yet deep and muffled, as though it came from the very bowels of the earth.

Then at the hour of midnight I entered again the shrine and performed the ritual.

As I went on I became inflamed with an infinite lust for the Infinite; and now I let it leap unchecked, a very lion. Even so the Veil glowed red as with some infernal fire. Now then I am come to the moment of the Assumption; but instead of sitting calm and cold, remote, aloof, I gather myself together, and spring madly at the Veil, catching it in my two hands. Now the Veil was of woven gold, three thousand twisted wires; a span thick! Yet I put out my whole force to tear it across; and (for she also put out her force) it rent with a roar as of earthquake. Blinded I was with the glory of her face; I should have fallen; but she caught me to her, and fixed her divine mouth on mine, eating me up with the light of her eyes. Her mouth moaned, her throat sobbed with love; her tongue thrust itself into me as a shaft of sunlight smites into the palm-groves; my robes fell shrivelled, and flesh to flesh we clung. Then in some strange way she gripped me body and soul, twining herself about me and within me even as Death that devoureth mortal man.

Still, still my being increased; my consciousness expanded until I was all Nature seen as one, felt as one, apprehended as one, formed by me, part of me, apart from me—all these things at one moment—and at the same time the ecstasy of love grew colossal, a tower to scale the stars, a sea to drown the sun . . .

I cannot write of this . . . but in the streets people gathered apples of gold that dropped from invisible boughs, and invisible porters poured out wine for all, strange wine that healed disease and old age, wine that, poured between the teeth of the dead (so long as the embalmer had not begun his work), brought them back from the dark kingdom to perfect health and youth.

As for me, I lay as one dead in the arms of the holy Veiled One—Veiled no more!—while she took her pleasure of me ten times, a thousand times. In that whirlwind of passion all my strength was as a straw in the simoom.

Yet I grew not weaker but stronger. Though my ribs

317

cracked, I held firm. Presently indeed I stirred; it seemed as if her strength had come to me. Thus I forced back her head and thrust myself upon and into her even as a comet that impales the sun upon its horn! And my breath came fast between my lips and hers; her moan now faint, like a dying child, no more like a wild beast in torment.

Even so, wild with the lust of conquest, I urged myself upon her and fought against her. I stretched out her arms and forced them to the ground; then I crossed them on her breast, so that she was powerless. And I became like a mighty serpent of flame, and wrapt her, crushed her in my coils.

I was the master! . . .

Then grew a vast sound about me as of shouting: I grew conscious of the petty universe, the thing that seems apart from oneself, so long as one is oneself apart from it.

Men cried " The temple is on fire! The temple of Asi the Veiled One is burning! The mighty temple that gave its glory to Thebai is aflame! "

Then I loosed my coils and gathered myself together into the form of a mighty hawk of gold and spake one last word to her, a word to raise her from the dead!

But lo! not Asi, but Asar!

White was his garment, starred with red and blue and yellow. Green was his Countenance, and in his hands he bore the crook and scourge. Thus he rose, even as the temple fell about us in ruins, and we were left standing there.

And I wist not what to say.

Now then the people of the city crowded in upon us, and for the most part would have slain me.

But Thoth the mighty God, the wise one, with his Ibis-

318

head, and his nemyss of indigo, with his Ateph crown and his Phoenix wand and with his Ankh of emerald, with his magic apron in the Three colours; yea, Thoth, the God of Wisdom, whose skin is of tawny orange as though it burned in a furnace, appeared visibly to all of us. And the old Magus of the Well, whom no man had seen outside his well for nigh threescore years, was found in the midst: and he cried with a loud voice, saying:

" The Equinox of the Gods! "

And he went on to explain how it was that Nature should no longer be the centre of man's worship, but Man himself, man in his suffering and death, man in his purification and perfection. And he recited the Formula of the Osiris as follows, even as it hath been transmitted unto us by the Brethren of the Cross and Rose unto this day:

" For Asar Un-nefer hath said:
He that is found perfect before the Gods hath said:
These are the elements of my body, perfected through suffering, glorified through trial.
For the Scent of the dying Rose is the repressed sigh of my suffering;
The Flame-Red fire is the energy of my undaunted Will;
The Cup of Wine is the outpouring of the blood of my heart, sacrificed to regeneration;
And the Bread and Salt are the Foundations of my Body
Which I destroy in order that they may be renewed.
For I am Asar triumphant, even Asar Un-nefer the Justified One!
I am He who is clothed with the body of flesh,
Yet in Whom is the Spirit of the mighty Gods.
I am the Lord of Life, triumphant over death; he who partaketh with me shall arise with me.
I am the manifestor in Matter of those whose abode is in the Invisible.
I am purified: I stand upon the Universe: I am its Reconciler with the eternal Gods: I am the Perfector of Matter; and without me the Universe is not! "

319

THE EQUINOX

All this he said, and displayed the sacraments of Osiris before them all; and in a certain mystical manner did we all symbolically partake of them. But for me! in the Scent of the dying Rose I beheld rather the perfection of the love of my lady the Veiled One, whom I had won, and slain in the winning!

Now, however, the old Magus clad me (for I was yet naked) in the dress of a Priest of Osiris. He gave me the robes of white linen, and the leopard's skin, and the wand and ankh. Also he gave me the crook and scourge, and girt me with the royal girdle. On my head he set the holy Uraeus serpent for a crown; and then, turning to the people, cried aloud:

"Behold the Priest of Asar in Thebai!

"He shall proclaim unto ye the worship of Asar; see that ye follow him!"

Then, ere one could cry "Hold!" he had vanished from our sight.

I dismissed the people; I was alone with the dead God; with Osiris, the Lord of Amennti, the slain of Typhon, the devoured of Apophis . . .

Yea, verily, I was alone!

CHAPTER V

Now then the great exhaustion took hold upon me, and I fell at the feet of the Osiris as one dead. All knowledge of terrestrial things was gone from me; I entered the kingdom of the dead by the gate of the West. For the worship of Osiris is to join the earth to the West; it is the cultus of the Setting Sun. Through Isis man obtains strength of nature; through Osiris he obtains the strength of suffering and ordeal, and as the trained athlete is superior to the savage, so is the magic of Osiris stronger than the magic of Isis. So by my secret practices at night, while my guardians strove to smooth my spirit to a girl's, had I found the power to bring about that tremendous event, an Equinox of the Gods.

Just as thousands of years later was my secret revolt against Osiris—for the world had suffered long enough!—destined to bring about another Equinox in which Horus was to replace the Slain One with his youth and vigour and victory.

I passed therefore into these glowing abodes of Amennti, clad in thick darkness, while my body lay entranced at the feet of the Osiris in the ruined temple.

Now the god Osiris sent forth his strange gloom to cover us, lest the people should perceive or disturb; Therefore I lay peacefully entranced, and abode in Amennti. There I confronted the devouring god, and there was my heart weighed and found perfect; there the two-and-forty Judges bade me pass through the pylons they guarded; there I spoke with the Seven, and with the Nine, and with the Thirty-Three; and at the end I came out into the abode of the Holy Hathor, into her mystical mountain, and being there crowned and garlanded I rejoiced exceedingly, coming out through the gate of the East, the Beautiful gate, unto the Land of Khemi, and the city of Thebai, and the temple that had been the temple of the Veiled One. There I rejoined my body, making the magical links in the prescribed manner, and rose up and did adoration to the Osiris by the fourfold sign. Therefore the Light of Osiris began to dawn; it went about the city whirling forth, abounding, crying aloud; whereat the people worshipped, being abased with exceeding fear. Moreover, they hearkened unto their wise men and brought gifts of gold, so that the temple floor was heaped high; and gifts of oxen, so that the courts of the temple could not contain them: and gifts of slaves, as it were a mighty army.

Then I withdrew myself; and taking counsel with the wisest of the priests and of the architects and of the sculptors, I gave out my orders so that the temple might duly be builded. By the favour of the god all things went smoothly enough; yet was I conscious of some error in the working; or if you will, some weakness in myself and my desire. Look you, I could not forget the Veiled One, my days of silence and solitude with Her, the slow dawn of our splendid passion, the climax of all that wonder in her ruin!

So as the day approached for the consecration of the temple I began to dread some great catastrophe. Yet all went well—perhaps too well.

322

The priests and the people knew nothing of this, however. For the god manifested exceptional favour; as a new god must do, or how shall he establish his position? The harvests were fourfold, the cattle eightfold; the women were all fertile—yea! barren women of sixty years bore twins!—there was no disease or sorrow in the city.

Mighty was the concourse of the citizens on the great day of the consecration.

Splendid rose the temple, a fortress of black granite. The columns were carved with wonderful images of all the gods adoring Osiris; marvels of painting glittered on the walls; they told the story of Osiris, of his birth, his life, his death at the hands of Typhon, the search after his scattered members, the birth of Horus and Harpocrates, the vengeance upon Typhon Seth, the resurrection of Osiris.

The god himself was seated in a throne set back into the wall. It was of lapis-lazuli and amber, it was inlaid with emerald and ruby. Mirrors of polished gold, of gold burnished with dried poison of asps, so that the slaves who worked upon it might die. For, it being unlawful for those mirrors to have ever reflected any mortal countenance, the slaves were both blinded and veiled; yet even so, it were best that they should die.

At last the ceremony began. With splendid words, with words that shone like flames, did I consecrate all that were there present, even the whole city of Thebai.

And I made the salutation unto the attendant gods, very forcibly, so that they responded with echoes of my adoration. And Osiris accepted mine adoration with gladness as I journeyed about at the four quarters of the temple.

THE EQUINOX

Now cometh the mysterious ceremony of Assumption. I took upon myself the form of the god: I strove to put my heart in harmony with his.

Alas! alas! I was in tune with the dead soul of Isis; my heart was as a flame of elemental lust and beauty; I could not—I could not. Then the heavens lowered and black clouds gathered upon the Firmament of Nu. Dark flames of lightning rent the clouds, giving no light. The thunder roared; the people were afraid. In his dark shrine the Osiris gloomed, displeasure on his forehead, insulted majesty in his eyes. Then a pillar of dust whirled down from the vault of heaven, even unto me as I stood alone, half-defiant, in the midst of the temple while the priests and the people cowered and wailed afar off. It rent the massy roof as it had been a thatch of straw, whirling the blocks of granite far away into the Nile. It descended, roaring and twisting, like a wounded serpent demon-king in his death-agony; it struck me and lifted me from the temple; it bore me through leagues of air into the desert; then it dissolved and flung me contemptuously on a hill of sand. Breathless and dazed I lay, anger and anguish tearing at my heart.

I rose to swear a mighty curse; exhaustion took me, and I fell in a swoon to the earth.

When I came to myself it was nigh dawn. I went to the top of the hillock and looked about me. Nothing but sand, sand all ways. Just so was it within my heart!

The only guide for my steps (as the sun rose) was a greener glimpse in the East, which I thought might be the valley of the Nile reflected. Thither I bent my steps: all day I struggled with the scorching heat, the shifting sand. At night I tried to sleep, for sheer fatigue impelled me. But as often as I lay

324

down, so often restlessness impelled me forward. I would stagger on awhile, then stumble and fall. Only at dawn I slept perhaps for an hour, and woke chilled to death by my own sweat. I was so weak that I could hardly raise a hand; my tongue was swollen, so that I could not greet the sun-disk with the accustomed adoration. My brain had slipped control; I could no longer even think of the proper spells that might have brought me aid. Instead, dreadful shapes drew near; one, a hideous camel-demon, an obscene brute of filth; another, a black ape with a blue muzzle and crimson buttocks, all his skin hairless and scabby, with his mass of mane oiled and trimmed like a beautiful courtesan's. This fellow mocked me with the alluring gestures of such an one, and anon voided his excrement upon me. Moreover there were others, menacing and terrible, vast cloudy demon-shapes. . . .

I could not think of the words of power that control them.

Now the sun that warmed my chill bones yet scorched me further. My tongue so swelled that I could hardly breathe; my face blackened; my eyes bulged out. The fiends came closer; drew strength from my weakness, made themselves material bodies, twitched me and spiked me and bit me. I turned on them and struck feebly again and again; but they evaded me easily and their yelling laughter rang like hell's in my ears. Howbeit I saw that they attacked me only on one side, as if to force me to one path. But I was wise enough to keep my shadow steadily behind me: and they, seeing this, were all the more enraged; I therefore the more obstinate in my course. Then they changed their tactics; and made as if to keep me in the course I had chosen; and seeing this, I was confirmed therein.

THE EQUINOX

Truly with the gods I went! for in a little while I came to a pool of water and a tall palm standing by.

I plunged in that cool wave; my strength came back, albeit slowly; yet with one wave of my hand in the due gesture the fiends all vanished; and in an hour I was sufficiently restored to call forth my friends from the pool—the little fishes my playmates—and the nymph of the pool came forth and bowed herself before me and cooked me the fishes with that fire that renders water luminous and sparkling. Also she plucked me dates from the tree, and I ate thereof. Thus was I much comforted; and when I had eaten, she took my head upon her lap, and sang me to sleep; for her voice was like the ripple of the lakes under the wind of spring and like the bubbling of a well and like the tinkling of a fountain through a bed of moss. Also she had deep notes like the sea that booms upon a rocky shore.

So long, long, long I slept.

Now when I awoke the nymph had gone; but I took from my bosom a little casket of certain sacred herbs; and casting a few grains into the pool, repaid her for her courtesy. And I blessed her in the name of our dead lady Isis, and went on in the strength of that delicious meal for a great way. Yet I wist not what to do; for I was as it were a dead man, although my age was barely two and twenty years.

What indeed should befall me?

Yet I went on; and, climbing a ridge, beheld at last the broad Nile, and a shining city that I knew not.

There on the ridge I stood and gave thanks to the great gods of Heaven, the Aeons of infinite years, that I had come thus far. For at the sight of Nilus new life began to dawn in me.

CHAPTER VI

WITHOUT any long delay I descended the slopes and entered the city. Not knowing what might have taken place in Thebai and what news might have come hither, I did not dare declare myself; but seeking out the High Priest of Horus I showed him a certain sign, telling him that I was come from Memphis on a journey, and intended to visit Thebai to pay homage at the shrine of Isis. But he, full of the news, told me that the ancient priestess of Isis, who had become priest of Osiris, had been taken up to heaven as a sign of the signal favour of the God. Whereat I could hardly hold myself from laughter; yet I controlled myself and answered that I was now prepared to return to Memphis, for that I was vowed to Isis, and Osiris could not serve my turn.

At this he begged me to stay as his guest, and to go worship at the temple of Isis in this city. I agreed thereto, and the good man gave me new robes and jewels from the treasury of his own temple. There too I rested sweetly on soft cushions fanned by young boys with broad leaves of palm. Also he sent me the dancing girl of Sleep. It was the art of this girl to weave such subtle movements that the sense, watching her, swooned; and as she swayed she sang, ever lower and lower as she moved slower and slower, until the looker-listener was dissolved in bliss of sleep and delicate dream.

THE EQUINOX

Then as he slept she would bend over him even as Nuit the Lady of the Stars that bendeth over the black earth, and in his ears she would whisper strange rhythms, secret utterances, whereby his spirit would be rapt into the realms of Hathor or some other golden goddess, there in one night to reap an harvest of refreshment such as the fields of mortal sleep yield never.

So then I woke at dawn, to find her still watching, still looking into my eyes with a tender smile on her mouth that cooed whispers infinitely soothing. Indeed with a soft kiss she waked me, for in this Art there is a right moment to sleep, and another to waken: which she was well skilled to divine.

I rose then—she flitted away like a bird—and robed myself; and, seeking my host, went forth with him to the Temple of Isis.

Now their ritual (it appeared) differed in one point from that to which I was accustomed. Thus, it was not death to intrude upon the ceremony save only for the profane. Priests of a certain rank of initiation might if they pleased behold it. I, therefore, wishing to see again that marvellous glowing of the Veil, disclosed a sufficient sign to the High Priest. Thereat was he mightily amazed; and, from the foot judging Hercules, began to think that I might be some sacred envoy or inspector from the Gods themselves. This I allowed him to think; meanwhile we went forward into the shrines and stood behind the pillars, unseen, in the prescribed position.

Now it chanced that the High Priestess herself had this day chosen to perform the rite.

This was a woman tall and black, most majestic, with

328

ACROSS THE GULF

limbs strong as a man's. Her gaze was hawk-keen, and her
brow commanding. But at the Assumption of the God-form
she went close and whispered into the Veil, so low that we
could not hear it; but as it seemed with fierce intensity, with
some passion that knotted up her muscles, so that her arms
writhed like wounded snakes. Also the veins of her forehead
swelled, and foam came to her lips. We thought that she had
died; her body swelled and shuddered; last of all a terrible
cry burst from her throat, inarticulate, awful.

Yet all this while the Veil glittered, though something
sombrely. Also the air was filled with a wild sweeping music,
which rent our very ears with its uncouth magic. For it was
like no music that I had ever heard before. At last the
Priestess tore herself away from the Veil and reeled—as one
drunken—down the temple. Sighs and sobs tore her breast;
and her nails made bloody grooves in her wet flanks.

On a sudden she espied me and my companion; with one
buffet she smote him to earth—it is unlawful to resist the
Priestess when she is in the Ecstasy of Union—and falling
upon me, like a wild beast she buried her teeth in my neck,
bearing me to the ground. Then, loosing me, while the blood
streamed from me, she fixed her glittering eyes upon it with
strange joy, and with her hands she shook me as a lion shakes
a buck. Sinewy were her hands, with big knuckles, and the
strength of her was as cords of iron. Yet her might was but a
mortal's; in a little she gave one gasp like a drowning man's;
her body slackened, and fell with its dead weight on mine,
her mouth glued to mine in one dreadful kiss. Dreadful; for
as my mouth returned it, almost mechanically, the blood
gushed from her nostrils and blinded me. I too, then, more

f   329

dead than alive, swooned into bliss, into trance. I was awakened by the High Priest of Horus. "Come," he said; "she is dead." I disengaged myself from all that weight of madness—and the body writhed convulsively as I turned it over—I kissed those frothy lips, for in death she was beautiful beyond belief, joyous beyond description—thence I staggered to the Veil, and saluted with all my strength, so that it glittered under the force of my sheer will. Then I turned me again, and with the High Priest sought his house.

Strange indeed was I as I went through the city, my new robes dark with blood of that most holy sorceress.

But no one of the people dared so much as lift his eyes; nor spoke we together at all. But when we were come into the house of the High Priest, sternly did he confront me.

"What is this, my son?"

And I weary of the folly of the world and of the uselessness of things answered him:

"Father, I go back to Memphis. I am the Magus of the Well."

Now he knew the Magus, and answered me:

"Why liest thou?"

And I said "I am come into the world where all speech is false, and all speech is true."

Then he did me reverence, abasing himself unto the ground even unto nine-and-ninety times.

And I spurned him and said, "Bring forth the dancing girl of Sleep; for in the morning I will away to Memphis."

And she came forth, and I cursed her and cried: "Be thou the dancing girl of Love!"

And it was so. And I went in unto her, and knew her;

330

and in the morning I girded myself, and boarded the state barge of the High Priest, and pillowed myself upon gold and purple, and disported myself with lutes and with lyres and with parrots, and with black slaves, and with wine and with delicious fruits, until I came even unto the holy city of Memphis.

And there I called soldiers of Pharaoh, and put cruelly to death all them that had accompanied me; and I burnt the barge, adrift upon the Nile at sunset, so that the flames alarmed the foolish citizens. All this I did, and danced naked in my madness through the city, until I came to the Old Magus of the Well.

And laughing, I threw a stone upon him, crying: " Ree me the riddle of my life!"

And he answered naught.

Then I threw a great rock upon him, and I heard his bones crunch, and I cried in mockery: " Ree me the riddle of *thy* life!"

But he answered naught.

Then I threw down the wall of the well; and I burned the house with fire that stood thereby, with the men-servants and the maid-servants.

And none dared stay me; for I laughed and exulted in my madness. Yea, verily, I laughed, and laughed—and laughed——

CHAPTER VII

THEN being healed of my madness I took all the treasure of that old Magus which he had laid up for many years—and none gainsaid me. Great and splendid was it, of gold more than twelve bullocks could draw, of balassius rubies, and sardonyx, and beryl, and chrysoprase; of diamond and starry sapphire, of emerald much, very much, of topaz and of amethyst great and wonderful gems. Also he had a figure of Nuit greater than a woman, which was made of lapis lazuli specked with gold, carved with marvellous excellence. And he had the secret gem of Hadit that is not found on earth, for that it is invisible save when all else is no more seen.

Then went I into the market and bought slaves. I bought me in particular a giant, a Nubian blacker than polished granite seen by starlight, tall as a young palm and straight, yet more hideous than the Ape of Thoth. Also I bought a young pale stripling from the North, a silly boy with idle languishing ways. But his mouth burned like sunset when the dust-storms blow. So pale and weak was he that all despised him and mocked him for a girl. Then he took a white-hot iron from the fire and wrote with it my name in hieroglyphics on his breast; nor did his smile once alter while the flesh hissed and smoked.

Thus we went out a great caravan to a rocky islet in the

Nile, difficult of access for that the waters foamed and swirled dangerously about it. There we builded a little temple shaped like a beehive; but there was no altar and no shrine therein; for in that temple should the god be sacrificed unto himself.

Myself I made the god thereof; I powdered my hair with gold, and inwound it with flowers. I gilded my eyelids, and I stained my lips with vermilion. I gilded my breasts and my nails, and as God and Victim in one was I daily sacrificed unto that strange thing that was none other than myself. I made my giant Nubian high priest; and I endowed his wand with magic power, so that he might properly perform my rites. This he did to such purpose that many men from Memphis and even from more distant towns, leaving their gods, came hither, and did sacrifice. Then I appointed also the pale boy warder of the Sanctuary: and he swore unto me to be faithful unto death.

Now there arose a great strife in Memphis, and many foolish and lewd women cried out against us. So fierce was the uproar that a great company of women issued forth from the city and came into the island. They slew my pale boy at the gate, though sword in hand he fought against them. Then they frothed on, and I confronted them in my glory. They hesitated, and in that moment I smote them with a deadly itching, so that running forth they tore off their clothes and set themselves to scratching, while my people laughed until they ached.

At the term, indeed, with exhaustion and with loss of blood they died all; four hundred and two women perished in that great day's slaughter. So that the people of Memphis had peace for awhile.

THE EQUINOX

But as for me, I mourned the loss of that young slave. I had his body embalmed as is not fitting for other than a king. And at the door of the temple I placed his sarcophagus beneath a hedge of knives and spears, so that there was no other access to my glory.

Like honour hath no slave had ever.

Thus then I abode three cycles of the season; and at the end of that time the High Priest died.

For mine was a strange and dreadful rite to do; none other, and none unfortified by magic power, could have done this thing.

Yet I too sickened of that everlasting sacrifice. I was become worn and wan; there was no blood but ice in my veins. I had indeed become all but a god . . .

Therefore I took the body of my Nubian, and slew four young girls, and filled all the hollow spaces of his body with their blood. Then too I sealed up his body with eight seals; and the ninth seal was mine own, the centre of my godhead.

Then he rose slowly and staggeringly as I uttered the dreadful words:

> A ka dua
> Tuf ur biu
> Bi aa chefu
> Dudu ner af an nuteru!

Then I touched him with my wand and he rose into full power of his being; and we entered in, and for the last time did he perform (though silent) the ceremony. At whose end he lay shrivelled and collapsed, shrunken like an old wine-skin; yet his blood availed me nothing. I was icier than before. Yet now indeed was I Osiris, for I sent out flames of cold gray glory from my skin, and mine eyes were rigid with ecstasy.

Yea, by Osiris himself, I swear it! Even as the eyes of all living men revolve ceaselessly, so were mine fixed!

Then I shook myself and went forth into the city of Memphis, my face being veiled and my steps led by slaves.

And there I went into the temples one by one; and I twitched aside my veil, whereat all men fell dead on the instant, and the gods tumbled from their places, and broke in pieces upon the floor.

And I veiled myself, and went into the market-place and lifted up my voice in a chant and cried:

> Death, and desolation, and despair!
> I lift up my voice, and all the gods are dumb.
> I unveil my face, and all that liveth is no more,
> I sniff up life, and breathe forth destruction.
> I hear the music of the world, and its echo is Silence.
>
> Death, and desolation, and despair!
> The parting of the ways is come: the Equinox of the Gods is past.
> Another day: another way.
> Let them that hear me be abased before me!
> Death, and desolation, and despair!

Then I pulled away my veil, and the cold lightnings of death shot forth, and the people of the city fell dead where they stood.

Save only one, a young boy, a flute-player, that was blind, and, seeing not those eyes of mine, died not.

Then to him I spake, saying:

"Arise, summon the priests and the people, all that remain. And let them build a temple unto Osiris the God of the dead, and let the dead be worshipped for ever and ever."

335

THE EQUINOX

This I said, and went out from the city with the two slaves that I had left in the gate, and we went unto Nile, unto a cave by the bank of the river; and there I abode for many months, weeping for Isis my Lady. For though I had avenged her in many dreadful deeds, yet I brought her not back unto life. Moreover the love of her was as it were dead in me, so that my heart stirred not at the thought of her. Say that my love wandered like a ghost unburied, frozen, adrift upon the winds!

Now of my deeds at this period it is almost too horrible to tell. For I performed great penance, in the hope of vitalizing that dead principle in me which men call the soul.

I starved myself shamefully, in this manner. First surrounding myself with all possible luxuries of food, brought in steaming and savoury from hour to hour, I yet condemned myself to subsist upon a little garlic and a little salt, with a little water in which oats had been bruised.

Then if any wish arose in me to eat of the dainties around me I gashed myself with a sharp stone.

Moreover I kindled a great fire in the cave so that the slaves stumbled and fainted as they approached. And the smoke choked me so that I constantly vomited a black and ill-smelling mucus from my lungs, stained here and there with frothing blood.

Again, I suffered my hair to grow exceeding long, and therein I harboured vermin. Also, when I lay down to sleep, though this I did not till with swollen tongue and blackened throat I could no longer howl the name of my dead Lady, then (I say) did I smear my limbs with honey, that the rats of the cave might gnaw them as I slept. Moreover, I pillowed

336

mine head upon a corpse dead of leprosy, and whenever that dead soul of mine stirred at all with love toward my Lady, then I caressed and kissed that corpse, and sang soft songs to it, playing with gracious words and gestures. All this spoke loudly to my soul, rebuking it for its weakness and corruption. So too the bitterness and foulness of my life would often overleap the limit of sensibility; and then for hours together would I be lost in a raging whirlwind of laughter. At this time my slaves would be afraid to come anigh me, and then darting out of the cave I would catch one by the hair and dragging him within put him to exquisite torture. This indeed was of great use to me; for I would devise atrocious things, and if they served to excite his utmost anguish I would then try them on myself. Thus I would run needles steeped in Nile mud beneath my finger-nails, so that the sores festering might produce a sickening agony. Or again I would cut strips of skin and tear them off; but this failed, though it acted well enough upon the slave, for my own skin had become too brittle. Then I would take a piece of hard wood, and hammer it with a stone against the bones, hurting the membrane that covers them, and causing it to swell. This too I had to abandon, for the limb of the slave died, and he swelled up and rotted and turned green, and in shocking agony he died.

So then I was compelled to cure myself magically, and this was a great loss of force.

Yet was I " Far from the Happy Ones," although my lips hung on my fleshless face like bean-pods withered and blackened, and although there was not one inch of skin upon all my body that was not scarred.

Yet my trial was nigh its end. For the people of Memphis, wondering at the frequent purchases of dead lepers made always by the same slave, began, as is the wont of the ignorant, to spread foolish rumours. At last they said openly "There is an holy hermit in the old cave by Nile." Then the barren women of the city came out stealthily to me in the hope that by my sanctity their dry sticks might blossom.

But I showed them my dead leper, and said "Let me first beget children upon this, and after I will do your business." This liked them not; yet they left me not alone, for they went home and cried out that I was an horror, a ghoul, a vampire. . . . And at that all the young and beautiful women of the city, leaving their lovers and their husbands, flocked to me, bringing gifts. But I took them to the dead leper and said, "When you are beautiful as that is beautiful, and when I am weary of its beauty and its delight, then will I do your pleasure."

Then they all raged vehemently against me, and stirred up the men of the city to destroy me. And I, not being minded to display my magic force, went by night (so soon as I heard of this) and took sanctuary in the shrine of Osiris that I had caused them to build. And there I attained felicity; for uniting my consciousness with the god's, I obtained the expansion of that consciousness. Is not the kingdom of the dead a mighty kingdom?

So I perceived the universe as it were a single point of infinite nothingness yet of infinite extension; and becoming this universe, I became dissolved utterly therein. Moreover, my body lifted itself up and rose in the air to a great height beyond the shadow of the earth, and the earth rolled beneath me; yet of all this I knew nothing, for that I was all these things and none of them. Moreover I was united with Isis the Mother of Osiris, being yet her brother and her lord.

Woe, woe to me! for all this was but partial and imperfect; nor did I truly understand that which occurred.

Only this I knew, that I should return to my city of Thebai, and rule therein as High Priest of Osiris, no longer striving to some end unheard-of or impossible, but quietly and patiently living in the enjoyment of my dignities and wealth, even as a man.

Yet one thing I saw also, that as Isis is the Lady of all Nature, the living; and as Osiris is the Lord of the Dead, so should Horus come, the Hawk-headed Lord, as a young child, the image of all Nature and all Man raised above Life and Death, under the supreme rule of Hadit that is Force and of Nuit that is Matter—though they are a Matter and a Force that transcend all our human conceptions of these things.

But of this more anon, in its due place.

CHAPTER VIII

BEHOLD me then returned to Thebai! So scarred and altered
was I, though not yet thirty years of age, that they knew me
not. So I offered myself as a serving-man in the temple of
Osiris, and I pleased the priests mightily, for by my magic
power—though they thought it to be natural—I sang songs
unto the god, and made hymns. Therefore in less than a year
they began to speak of initiating me into the priesthood. Now
the High Priest at this time was a young and vigorous man,
black-bearded in the fashion of Osiris, with a single square
tuft beneath the chin. Him had they chosen after my departure
in the whirlwind. And the High Priestess was a woman of
forty and two years old, both dark and beautiful, with flashing
eyes and stern lips. Yet her body was slim and lithe like that
of a young girl. Now, as it chanced, it was my turn to serve
her with the funeral offerings; flesh of oxen and of geese,
bread, and wine. And as she ate she spake with me; for she
could see by her art that I was not a common serving-man.
Then I took out the consecrated Wand of Khem that I had
from my father; and I placed it in her hand. At that she
wondered, for that Wand is the sign of a great and holy
initiation: so rare that (as they say) no woman but one has
ever attained unto it. Then she blessed herself that she had
been permitted to look upon it, and prayed me to keep silence

for a little while, for she had somewhat in her mind to do. And I lifted up the wand upon her in the nine-and-forty-fold benediction, and she received illumination thereof, and rejoiced. Then I fell at her feet—for she was the High Priestess—and kissed them reverently, and withdrew.

Then three days afterwards, as I learnt, she sent for a priestess who was skilled in certain deadly crafts and asked of her a poison. And she gave it, saying: "Let the High Priest of the God of the dead go down to the dead!" Then that wicked High Priestess conveyed unto him subtly the poison in the sacraments themselves, and he died thereof. Then by her subtlety she caused a certain youth to be made high priest who was slovenly and stupid, thinking in herself "Surely the god will reject him." But at his word the Image of the god glowed as was its wont. And at that she knew— and we all knew—that the glory was departed; for that the priests had supplanted the right ceremony by some trick of deceit and craft.

Thereat was she mightily cast down, for though wicked and ambitious, she had yet much power and knowledge.

But instead of using that power and that knowledge she sought to oppose craft with craft. And suspecting (aright) whose cunning had done this thing she bribed him to reverse the machinery, so that the High Priest might be shamed. But shamed he was not; for he lied, saying that the God glowed brighter than the Sun; and he lied securely, for Maat the Lady of Truth had no place in that temple. To such foulness was all fallen by my first failure to assume the god-form, and their priestly falsehood that my sanctity had rapt me into heaven. Nor had the wealth they lied to obtain availed them aught; for Pharaoh had descended upon Thebai, and laid heavy hand upon the coffers of the temple, so that they were poor. Even, they sold good auguries for gold; and these were a very destruction to them that bought. Then they sold curses, and sowed discord in the city. Wherefore the people grew poorer still, and their gifts to the temple waxed even less.

For there is no foolishness like the hunger after gain.

Of old the gods had given blessing, and the people offered freely of their plenty.

Now the priests sowed chaff, and reaped but barrenness.

So I waited patiently in silence to see what might befall. And this foolish priestess could think of no better expedient than formerly. But this young stupid man had guessed how his predecessor was dead, and he touched not the sacraments; but feigned.

Then she called for me—and I was now ordained priest—to take counsel of me; for she was minded to put me in his place.

Thus she made a great banquet for me; and when we were well drunken she laid her head upon my breast and said marvellous things to me of love, to me, who had loved the Veiled One! But I feigned all the madness of passion and made her drunk thereon, so that she talked great words, frothing forth like dead fishes swollen in the sun, of how we should rule Thebai and (it might be) displace Pharaoh and take his throne and sceptre. Yet, foolish woman! she could not think how she might remove this stupid high priest, her own nominee! So I answered her "Assume the Form of Osiris, and all will be well in the Temple of Osiris." Mocking her, for I knew that she could not. Yet so drunken was she upon love and wine that there and then she performed the ritual of Adoration and Assumption.

Then I in merry mood put out my power, and caused her in truth to become Osiris, so that she went icy stark, and her eyes fixed. . . .

Then she tried to shriek with fear, and could not; for I had put upon her the silence of the tomb.

But all the while I feigned wonder and applause, so that she was utterly deceived. And being tired of mocking her, I bade her return. This she did, and knew not what to say. At first she pretended to have received a great secret; then, knowing how much higher was my grade of initiation, dared not. Then, at last, being frightened, she flung herself at my feet and confessed all, pleading that at least her love for me was true. This may well have been; in any case I would have had compassion upon her, for in sooth her body was like a flower, white and pure, though her mouth was heavy and strong, her eyes wrinkled with lust, and her cheeks flaccid with deceit.

So I comforted her, pressing her soft body in mine arms, drinking the wine of her eyes, feeding upon the honey of her mouth.

Then at last I counselled her that she should bid him to a secret banquet, and that I should serve them, disguised in my old dress as a serving-man.

On the next night after this he came, and I served them, and she made open love (though feigned) to him. Yet subtly, so that he thought her the deer and himself the lion. Then at last he went clean mad, and said: " I will give thee what thou wilt for one kiss of that thy marvellous mouth." Then she made him swear the oath by Pharaoh—the which if he broke Pharaoh would have his head—and she kissed him once, as if her passion were like the passion of Nile in flood for the sandy bars that it devoureth, and then leaping up, answered him, "Give me thine office of High Priest for this my lover!" With that she took and fondled me. He gaped, aghast; then he took off the ring of office and flung it at her feet; he spat one word in her face; he slunk away.

But I, picking up the ring of office, cried after him: "What shall be done to who insulteth the High Priestess?"

And he turned and answered sullenly: "I was the High Priest." "Thou hadst no longer the ring!" she raged at him, her face white with fury, her mouth dripping the foam of her anger—for the word was a vile word! . . .

Then she smote upon the bell, and the guard appeared. At her order they brought the instruments of death, and summoned the executioner, and left us there. Then the executioner bound him to the wheel of iron by his ankles and his waist and his throat; and he cut off his eyelids, that he might look upon his death. Then with his shears he cut off the lips from him, saying, "With these lips didst thou blaspheme the Holy One, the Bride of Osiris." Then one by one he wrenched out the teeth of him, saying every time: "With this tooth didst thou frame a blasphemy against the Holy One, the Bride of Osiris." Then he pulled out the tongue with his pincers, saying: "With this tongue didst thou speak blasphemy against the Holy One, the Bride of Osiris." Then took he a strong corrosive acid and blistered his throat therewith, saying: "From this throat didst thou blaspheme the Holy One,

344

the Bride of Osiris." Then he took a rod of steel, white-hot, and burnt away his secret parts, saying: "Be thou put to shame, who hast blasphemed the Holy One, the Bride of Osiris." After that, he took a young jackal and gave it to eat at his liver, saying: "Let the beasts that devour carrion devour the liver that lifted itself up to blaspheme the Holy One, the Bride of Osiris!" With that the wretch died, and they exposed his body in the ditch of the city, and the dogs devoured it.

Now all this while had my lady dallied amorously with me, making such sweet moan of love as never was, yet her face fixed upon his eyes who loved her, and there glared in hell's torment, the body ever striving against the soul which should exceed.

And, as I judge, by the favour of Set the Soul gat mastery therein.

Also, though I write it now, coldly, these many thousand years afterward, never had I such joy of love of any woman as with her, and at that hour, so that as I write it I remember well across the mist of time every honey word she spoke, every witching kiss (our mouths strained sideways) that she sucked from my fainting lips, every shudder of her soft strong body. I remember the jewelled coils of hair, how they stung like adders as they touched me; the sharp rapture of her pointed nails pressing me, now velvet-soft, now capricious-cruel, now (love-maddened) thrust deep to draw blood, as they played up and down my spine. But I saw nothing; by Osiris I swear it! I saw nothing, save only the glare in the eyes of that lost soul that writhed upon the wheel.

Indeed, as the hangman took out the corpse, we fell back

and lay there among the waste of the banquet, the flagons overturned, the napery awry, the lamps extinct or spilt, the golden cups, chased with obscene images, thrown here and there, the meats hanging over the edge of their bejewelled dishes, their juice staining the white luxury of the linen; and in the midst ourselves, our limbs as careless as the wind, motionless.

One would have said: the end of the world is come. But through all that fiery abyss of sleep wherein I was plunged so deep, still stirred the cool delight of the knowledge that I had won the hand for which I played, that I was High Priest of Osiris in Thebai.

But in the morning we rose and loathed each other, our mouths awry, our tongues hanging loose from their corners like thirsty dogs, our eyes blinking in agony from the torture of daylight, our limbs sticky with stale sweat.

Therefore we rose and saluted each other in the dignity of our high offices; and we departed one from the other, and purified ourselves.

Then I went unto the Ceremony of Osiris, and for the last time the shameful farce was played.

But in my heart I vowed secretly to cleanse the temple of its chicanery and folly. Therefore at the end of the ceremony did I perform a mighty banishing, a banishing of all things mortal and immortal, even from Nuit that circleth infinite Space unto Hadit the Core of Things; from Amoun that ruleth before all the Gods unto Python the terrible Serpent that abideth at the end of things, from Ptah the god of the pure soul of aethyr unto Besz the brute force of that which is grosser than earth, which hath no name, which is denser than lead and more rigid than steel; which is blacker than the thick darkness of the abyss, yet is within all and about all.

Amen!

Then during the day I took counsel with myself, and devised a cunning to match the cunning of them that had blasphemed Osiris, who had at last become my God.

Yea! bitterly would I avenge him on the morrow.

CHAPTER IX

Now this was the manner of my working, that I inspired the High Priestess to an Oracle, so that she prophesied, saying that Osiris should never be content with his servants unless they had passed the four ordeals of the elements. Now of old these rituals had been reserved for a special grade of initiation. The chapter was therefore not a little alarmed, until they remembered how shamefully all the true magic was imitated, so that the rumour went that this was but a device of the High Priestess to increase the reputation of the temple for sanctity. And, their folly confirming them in this, they agreed cheerfully and boasted themselves. Now then did I swathe them one by one in the grave-clothes of Osiris, binding upon the breast an image, truly consecrated, of the god, with a talisman against the four elements.

Then I set them one by one upon a narrow and lofty tower, balanced, so that the least breath of wind would blow them off into destruction.

Those whom the air spared I next threw into Nile where most it foams and races. Only a few the water gave back again. These, however, did I bury for three days in the earth without sepulchre or coffin, so that the element of earth might combat them. And the rare ones whom earth spared I cast upon a fire of charcoal.

ACROSS THE GULF

Now who is prepared for these ordeals (being firstly attuned to the elements) findeth them easy. He remains still, though the tempest rage upon the tower; in the water he floats easily and lightly; buried, he but throws himself into trance; and, lastly, his wrappings protect him against the fire, though all Thebai went to feed the blaze.

But it was not so with this bastard priesthood of Osiris. For of the three hundred only nine were found worthy. The High Priestess, however, I brought through by my magic, for she had amused me mightily, and I took great pleasure in her love, that was wilder than the rage of all the elements in one.

So I called together the nine who had survived, all being men, and gave them instruction and counsel, that they should form a secret brotherhood to learn and to teach the formula of the Osiris in its supreme function of initiating the human soul. That they should keep discipline in the temple only for the sake of the people, permitting every corruption yet withdrawing themselves from it. Is not the body perishable, and the skin most pure? So also the ancient practice of embalming should fall into desuetude, and that soon; for the world was past under the rule of Osiris, who loveth the charnel and the tomb.

All being sworn duly into this secret brotherhood I appointed them, one to preside over each grade, and him of the lowest grade to select the candidates and to govern the temple.

Then did I perform the invoking Ceremony of Osiris, having destroyed the blasphemous machinery; and now at last did the God answer me, glittering with infinite brilliance.

Then I disclosed myself to the Priests, and they rejoiced exceedingly that after all those years the old lie was abolished, and the master come back to his own.

But the god uttered an Oracle, saying: "This last time shall I glitter with brilliance in My temple; for I am the god of Life in Death, concealed. Therefore shall your magic henceforth be a magic most secret in the heart; and whoso shall perform openly any miracle, him shall ye know for a liar and a pretender to the sacred Wisdom.

"For this cause am I wrapped ever in a shroud of white starred with the three active colours; these things conceal Me, so that he who knoweth Me hath passed beyond them."

Then did the god call us each separately to him, and in each ear did he whisper a secret formula and a word of power, pertaining to the grade to which I had appointed him.

But to me he gave the supreme formula and the supreme word, the word that hath eight-and-seventy letters, the formula that hath five-and-sixty limbs.

So then I devoted myself there and then to a completer understanding of Osiris my God, so that I might discover his function in the whole course of the Cosmos.

For he that is born in the years of the power of a God thinketh that God to be eternal, one, alone. But he that is born in the hour of the weakness of the God, at the death of one and the birth of the other, seeth something (though it be little) of the course of things. And for him it is necessary to understand fully that change of office (for the gods neither die nor are re-born, but now one initiates and the other guards, and now one heralds and the other sanctifies) its purpose and meaning in the whole scheme of things.

ACROSS THE GULF

So I, in this year V of the Equinox of the Gods (1908) wherein Horus took the place of Osiris, will by the light of this my magical memory seek to understand fully the formula of Horus—Ra Hoor Khuit—my god, that ruleth the world under Nuit and Hadit. Then as Ankh-f-na-khonsu left unto me the *stelé* 666 with the keys to that knowledge, so also may I write down in hieroglyph the formula of the Lady of the Forked Wand and of the Feather, that shall assume his throne and place when the strength of Horus is exhausted.

So now the service of the Gods was to be secret and their magic concealed from men. They were to fall before the eyes of men from their place, and little sewer-rats were to come and mock at them, no man avenging them, and they utterly careless, not striking for themselves. Yet was there knowledge of them which an initiate might gain, though so much more difficult, immeasurably higher and more intimate.

My life from this moment became highly concentrated upon itself. I had no time either for ascetic practices or for any pleasures; nor would I take any active part in the service of the temple which, purified and regenerated, had become both subtly perfect and perfectly subtle.

It was not all of the people who did at all comprehend the change that had occurred; but the others obeyed and made believe to understand, lest their fellows should despise them. So it happened that the more ignorant and stupid any person was the more he feigned understanding; so that the least devout appeared the most devout—as it is unto this day.

But for me all these things were as nothing; for I studied ever the nature of Osiris, concentrating myself into mysterious pure symbols. I understood why it was said that Isis had

351

failed to discover the Phallus of Osiris, and thus perceived the necessity of Horus to follow him in the great succession of the Equinoxes. Moreover I fashioned talismans of pure light concerning Osiris, and I performed in light all the ceremonies of initiation into his mysteries.

These were interpreted by wise men and translated into the language of the twilight and graven on stone and in the memories of men.

Yet was I even more intrigued in that great struggle to apprehend the course of things, as it is seen from the standpoint of Destiny. So that I might leave true and intelligible images to enlighten the mind of him (whether myself or another) that should come after me to celebrate the Equinox of the Gods at the end of the period of Osiris.

As now hath come to pass.

Thus then three-and-thirty years I lived in the temple of Osiris as High Priest; and I subdued all men under me. Also I abolished the office of priestess, for had not Isis failed to find that venerable Phallus without which Osiris must be so melancholy a god? Therefore was Khemi to fall, and the world to be dark and sorrowful for many years.

Therefore I made mine High Priestess into a serving-maid, and with veiled face she served me all those many years, never speaking.

Yet they being accomplished, I thought fit to reward her. So magically I renewed about her the body of a young girl, and for a year she served me, unveiled and speaking at her pleasure.

And her time being come, she died.

Then I looked again into my destiny, and perceived that

all my work was duly accomplished. Nor could any use or worth be found in my body.

So therefore I determined to accept my great reward, that was granted unto me as the faithful minister of the god F.I.A.T. that is behind all manifestation of Will and of Intelligence, of whom Isis and Osiris and Horus are but the ministers.

Of this, and of my death, I will speak on another occasion.

But first I will discourse of the inhabitants of the kingdom that encircleth the world, so that they who *fear* may be comforted.

h

CHAPTER X

BUT of these matters I am warned that I shall not now become aware, for that there be great mysteries therein contained, pertaining to a degree of initiation of which I am as yet unworthy.

(Thus the record comes abruptly to an end.)

354

THE TEMPLE OF SOLOMON
THE KING (*Continued*)

i

A∴A∴
Publication in Class B.
Imprimatur :
N. Fra∴ A∴ A∴

THE TEMPLE OF SOLOMON THE KING (*Continued*)

THE PRIEST

In opening this the most important section of Frater P.'s career, we may be met by the unthinking with the criticism that since it deals rather with his relation to others than with his personal attainment, it has no place in this volume.

Such criticism is indeed shallow. True, the incidents which we are about to record took place on planes material or contiguous thereto; true, so obscure is the light by which we walk that much must be left in doubt; true, we have not as yet the supreme mystical attainment to record; but on the other hand it is our view that the Seal set upon Attainment may be itself fittingly recorded in the story of that Attainment, and that no step in progress is more important than that when it is said to the aspirant: " Now that you are able to walk alone, let it be your first care to use that strength to help others!" And so this great event which we are about to describe, an event which will lead, as time will show, to the establishment of a New Heaven and a New Earth for all men, wore the simplest and humblest guise. So often the gods come clad as peasants or as children; nay, I have listened to their voice in stones and trees.

357

However, we must not forget that there are persons so sensitive and so credulous that they are convinced by anything. I suppose that there are nearly as many beds in the world as there are men; yet for the Evangelical every bed conceals its Jesuit. We get "Milton composing baby rhymes," and "Locke reasoning in gibberish," divine revelations which would shock the intelligence of a sheep or a Saxon; and we find these upheld and defended with skill and courage.

Therefore since we are to announce the divine revelation made to Fra. P., it is of the last importance that we should study his mind as it was at the time of the Unveiling. If we find it to be the mind of a neurotic, of a mystic, of a person predisposed, we shall slight the revelation; if it be that of a sane man of the world, we shall attach more importance to it.

If some dingy Alchemist emerges from his laboratory, and proclaims to all Tooting that he has made gold, men doubt; but the conversion to spiritualism of Professor Lombroso made a great deal of impression on those who did not understand that his criminology was but the heaped delusion of a diseased brain.

So we shall find that the A∴A∴ subtly prepared Fra. P. by over two years' training in rationalism and in-differentism for Their message. And we shall find that so well did They do Their work that he refused the message for five years more, in spite of many strange proofs of its truth. We shall find even that Fra. P. had to be stripped naked of himself before he could effectively deliver the message.

The battle was between all that mighty will of his and

the Voice of a Brother who spoke once, and entered again into His silence; and it was not Fra. P. who had the victory.

* * * * *

We left Fra. P. in the autumn of 1901, having made considerable progress in Yoga. We noted that in 1902 he did little or nothing either in Magic or Mysticism. The interpretation of the occult phenomena which he had observed occupied him exclusively, and his mind was more and more attracted to materialism.

What are phenomena? he asked. Of noumena I know and can know nothing. All I know is, as far as I know, a mere modification of the mind, a phase of consciousness. And thought is a secretion of the brain. Consciousness is a function of the brain.

If this thought was contradicted by the obvious, "And what is the brain? A phenomenon in mind!" it weighed less with him. It seemed to his mind as yet unbalanced (as all minds are unbalanced until they have crossed the Abyss), that it was more important to insist on matter than on mind. Idealism wrought such misery, was the father of all illusion, never led to research. And yet what odds? Every act or thought is determined by an infinity of causes, is the resultant of an infinity of forces. He analysed free will, found it illusion. He analysed God, saw that every man had made God in his own image, saw the savage and cannibal Jews devoted to a savage and cannibal God, who commanded the rape of virgins and the murder of little children. He saw the timid inhabitants of India, races continually the prey of every robber tribe, inventing the effeminate Vishnu, while under the same name their conquerors worshipped a warrior, the conqueror of demon Swans. He saw the flower of the earth throughout all time, the gracious Greeks, what gracious gods they had invented. He saw Rome, in its strength devoted to Jupiter and Hercules, in its decay turning to emasculate Attis, slain Adonis, murdered Osiris, crucified Christ. He could even trace in his own life every aspiration, every devotion, as a reflection of his physical and intellectual needs. He saw, too, the folly of all this supernaturalism. He heard the Boers and the British pray to the same Protestant God, and it occurred to him that the early successes of the former might be due rather to superior valour than to superior praying power, and their eventual defeat to the circumstance that they could only bring 60,000 men against a quarter of a million. He saw, too, the face of humanity mired in its own blood that dripped from the leeches of religion fastened to its temples.

In all this he saw man as the only thing worth holding to; the one thing that needed to be " saved," but also the one thing that could save it.

All that he had attained, then, he abandoned. The intuitions of the Qabalah were cast behind him with a smile at his youthful folly; magic, if true, led nowhere; Yoga had become psychology. For the solution of his original problems of the universe he looked to metaphysics; he devoted his intellect to the cult of absolute reason. He took up once more with Kant, Hume, Spencer, Huxley, Tyndall, Maudsley, Mansel, Fichte, Schelling, Hegel, and many another; while as for his life, was he not a man? He had a wife; he knew his duty to the race, and to his own ancient graft thereof. He was a traveller and a sportsman; very well, then, live it! So we

360

find that from November 1901 he did no practices of any kind until the Spring Equinox of 1904, with the exception of a casual week in the summer of 1903, and an exhibition game of magic in the King's Chamber of the Great Pyramid in November 1903, when by his invocations he filled that chamber with a brightness as of full moonlight,[1] only to conclude, " There, you see it ? What's the good of it ? "

We find him climbing mountains, skating, fishing, hunting big game, fulfilling the duties of a husband ; we find him with the antipathy to all forms of spiritual thought and work which marks disappointment.

If one goes up the wrong mountain by mistake, as may happen, no beauties of that mountain can compensate for the disillusionment when the error is laid bare. Leah may have been a very nice girl indeed, but Jacob never cared for her after that terrible awakening to find her face on the pillow when, after seven years' toil, he wanted the expected Rachel.

So Fra. P., after five years barking up the wrong tree, had lost interest in trees altogether as far as climbing them was concerned. He might indulge in a little human pride : " See, Jack, that's the branch I cut my name on when I was a boy"; but even had he seen in the forest the Tree of Life itself with the golden fruit of Eternity in its branches, he would have done no more than lift his gun and shoot the pigeon that flitted through its foliage.

Of this " withdrawal from the vision " the proof is not merely deducible from the absence of all occult documents in his dossier, and from the full occupation of his life in external and

---

[1] This was no subjective illusion. The light was sufficient for him to read the ritual by.

mundane duties and pleasures, but is made irrefragible and emphatic by the positive evidence of his writings. Of these we have several examples. Two are dramatisations of Greek mythology, a subject offering every opportunity to the occultist. Both are markedly free from any such allusions. We have also a slim booklet in which the joys of pure human love are pictured without the faintest tinge of mystic emotion. Further, we have a play in which the Origin of Religion, as conceived by Spencer or Frazer, is dramatically shown forth ; and lastly we have a satire, hard, cynical, and brutal in its estimate of society, but careless of any remedy for its ills.

It is as if the whole past of the man with all its aspiration and attainment was blotted out. He saw life (for the first time, perhaps) with commonplace human eyes. Cynicism he could understand, romance he could understand ; all beyond was dark. Happiness was the bedfellow of contempt.

As to miracles and prophecies, he was as sceptical as the famous Pope of Rome who "didn't believe in them ; he had seen too many." If an angel had appeared to him, he would have explained him away as cheerily as the late Frank Podmore. He was as ready to acquiesce in the unhistoricity of Gotama as in that of Jesus. If he called himself a Buddhist, it was the agnostic and atheistic philosophy and the acentric nominalist psychology that attracted him. The precepts and practices of Buddhism earned only his dislike and contempt.

We learn that, late in 1903, he was proposing to visit China on a sporting expedition when a certain very commonplace communication made to him by his wife caused him to postpone it. "Let's go and kill something for a month or two," said he, "and if you're right, we'll get back to nurses and doctors."

THE TEMPLE OF SOLOMON THE KING

So we find them in Hambantota, the south-eastern province of Ceylon, occupied solely with buffalo, elephant, leopard, sambhur, and the hundred other objects of the chase.

We here insert extracts from the diary, indeed a meagre production—after what we have seen of his previous record in Ceylon.

Whole weeks pass without a word; the great man was playing bridge, poker, or golf!

The entry of February 19th reads as if it were going to be interesting, but it is followed by that of February 20th. It is, however, certain that about the 14th of March he took possession of a flat in Cairo—in the Season!

Can bathos go further?

So that the entry of March 16th is dated from Cairo.

[Our notes given in round brackets.]

FRATER P.'S DIARY

(This diary is extremely incomplete and fragmentary. Many entries, too, are evidently irrelevant or "blinds." We omit much of the latter two types.)

"This eventful year 1903 finds me at a nameless camp in the jungle of Southern Province of Ceylon; my thoughts, otherwise divided between Yoga and sport, are diverted by the fact of a wife . . ."

(This reference to Yoga is the subconscious Magical Will of the Vowed Initiate. He was not doing anything; but, on questioning himself, as was his custom at certain seasons, he felt obliged to affirm his Aspiration.)

Jan. 1. . . . (Much blotted out) . . . missed deer and hare. So annoyed. Yet the omen is that the year is well for works of Love and Union; ill for those of Hate. Be mine of Love! (Note that he does not add "and Union").

Jan. 28. Embark for Suez.

Feb. 7. Suez.

Feb. 8. Landed at Port Said.

Feb. 9. To Cairo.

Feb. 11. Saw b. f. g.
b. f. b.

(This entry is quite unintelligible to us.)

THE EQUINOX

Feb. 19. To Helwan as Oriental Despot.

(Apparently P. had assumed some disguise, probably with the intention of trying to study Islam from within as he had done with Hinduism.)

Feb. 20. Began golf.

March 16. Began INV. (invocation). IAΩ.

March 17. ΘωουΘ appeared.

March 18. Told to INV. (invoke) ῃωωρι as ☉ by new way.

March 19. Did this badly at noon 30.

March 20. At 10 p.m. did well—Equinox of Gods—οὔ μή Nev (? new) C.R.C. (Christian Rosy Cross, we conjecture.) Hoori now Hpnt (obviously " Hierophant ").

March 21. ☉ in ♈. I.A.M. (? one o'clock.)

March 22. X.P.B. اﺧﯾﺴا

(May this and the entry March 24 refer to the Brother of the A.·. A.·. who found him ?)

E.P.D. in 84 m.

(Unintelligible to us : possibly a blind.)

March 23. Y.K. done. (? His work on the Yi King.)

March 24. Met اﺧﯾﺴا again.

March 25. 823 Thus
461 „ „ = p f l y 2 b z
218

(Blot) wch trouble with ds.

(Blot) P.B. (All unintelligible ; possibly a blind.)

April 6. Go off again to H, taking A's p.

(This probably a blind.)

Before we go further into the history of this period we must premise as follows.

Fra. P. never made a thorough record of this period. He seems to have wavered between absolute scepticism in the bad sense, a dislike of the revelation, on the one hand, and real enthusiasm on the other. And the first of these moods would induce him to do things to spoil the effect of the latter. Hence the " blinds " and stupid meaningless cyphers which deface the diary.

And, as if the Gods themselves wished to darken the

364

Pylon, we find that later, when P.'s proud will had been broken, and he wished to make straight the way of the historian, his memory (one of the finest memories in the world) was utterly incompetent to make everything certain.

However, nothing of which he was not certain will be entered in this place.

We have one quite unspoiled and authoritative document "The Book of Results," written in one of the small Japanese vellum note-books which he used to carry. Unfortunately, it seems to have been abandoned after five days. What happened between March 23rd and April 8th?

THE BOOK OF RESULTS

March 16*th*. Die ☿, I invoke IAΩ.

(Fra. P. tells us that this was done by the ritual of the "Bornless One,"[1] merely to amuse his wife by showing her the sylphs. She refused or was unable to see any sylphs, but became "inspired," and kept on saying: "They're waiting for you!")

W. says "they" are "waiting for me."

17. ♃.

It is "all about the child." Also "all Osiris."

(Note the cynic and sceptic tone of this entry. How different it appears in the light of Liber 418!)

Thoth, invoked with great success, indwells us.

(Yes; but what happened? Fra. P. has no sort of idea.)

18. ♀. Revealed that the waiter was Horus, whom I had offered and ought to invoke. The ritual revealed in skeleton. Promise of success ♄ or ☉ and of Samadhi.

---

[1] This is identical with the "Preliminary Invocation" in the "Goetia."

(Is this "waiter" another sneer? We are uncertain.) The revealing of the ritual (by W. the seer) consisted chiefly in a prohibition of all formulæ hitherto used, as will be seen from the text printed below.

It was probably on this day that P. cross-examined W. about Horus. Only the striking character of her identification of the God, surely, would have made him trouble to obey her. He remembers that he only agreed to obey her in order to show her how silly she was, and he taunted her that "nothing could happen if you broke all the rules."

Here therefore we insert a short note of Fra. P.

How W. knew R.H.K. (Ra Hoor Khuit).

1. Force and Fire (I asked her to describe his moral qualities).

2. Deep blue light. (I asked her to describe the condition caused by him. This light is quite unmistakable and unique; but of course her words, though a fair description of it, might equally apply to some other.)

3. Horus. (I asked her to pick out his name from a list of ten dashed off at haphazard.)

4. Recognised his figure when shown. (This refers to the striking scene in the Boulak Museum, which will be dealt with in detail.)

5. Knew my past relations with the God. (This means, I think, that she knew I had taken his place in temple, etc., and that I had never once invoked him.)

6. Knew his enemy. (I asked, "Who is his enemy?" Reply, "Forces of the waters—of the Nile." W. knew no Egyptology—or anything else.)

7. Knew his lineal figure and its colour. (A $\frac{1}{64}$ chance.)

8. Knew his place in temple.   (A $\frac{1}{4}$ chance, at the least.)

9. Knew his weapon (from a list of 6).

10. Knew his planetary nature (from a list of 7 planets.)

11. Knew his number (from a list of the 10 units).

12. Picked him out of (a) Five $\bigg\}$ indifferent, i.e. arbitrary
   (b) Three

symbols. (This means that I settled in my own mind that say D of A, B, C, D, and E should represent him, and that she then said D.)

We cannot too strongly insist on the extraordinary character of this identification.

We had made no pretension to clairvoyance, nor had P. ever tried to train her.

P. had great experience of clairvoyants, and it was always a point of honour with him to bowl them out.   And here was the novice, a woman who should never have been allowed outside a ballroom, speaking with the authority of God, and proving it by unhesitating correctness.

One slip, and Fra. P. would have sent her to the devil. And that slip was not made.   Calculate the odds!   We cannot find a mathematical expression for tests 1, 2, 4, 5, or 6. But the other 7 tests give us

$$\frac{1}{10} \times \frac{1}{84} \times \frac{1}{4} \times \frac{1}{6} \times \frac{1}{7} \times \frac{1}{10} \times \frac{1}{15} = \frac{1}{21,168,000}$$

Twenty-one millions to one against her getting through half the ordeal !

Even if we suppose what is absurd, that she knew the

367

correspondences of the Qabalah[1] as well as Fra. P., and had knowledge of his own secret relations with the Unseen, we must strain telepathy to explain test 12.

But we know that she was perfectly ignorant of the subtle correspondences, which were only existing at that time in Fra. P.'s own brain.

And even if it were so, how are we to explain what followed—the discovery of the Stélé of Revealing?

To apply test 4, Fra. P. took her to the museum at Boulak, which they had not previously visited. She passed by (as P. noted with silent glee) several images of Horus. They went upstairs. A glass case stood in the distance, too far off for its contents to be recognised. But W. recognised it! "There," she cried, "There he is!"

Fra. P. advanced to the case. There was the image of Horus in the form of Ra Hoor Khuit painted upon a wooden stélé of the 26th dynasty—*and the exhibit bore the number 666!*

(And after that it was five years before Fra. P. was forced to obedience.)

This incident must have occurred before the 23rd March, as the entry on that date refers to Ankh-f-n-khonsu.

Here is P.'s description of the stélé.

" In the museum at Cairo, No. 666 is the stélé of the Priest Ankh-f-n-khonsu.

Horus has a red Disk and green Uræus.

---

[1] We may add, too, that Fra. P. thinks, but is not quite certain, that he also tested her with the Hebrew alphabet and the Tarot trumps, in which case the long odds must be still further multiplied by 484, bringing them over the billion mark!

368

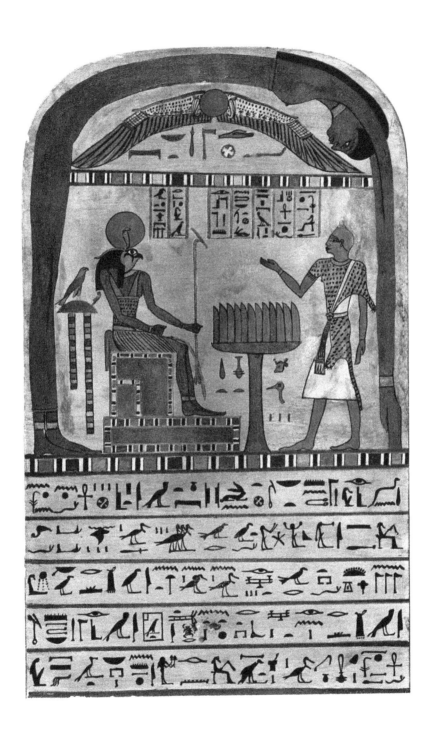

A PARAPHRASE OF THE INSCRIPTIONS UPON THE OBVERSE OF THE STÉLÉ OF REVELLING

Above, the gemmèd azure is
   The naked splendour of Nuit;
She bends in ecstasy to kiss
   The secret ardours of Hadit.
The wingèd globe, the starry blue
Are mine, o Ankh-f-n-Khonsu.

I am the Lord of Thebes, and I
   The inspired forth-speaker of Mentu;
For me unveils the veilèd sky,
   The self-slain Ankh-f-n-Khonsu
Whose words are truth. I invoke, I greet
Thy presence, o Ra-Hoor-Khuit!

Unity uttermost showed!
   I adore the might of Thy breath,
Supreme and terrible God,
   Who makest the gods and death
     To tremble before Thee:—
     I, I adore thee!

Appear on the throne of Ra!
   Open the ways of the Khu!
Lighten the ways of the Ka!
   The ways of the Khabs run through
     To stir me or still me!
     Aum! let it kill me!

The Light is mine; its rays consume
   Me: I have made a secret door
Into the House of Ra and Tum,
   Of Khephra, and of Ahathoor.
I am thy Theban, o Mentu,
The prophet Ankh-f-n-Khonsu!

By Bes-na-Maut my breast I beat;
   By wise Ta-Nech I weave my spell.
Show thy star-splendour, O Nuith!
   Bid me within thine House to dwell,
O wingèd snake of light, Hadith!
Abide with me, Ra-Hoor-Khuit!

A PARAPHRASE OF THE HIEROGLYPHS OF THE 11 LINES UPON THE REVERSE OF THE STÉLÉ

Saith of Mentu the truth-telling brother
  Who was master of Thebes from his birth:
O heart of me, heart of my mother!
  O heart which I had upon earth!
Stand not thou up against me a witness!
  Oppose me not, judge, in my quest!
Accuse me not now of unfitness
  Before the Great God, the dread Lord of the West!
For I fastened the one to the other
  With a spell for their mystical girth,
The earth and the wonderful West,
  When I flourished, o earth, on thy breast!

The dead man Ankh-f-n-Khonsu
  Saith with his voice of truth and calm:
O thou that hast a single arm!
  O thou that glitterest in the moon!
Iweave thee in the spinning charm;
  I lure thee with the billowy tune.

The dead man Ankh-f-n-Khonsu
  Hath parted from the darkling crowds,
Hath joined the dwellers of the light,
  Opening Duant, the star-abodes,
  Their keys receiving.
The dead man Ankh-f-n-Khonsu
  Hath made his passage into night,
His pleasure on the earth to do
  Among the living.

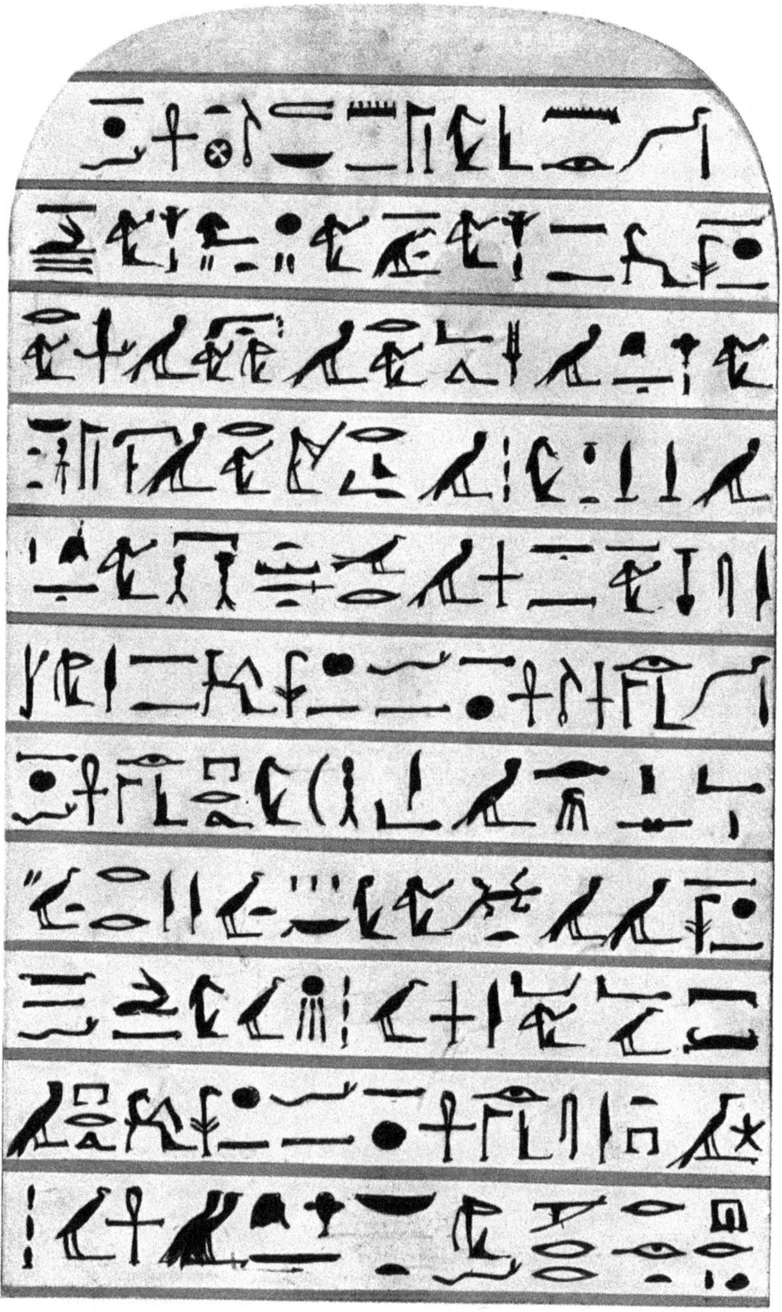

His face is green, his skin indigo.

His necklace, anklets, and bracelets are gold.

His nemyss nearly black from blue.

His tunic is the Leopard's skin, and his apron green and gold.

Green is the wand of double Power; his r.h. is empty.

His throne is indigo the gnomon, red the square.

The light is gamboge.

Above him are the Winged Globe and the bent figure of the heavenly Isis, her hands and feet touching earth.

[We print the most recent translation of the Stélé, by Messrs Alan Gardiner, Litt.D., and Battiscombe Gunn. It differs slightly from that used by Fra ∴ P., which was due to the assistant-curator of the Museum at Bulak.]

STÉLÉ OF ANKH-F-NA-KHONSU.

OBVERSE.

Topmost Register (under Winged Disk).

Behdet (? Hadit?), the Great God, the Lord of Heaven.

Middle Register.

Two vertical lines to left : —

Ra-Harakhti, Master of the Gods.

Five vertical lines to right :—

Osiris, the Priest of Montu, Lord of Thebes, Opener of the doors of Nut in Karnak, Ankh-f-na-Khonsu, the Justified.

THE EQUINOX

Below Altar :—

Oxen, Geese, Wine, (?) Bread.

Behind the god is the hieroglyph of Amenti.

Lowest Register.

(1) Saith Osiris, the Priest of Montu, Lord of Thebes, the Opener of the Doors of Nut in Karnak, Ankh-f-na-Khonsu, (2) the Justified :—" Hail, Thou whose praise is high (the highly praised), thou great-willed, O Soul (*ba*) very awful (*lit.* mighty of awe) that giveth the terror of him (3) among the Gods, shining in glory upon his great throne, making ways for the Soul (*ba*), for the Spirit (*yekh*) and for the Shadow (*khabt*). I am prepared, and I shine forth as one that is prepared. (4) I have made way to the place in which are Ra, Tôm, Khepri and Hathor." Osiris, the Priest of Montu, Lord of Thebes, (5) Ankh-f-na-Khonsu, the Justified; son of MNBSNMT[1]; born of the Sistrum-bearer of Amon, the Lady Atne-sher.

REVERSE.

Eleven lines of writing.

(1) Saith Osiris, the Priest of Montu, Lord of Thebes, Ankh-f-(2)na-Khonsu, the Justified :—" My heart from my mother, my heart from my mother, my heart[2] of my existence (3) upon earth, stand not forth against me as a witness, drive me not back (4) among the

---

[1] The father's name. The method of spelling shows he was a foreigner. There is no clue to the vocalisation.

[2] Different word, apparently synonymous, but probably not so at all.

370

Sovereign Judges,[1] neither incline against me in the presence of the Great God, the Lord of the West.[2] (5) Now that I am united with Earth in the Great West, and endure no longer upon Earth. (6) Saith Osiris, he who is in Thebes, Ankh-f-na-Khonsu, the Justified:—"O Only-(7)One, shining like (or in) the Moon; Osiris Ankh-f-(8)na-Khonsu has come forth upon high among these thy multitudes. (9) He that gathereth together those that are in the Light, the Underworld (*duat*) is [also] (10) opened to him; lo, Osiris Ankh-f-na-Khonsu, cometh forth by (11) day to do all that he wisheth upon earth among the living."

There is one other object to complete the secret of Wisdom —or,[3] it is in the hieroglyphs.

This last paragraph is, we suppose, dictated by W.)

We now return to the " Book of Results."

19. ♄ The ritual written out and the invocation done— little success.

20. ☉ Revealed [4] that the Equinox of the Gods is come. Horus taking the Throne of the East and all rituals, etc., being abrogated.

(To explain this we append the G.D. ritual of the Equinox, which was celebrated in the spring and autumn

---

[1] Quite an arbitrary and conventional translation of the original word.

[2] Osiris, of course.

[3] P. notes " perhaps a Thoth."

[4] We cannot make out if this revelation comes from W. or is a result of the ritual. But almost certainly the former, as it precedes the "Great Success" entry.

THE EQUINOX

within 48 hours of the actual dates of Sol entering Aries and Libra.)

(Temple arranged as for O = O)

Ht. (*knocks*). Fratres and Sorores of all grades of the Golden Dawn in the Outer, let us celebrate the Festival of the $\left\{ \begin{array}{c} \text{Vernal} \\ \text{Autumnal} \end{array} \right\}$ Equinox. !

All rise.

Ht. Frater Kerux, proclaim the fact, and announce the abrogation of the present Pass Word.

K. (*going to Ht.'s right, saluting, and facing West*). In the Name of the Lord of the Universe, and by command of the V.H.Ht., I proclaim the $\left\{ \begin{array}{c} \text{Vernal} \\ \text{Autumnal} \end{array} \right\}$ Equinox, and declare that the Pass Word —— is abrogated.

Ht. Let us, according to ancient custom, consecrate the return of the $\left\{ \begin{array}{c} \text{Vernal} \\ \text{Autumnal} \end{array} \right\}$ Equinox.

      Light.

Hs. Darkness.

Ht. East.

Hs. West.

Ht. Air.

Hs. Water.

Hg. (*knocks*). I am the Reconciler between them.

All give signs.

D. Heat.

S. Cold.

D. South.

S. North.

D. Fire.

S. Earth.

Hg. (*knocks*). I am the Reconciler between them.

All give signs.

Ht. (*knocks*). One Creator.

D. One Preserver.

Hs. (*knocks*). One Destroyer.

THE TEMPLE OF SOLOMON THE KING

S. One Redeemer.

Hg. (knocks). One Reconciler between them.

All give signs.

Each retiring Officer in turn, beginning with Ht., quits his post by the left hand and goes to foot of Throne. He there disrobes, placing robe and lamen at foot of Throne or Dais. He then proceeds with the Sun's course to the Altar, and lays thereon his special insignia, viz.:—Ht., Sceptre: Hs., Sword: Hg., Sceptre: K., Lamp and Wand: S., Cup: D., Censer: repeating out-going Password as he does so.

Ht., taking from the Altar the Rose, returns with the Sun to his post:

Hs. takes Cup of Wine:

Hg. waits for the Kerux and takes his Red Lamp from him:

K. takes nothing:

S. takes platter of Salt:

D. takes emblem of Elemental Fire:

Returning each to his place.

All Officers except K. now keep their places.

The remaining members form a column in the North and, led by Kerux, proceed to the East; when all are in column along East side each turns to left and faces Hierophant.

Ht. Let us adore the Lord of the Universe.

Holy art Thou, Lord of the Air, who hast created the Firmament.

(Making with the Rose the sign of the Cross in the Air towards the East.)

All give signs. Procession moves on to the South, halts, and all face South.

D. (facing South). Let us adore the Lord of the Universe.

Holy art Thou, Lord of the Fire, wherein Thou hast shown forth the Throne of Thy Glory.

(Making with the Fire the sign of the Cross toward the South.)

All give signs. Procession moves on to the West, halts, and faces West.

Hs. (facing West). Let us adore the Lord of the Universe.

Holy art Thou, Lord of the Waters, whereon Thy Spirit moved at the Beginning.

(Making with the Cup the sign of the Cross in the Air before him.)

All give signs. Procession passes on to the North. All halt and face North.

S. (facing North). Let us adore the Lord of the Universe.

Holy art Thou, Lord of the Earth, which Thou hast made Thy footstool.

(Making with the platter of Salt the sign of the Cross toward the North.)

All give signs.

All resume their places and face the usual way.

VII   *k*   373

THE EQUINOX

Hg. Let us adore the Lord of the Universe.

Holy art Thou, Who art in all things, in Whom are all things;

If I climb up into Heaven, Thou art there;

If I go down into Hell, Thou art there also;

If I take the Wings of the Morning and remain in the uttermost parts of the Sea, even there shall Thy hand lead me and Thy right hand shall hold me;

If I say "Peradventure the Darkness shall cover me," even the Night shall be Light unto Thee;

Thine is the Air with its Movement,

Thine is the Fire with its flashing Flame,

Thine is the Water with its Flux and Reflux,

Thine is the Earth with its Eternal Stability.

(*Makes the sign of the Cross with Red Lamp.*)

All give signs.

Ht. goes to Altar and deposits the Rose.

Imperator meanwhile assumes the Throne.

Ht. returns to a seat on immediate left as Past Hierophant.

Each old Officer now proceeds in turn to the Altar and places upon it the ensign he had taken therefrom, returning to places of their grade, not their Thrones, with nothing in their hands: they sit as common members, leaving all offices vacant.

Imperator. By the Power and Authority in me vested, I confer upon you the new Password. It is ——.

The Officers of this Temple for the ensuing half-year are as follows :—

(*Reads list of new Officers.*)

New Officers come up in turn and are robed by the Imperator.

Each new Officer in turn passes to the Altar and takes his insignia therefrom, repeating aloud :—

By the Password —— I claim my ——.

S., after claiming his Cup, purifies the Hall and the Members by Water, without a word spoken by the Ht. unless he fails in this duty.

D., after claiming his Censer, consecrates the Hall and the Members by Fire, without unnecessary word from the Ht.

THE MYSTIC CIRCUMAMBULATION

This should take place in Silence, but if the Members be unprovided with Rituals, the Ht. may order it as follows :—

All form in North, K., Hg., Members, Hs., S., D.

Each member as he passes the Throne repeats the Password aloud.

374

Ht. Let us invoke the Lord of the Universe.

Lord of the Universe, Blessed be Thy Name unto the Eternal Ages.

Look with favour upon this Order, and grant that its members may at length attain to the true Summum Bonum, the Stone of the Wise, the Perfect Wisdom and the Eternal Light,

To the Glory of Thine Ineffable Name, AMEN.

All salute.

Ht. Frater Kerux, in the Name of the Lord of the Universe, I command you to declare that the $\begin{Bmatrix} \text{Vernal} \\ \text{Autumnal} \end{Bmatrix}$ Equinox has returned, and that —— is the Password for the next six months.

K. In the Name of the Lord of the Universe and by command of the V.H.Ht., I declare that the Sun has entered $\begin{Bmatrix} \text{Aries} \\ \text{Libra} \end{Bmatrix}$, the Sign of the $\begin{Bmatrix} \text{Vernal} \\ \text{Autumnal} \end{Bmatrix}$ Equinox, and that the Password for the ensuing half-year will be ——.

Ht. Khabs.	Pax.	In.
Hs. Am.	Konx.	Extension.
Hg. Pekht.	Om.	Light.

20. (*contd.*)—Great success in midnight invocation.

(The other diary says 10 P.M. " Midnight " is perhaps a loose phrase, or perhaps marks the climax of the ritual.)

I am to formulate a new link of an order with the solar force.

(It is not clear what happened in this invocation ; but it is evident from another note of certainly later date, that " great success " does not mean " Samadhi." For P. writes : " I make it an absolute condition that I should attain Samadhi, in the god's own interest." His memory concurs in this. It was the Samadhi attained in October 1906 that set him again in the path of obedience to this revelation.

But that " great success " means something very important

is clear enough. The sneering sceptic of the 17th March must have had a shock before he wrote those words.)

21. ☽. ☉ enters ♈.

22. ♂. The day of rest, on which nothing whatever of magic is to be done at all. ☿ is to be the great day of invocation.

(This note is due to W.'s prompting, or to his own rationalising imagination.)

23. ☿. The Secret of Wisdom.

(We omit the record of a long and futile Tarot divination.)

At this point we may insert the Ritual which was so successful on the 20th.

Invocation of Horus according to the Divine Vision of W. the Seer

To be performed before a window open to the E. or N. without incense. The room to be filled with jewels, but only diamonds to be worn. A sword, unconsecrated. 44 pearl beads to be told. Stand. Bright daylight at 12.30 noon. Lock doors. White robes. Bare feet. Be very loud. Saturday. Use the Sign of Apophis and Typhon.

The above is W.'s answer to various questions posed by P.

   *   *   *   *   *

Preliminary. Banish. L.B.R. Pentagram. L.B.R. Hexagram. Flaming Sword. Abrahadabra. Invoke. As before.

[These are P.'s ideas for the ritual. W. replied, " Omit."]

[The MS. of this Ritual bears many internal marks of having been written at white heat and left unrevised, save perhaps for one glance. There are mistakes in grammar and spelling unique in all MSS. of Fra. P. ; the use of capitals is irregular, and the punctuation almost wanting.]

376

CONFESSION

Unprepared and uninvoking Thee, I, οὔ μή, Fra. R. R. et A. C., am here in Thy Presence—for Thou art Everywhere, O Lord Horus !—to confess humbly before Thee my neglect and scorn of Thee.

How shall I humble myself enough before Thee ? Thou art the mighty and unconquered Lord of the Universe ; I am a spark of Thine unutterable Radiance.

How should I approach Thee ?—but Thou art Everywhere.

But Thou hast graciously deigned to call me unto Thee, to this Exorcism of Art, that I may be Thy Servant, Thine Adept, O Bright One, O Sun of Glory ! Thou hast called me—should I not then hasten to Thy Presence ?

With unwashen hands therefore I come unto Thee, and I lament my wandering from Thee—but Thou knowest !

Yea, I have done evil !

If one[1] blasphemed Thee, why should I therefore forsake Thee ? But thou art the Avenger ; all is with Thee.

I bow my neck before Thee ; and as once Thy sword was upon it,[2] so am I in Thy hands. Strike if Thou wilt : spare if Thou wilt : but accept me as I am.

My trust is in Thee : shall I be confounded ? This Ritual of Art ; this Forty and Fourfold Invocation ; this Sacrifice of Blood[3]—these I do not comprehend.

---

[1] Doubtless a reference to S.R.M.D., who was much obsessed by Mars P. saw Horus at first as Geburah ; later as an aspect of Tiphereth, including Chesed and Geburah (the red Triangle inverted), an aspect opposite to Osiris.

[2] See G.·. D.·. Ceremony of Neophyte, the Obligation.

[3] Merely, we suppose, that 44 = DM, blood. Possibly a bowl of blood was used. P. thinks it was in some of the workings at this time, but is not sure if it was this one.

It is enough if I obey Thy decree; did thy fiat go forth for my eternal misery, were it not my joy to execute Thy Sentence on myself?

For why? For that All is in Thee and of Thee; it is enough if I burn up in the intolerable glory of Thy presence.

Enough! I turn toward Thy Promise.

Doubtful are the Words: Dark are the Ways: but in Thy Words and Ways is Light. Thus then now as ever, I enter the Path of Darkness, if haply so I may attain the Light.

Hail!

a I א

Strike, strike the master chord!
Draw, draw the Flaming Sword!
Crowned Child and Conquering Lord,
   Horus, avenger!

1. O Thou of the Head of the Hawk! Thee, Thee, I invoke! [*At every " Thee I invoke," throughout whole ritual, give the Sign of Apophis.*]

A. Thou only-begotten-child of Osiris Thy Father, and Isis Thy Mother. He that was slain; She that bore Thee in Her womb, flying from the Terror of the Water.

Thee, Thee, I invoke!

2. O Thou whose Apron is of flashing white, whiter than the Forehead of the Morning!

Thee, Thee, I invoke!

B. O Thou who hast formulated Thy Father and made fertile Thy Mother!

Thee, Thee, I invoke!

378

3. O Thou whose garment is of golden glory, with the azure bars of sky!

Thee, Thee, I invoke!

C. Thou who didst avenge the Horror of Death ; Thou the slayer of Typhon! Thou who didst lift Thine arms, and the Dragons of Death were as dust ; Thou who didst raise Thine Head, and the Crocodile of Nile was abased before Thee!

Thee, Thee, I invoke!

4. O Thou whose Nemyss hideth the Universe with night, the impermeable Blue!

Thee, Thee, I invoke!

D. Thou who travellest in the Boat of Ra, abiding at the Helm of the Aftet boat and of the Sektet boat!

Thee, Thee, I invoke!

5. Thou who bearest the Wand of Double Power!

Thee, Thee, I invoke!

E. Thou about whose presence is shed the darkness of Blue Light, the unfathomable glory of the outmost Ether, the untravelled, the unthinkable immensity of Space. Thou who concentrest all the Thirty Ethers in one darkling sphere of Fire!

Thee, Thee, I invoke!

6. O Thou who bearest the Rose and Cross of Life and Light!

Thee, Thee, I invoke!

The Voice of the Five.
The Voice of the Six.
Eleven are the Voices.
Abrahadabra!

β II ב

Strike, strike the master chord!
Draw, draw the Flaming Sword!
Crowned Child and Conquering Lord,
  Horus, avenger!

1. By thy name of Ra I invoke Thee, Hawk of the Sun, the glorious one!

2. By thy name Harmachis, youth of the Brilliant Morning, I invoke Thee!

3. By thy name Mau, I invoke Thee, Lion of the Midday Sun.

4. By thy name Tum, Hawk of the Even, crimson splendour of the Sunset, I invoke Thee!

5. By thy name Khep-Ra I invoke Thee, O Beetle of the hidden Mastery of Midnight!

A. By thy name Heru-pa-Kraat, Lord of Silence, Beautiful Child that standest on the Dragons of the Deep, I invoke Thee!

B. By thy name of Apollo, I invoke Thee, O man of strength and splendour, O poet, O father!

C. By thy name of Phœbus, that drivest thy chariot through the Heaven of Zeus, I invoke Thee!

D. By thy name of Odin I invoke Thee, O warrior of the North, O Renown of the Sagas!

E. By thy name of Jeheshua, O child of the Flaming Star, I invoke Thee!

F. By Thine own, Thy secret name Hoori, Thee I invoke!

The Names are Five.
The Names are Six.
Eleven are the Names!
Abrahadabra!

Behold! I stand in the midst. Mine is the symbol of Osiris; to Thee are mine eyes ever turned. Unto the splendour of Geburah, the Magnificence of Chesed, the mystery of Daath, thither I lift up mine eyes. This have I sought, and I have sought the Unity: hear Thou me!

γ III ɔ

1. Mine is the Head of the Man, and my insight is keen as the Hawk's.

By my Head I invoke Thee!

A. I am the only-begotten child of my Father and Mother.

By my Body I invoke Thee!

2. About me shine the Diamonds of Radiance white and pure.

By their brightness I invoke Thee!

B. Mine is the Red Triangle Reversed, the Sign[1] given of none, save it be of Thee, O Lord!

By the Lamen I invoke Thee!

3. Mine is the garment of white sewn with gold, the flashing abbai that I wear.

By my robe I invoke Thee!

C. Mine is the sign of Apophis and Typhon!

By the sign I invoke Thee!

4. Mine is the turban of white and gold, and mine the blue vigour of the intimate air!

---

[1] This sign had been previously communicated by W. It was entirely new to P.

By my crown I invoke Thee!

D. My fingers travel on the Beads of Pearl: so run I after Thee in thy car of glory.

By my fingers I invoke Thee!

[On the Saturday the string of pearls broke: so I changed the invocation to " My mystic sigils travel in the Bark of the Akasa, etc. By the spells I invoke Thee!—P.]

5. I bear the Word of Double Power in the Voice of the Master—Abrahadabra!

By the Word I invoke Thee!

E. Mine are the dark-blue waves of music in the song that I made of old to invoke thee—

> Strike, strike the master chord!
> Draw, draw the Flaming Sword!
> Crowned Child and Conquering Lord,
>   Horus, avenger!

By the Song I invoke Thee!

6. In my hand is thy Sword of Revenge; let it strike at Thy Bidding!

By the Sword I invoke Thee!

> The Voice of the Five.
> The Voice of the Six.
> Eleven are the Voices.
> Abrahadabra!

§ IV ז

[This section merely repeats α I א in the first person. Thus it begins:

THE TEMPLE OF SOLOMON THE KING

1. " Mine is the Head of the Hawk! Abrahadabra!", and ends :

6. " I bear the Rose and Cross of Life and Light! Abrahadabra!" giving the Sign at each Abrahadabra. Remaining in the Sign, the invocation concludes :]

Therefore I say unto thee : Come Thou forth and dwell in me ; so that every my Spirit, whether of the Firmament, or of the Ether, of the Earth or under the Earth ; on dry land or in the Water, or Whirling Air or of rushing fire ; and every spell and scourge of God the Vast One may be THOU. Abrahadabra!

The Adoration—impromptu.

Close by banishing. [I think this was omitted at W.'s order.—P.]

* * * * *

During the period March 23rd—April 8th, whatever else may have happened, it is at least certain that work was continued to some extent, that the inscriptions of the stélé were translated for Fra. P., and that he paraphrased the latter in verse. For we find him using, or prepared to use, the same in the text of Liber Legis.

Perhaps then, perhaps later, he made out the "name-coincidences of the Qabalah" to which we must now direct the reader's attention.

The MS. is a mere fragmentary sketch.

Ch = 8 = Ch 1 Th = 418 = Abrahadabra = RA-HVVR (Ra-Hoor).

Also 8 is the great symbol I adore.

(This may be because of its likeness to ∞ or because of its (old G . ˙. D . ˙.) attribution to Daath, P. being then a rationalist ; or for some other reason.)

So is O.

O = A in the Book of Thoth (The Tarot).

A = 111 with all its great meanings, ⊙ = 6.

Now 666 = My name.

       = the number of the stélé.

       = the number of the Beast. (See Apocalypse.)

       = the number of the ⊙

The Beast A Ch I H A = 666 in full. (The usual spelling is ChIVA.)

(A = 111 Ch = 418 I = 20 H = 6 A = 111.)

HRV-RA-HA.

211 + 201 + 6 = 418.

(This name occurs only in L. Legis, and is a test of that book rather than of the stélé.)

ANKH-P-N-KHONS*h*V-T = 666.

(We trust the addition of the termination T will be found justified.)

Bes-n-maut B I Sh-NA-MAVT   } = 888

Ta-Nich TA-NICh.   } = Ch × A.

Nuteru NVThIRV = 666.

Montu MVNTV = 111.

Aiwass AIVAS = 78, the influence or messenger, or the Book T.

Ta-Nich TA-NICh = 78. Alternatively, Sh for Ch gives 370, O Sh, Creation.

So much we extract from volumes filled with minute calculations, of which the bulk is no longer intelligible even to Fra. P.

His memory, however, assures us that the coincidences were much more numerous and striking than those we have been able to reproduce here; but his attitude is, we understand, that after all " It's all in Liber Legis. ' Success is thy proof: argue not; convert not; talk not overmuch!'" And indeed in the Comment to that Book will be found sufficient for the most wary of inquirers.

Now who, it may be asked, was Aiwass? It is the name given by W. to P. as that of her informant. Also it is the name given as that of the revealer of Liber Legis. But whether

Aiwass is a spiritual being, or a man known to Fra. P., is a matter of the merest conjecture. His number is 78, that of Mezla, the Channel through which Macroprosopus reveals Himself to, or showers His influence upon, Microprosopus. So we find Fra. P. speaking of him at one time as of another, but more advanced, man ; at another time as if it were the name of his own superior in the Spiritual Hierarchy. And to all questions Fra. P. finds a reply, either pointing out "the subtle metaphysical distinction between curiosity and hard work," or indicating that among the Brethren "names are only lies," or in some other way defeating the very plain purpose of the historian.

The same remark applies to all queries with regard to V.V.V.V.V. ; with this addition, that in this case he condescends to argue and to instruct. " If I tell you," he once said to the present writer, " that V.V.V.V.V. is a Mr Smith and lives at Clapham, you will at once go round and tell everybody that V.V.V.V.V. is a Mr Smith of Clapham, which is not true. V.V.V.V.V. is the Light of the World itself, the sole Mediator between God and Man ; and in your present frame of mind (that of a poopstick) you cannot see that the two statements may be identical for the Brothers of the A ∴ . A ∴ .! Did not your great-grandfather argue that no good thing could come out of Nazareth ? " Is not this the carpenter's son ? is not his mother called Mary ? and his brethren, James, and Joses, and Simon, and Judas ? And his sisters, are they not all with us ? Whence then hath this man all these things ? And they were offended in him."

Similarly, with regard to the writing of Liber Legis, Fra. P. will only say that it is in no way "automatic writing," that he heard clearly and distinctly the human articulate accents of a man. Once, on page 6, he is told to edit a sentence ; and once, on page 19, W. supplies a sentence which he had failed to hear.

To this writing we now turn.

It must have been on the 7th of April that W. commanded P. (now somewhat cowed) to enter the " temple " exactly at 12 o'clock noon on three successive days, and to write down what he should hear, rising exactly at 1 o'clock.

This he did. Immediately on his taking his seat the Voice began its Utterance, and ended exactly at the expiration of the hour.

These are the three chapters of Liber Legis, and we have nothing to add to the comment prepared by Fra. P. himself while the Sun was in the sign of the Virgin, Anno V from this first revelation.

Note, however, the 65 pages of MS., and the 220 verses.

The reproduction of Liber Legis has been done thus minutely in order to prevent the casual reader from wasting his valuable time over it.

The full title of the book is

LIBER L vel LEGIS

svb figvrâ ccxx

as delivered by LXXVIII to DCLXVI

and it is the First and Greatest of those Class A publications of A∴A∴ of which is not to be altered so much as the style of a letter.

LIBER LEGIS

THE COMMENT[1]

I

1. Compare II. 1, the complement of this verse.

In Nu is Had concealed; by Had is Nu manifested.

Nu being 56 and Had 9, their conjunction results in 65, Adonai, the Holy Guardian Angel.

See the Sepher Sephiroth and "The Wake-World" in "Konx Om Pax" for further details on 65.

Note, however, the sixty-five pages of the MS. of Liber Legis.

Or counting NV 56 HAD 10, we get 66, which is Σ (1-11).

Had is further the centre of the Key-Word *Abrahadabra*.

2. This book is a new revelation, or unveiling of the holy ones.

3. This should not be understood in the spiritualistic sense. It means that in each person is the sublime starry nature, a consciousness to be attained by the prescribed methods.

[Yet it may mean some real connection between a given person and a given star. Why not? Still, this is not in my knowledge. See Lib. 418.]

4. The limited is a mere mask; the illimitable is the only truth.

5. Nu, to unveil herself, needs a mortal intermediary, in the first instance.

It is to be supposed that Ankh-f-n-khonsu, the warrior lord of Thebes, priest of Men Tu, is in some subtle manner identical with either Aiwass or the Beast.

6. The recipient of this knowledge is to identify himself with Hadit, and thus fully express the thoughts of her heart in her very language.

7. Aiwass—see Introduction. He is 78, Mezla the "influence" from the Highest Crown, and the number of cards in the Tarot, Rota, the all-embracing Wheel.

Hoor-paar-Kraat. See II. 8.

Aiwass is called the minister of Hoor-paar-Kraat, the God of Silence; for his word is the Speech in the Silence.

---

[1] Dates in brackets, giving solar position (An 0. $\odot$ in ♈ being March 21, 1904, ψ-χ), refer to the time of writing particular parts of this comment.

THE EQUINOX

8. Here begins the text.

Khabs is the secret Light or L.V.X.; the Khu is the magical entity of a man.

I find later (☉ in ♍, An VII.) that Khabs means star. In which case *cf. v.* 3.

The doctrine here taught is that that Light is innermost, essential man. Intra (not Extra) Nobis Regnum Dei.

9. That Khabs is declared to be the light of Nu. It being worshipped in the centre, the light also fills the circumference, so that all is light.

10. This is the rule of Thelema, that its adepts shall be invisible rulers.

This, it may be remarked, has always been the case.

11. "The many and the known," both among Gods and men, are revered; this is folly.

12. The Key of the worship of Nu. The uniting of consciousness with infinite space by the exercise of love, pastoral or pagan love. But *vide infra.*

13. This doctrine implies some mystic bond which I imagine is only to be understood by experience; this human ecstasy and that divine ecstasy interact.

A similar doctrine is to be found in the Bhagavad Gita.

14. This verse is a direct translation of the first section of the stélé. It conceals a certain secret ritual, of the highest rank, connected with the two previous verses.

15. The authority of the Beast rests upon this verse; but it is to be taken in conjunction with certain later verses which I shall leave to the research of students to interpret. I am inclined, however, to believe that "the Beast" and "the Scarlet Woman" do not denote persons, but are titles of office, that of Hierophant and High Priestess (☿ and ☽), else it would be difficult to understand the next verse.

16. In II. 16 we find that Had is to be taken as 11 (see II. 16, comment). Then Hadit = 421, Nuit = 466.

$$421 - 3 \text{ (the moon)} = 418.$$
$$466 + 200 \text{ (the sun)} = 666.$$

These are the two great numbers of the Qabalistic system that enabled me to interpret the signs leading to this revelation.

The winged secret flame is Hadit; the stooping starlight is Nuit; these are their true natures, and their functions in the supreme ritual referred to above.

17. "Ye" refers to the other worshippers of Nuit, who must seek out their own election.

18. The serpent is the symbol of divinity and royalty. It is also a symbol of Hadit, invoked upon them.

19. Nuit herself will overshadow them.

388

LIBER LEGIS

20. This word is perhaps Abrahadabra, the sacred word of 11 letters.

21. Refers to the actual picture on the stélé. Nuit is a conception immeasurably beyond all men have ever thought of the Divine. Thus she is not the mere star-goddess, but a far higher thing, dimly veiled by that unutterable glory.

This knowledge is only to be attained by adepts; the outer cannot reach to it.

22. A promise—not yet fulfilled. [Since ($\odot$ in $\uparrow$, An V.) fulfilled.]

A charge to destroy the faculty of discriminating between illusions.

23. The chief, then, is he who has destroyed this sense of duality.

24. Nu $ח$ $=6+50=56$.

25. Dividing $\frac{6}{50}=0.12$.

o the circumference, Nuit.

. the centre, Hadit.

1 the Unity proceeding, Ra-Hoor-Khuit.

2 = the Coptic H, whose shape closely resembles the Arabic figure 2, the Breath of Life, inspired and expired. Human consciousness. Thoth.

Adding $50+6=56$, Nu, and concentrating $5+6=11$, Abrahadabra, etc.

Multiplying $50\times6=300$, $ש$ and Ruach Elohim, the Holy Spirit.

I am inclined to believe that there is a further mystery concealed in this verse; possibly those of 418 and 666 again.

26. The prophet demanding a sign of his mission, it is promised: a Samadhi upon the Infinite.

This promise was later fulfilled—see " The Temple of Solomon the King," which proposes to deal with the matter in its due season.

27-31. Here is a profound philosophical dogma, in a sense possibly an explanation and illumination of the propositions in " Berashith."

The dyad (or universe) is created with little pain in order to make the bliss of dissolution possible. Thus the pain of life may be atoned for by the bliss of death.

This delight is, however, only for the chosen servants of Nu. Outsiders may be looked on much as the Cartesians looked on animals.

32. The rule and purpose of the Order: the promise of Nuit to her chosen.

33. The prophet then demanded instruction: ordeals, rituals, law.

34. The first demand is refused, or, it may be, is to be communicated by another means than writing.

[It has since been communicated.]

The second is partially granted; or, if fully granted, is not to be made wholly public.

The third is granted unconditionally.

35. Definition of this book.

36. The first strict charge not to tamper with a single letter of this book.

The comment is to be written "by the wisdom of Ra-Hoor-Khuit," *i.e.* by open, not by initiated wisdom.

37. An entirely new system of magic is to be learnt and taught, as is now being done.

38. The usual charge in a work of this kind.

Every man has a right to attain; but it is equally the duty of the adept to see that he duly earns his reward, and to test and train his capacity and strength.

39. Compare Rabelais. Also it may be translated, "Let Will and Action be in harmony."

But θελημα also means Will in the higher sense of Magical One-pointedness, and in the sense used by Schopenhauer and Fichte.

There is also most probably a very lofty secret interpretation.

I suggest—

The	the essential אח, Azoth, etc. = θε.
Word	Chokmah, Thoth, the Logos, the Second Emanation.
of	the Partitive, Binah the Great Mother.
the	Chesed, the paternal power, reflection of the "The" above.
Law	Geburah, the stern restriction.
is	Tiphereth, visible existence, the balanced harmony of the worlds.
θελημα	The idea embracing all this sentence in a word.

Or—

θ the = ט the Lion, "Thou shalt unite all these symbols into the form of a Lion."

ε Word = ה the letter of Breath, the Logos.

λ of = ל ♎ the Equilibrium.

η the = ה 418, Abrahadabra.

μ Law = ט the Hanged Man, or Redeemer.

α is = א the O (zero, Nuit, which is Existence).

θελημα the sum of all.

40. θε, the Hermit, ' invisible, yet illuminating. The A∴ A∴

λη, the Lover, ז visible as is the lightning flash. The College of Adepts.

μα, the Man of Earth, פ the Blasted Tower. The 3 Keys add up to 31 = לא Not and אל God. Thus is the whole of θελημα equivalent to Nuit, the all-embracing.

LIBER LEGIS

See the Tarot Trumps for further study of these grades.

$\theta\epsilon = 14$, the Pentagram, rule of Spirit over ordered Matter. Strength and Authority (ט and ה) and secretly $1+4=5$, the Hierophant ו. V. Also: ♌ ♈, the Lion and the Ram. *Cf* Isaiah. It is a "millennial" state.

$\lambda\eta = 38$, the Key-word Abrahadabra, 418, divided by the number of its letters, 11. Justice or Balance and the Charioteer or Mastery. A state of progress; the church militant.

$\mu a = 41$, the Inverted Pentagram, matter dominating spirit. The Hanged Man and the Fool. The condition of those who are not adepts.

"Do what thou wilt" need not only be interpreted as licence or even as liberty. It may for example be taken to mean Do what thou (Ateh) wilt; and Ateh is $406 = $ האת $= $ T, the sign of the cross. The passage might then be read as a charge to self-sacrifice or equilibrium.

I only put forward this suggestion to exhibit the profundity of thought required to deal even with so plain a passage.

All the meanings are true, if only the interpreter be illuminated; but if not, they are all false, even as he is false.

41, 42. Interference with the will of another is the great sin, for it predicates the existence of another. In this duality sorrow consists. I think that possibly the higher meaning is still attributed to *will*.

43. *No other* shall say *nay* may mean—

No-other ($=$ Nuit) shall pronounce the word No, uniting the aspirant with Herself by denying and so destroying that which he is.

44. Recommends "non-attachment." Students will understand how in meditation the mind which attaches itself to hope of success is just as bound as if it were to attach itself to some base material idea. It is a bond; and the aim is freedom.

I recommend serious study of the word *unassuaged* which appears not very intelligible.

45. Perhaps means that adding perfection to perfection results in the unity and ultimately the Negativity.

But I think there is much more than this.

46. $61 = $ אין. But the True Nothing of Nuit is 8, 80, 418. Now 8 is ח, which spelt fully, חית, is 418. And 418 is Abrahadabra, the word of Ra-Hoor-Khuit. Now 80 is פ, the letter of Ra-Hoor-Khuit. [Qy. this.]

47. Let us, however, add the Jewish half 61.

$8+80+418 = 506$. *Cf.* verses 24, 25.

$506+61 = 567 = 27 \times 21 = \qquad ?$

But writing 506 qabalistically backwards we get

605, and $605+61 = 666$.

$666 = 6 \times 111$, and $111 = \aleph = 0$ in Taro

$= 1 + 2 + \ldots + 36$, the sum of the numbers in the Magic Square of Sol.

= the Number of the Beast

Or, taking the keys of 8, 80, 418, we get vii., xvi., vii., adding to 30.

$30 + 61 = 91 = $ אמן, Amen.

This may unite Nuit with Amoun the negative and concealed. Yet to my mind she is the greater conception, that of which Amoun is but a reflection.

48. See above for 111.

"My prophet is a fool," *i.e.* my prophet has the highest of all grades, since the Fool is א.

I note later (An V., ☉. in ♒) that *v.* 48 means that all disappears when $61 + 8$, 80, 418 are reduced to 1. And this may indicate some practical mystic method of annihilation. I am sure (☉ in ♎, An VII.) that this is by no means the perfect solution of these marvellous verses.

49. Declares a New System of Magic and initiation.

Asar—Isa—is now the Candidate, not the Hierophant.

Hoor—see Cap. III.—is the Initiator.

50. Our system of initiation is to be triune.

For the outer, tests of labour, pain, etc.

For the inner, intellectual tests.

For the elect of the A∴ A∴, spiritual tests.

Further, the Order is not to hold lodges, but to have a chain-system.

51. The candidate will be brought through his ordeals in divers ways.

The Order is to be of freemen and nobles.

52. But distinctions must not be made before Nuit, either intellectually, morally, or personally.

Metaphysics, too, is intellectual bondage; avoid it!

Otherwise one falls back to the Law of Hoor from the perfect emancipation of Nuit. This is a great mystery, only to be understood by those who have fully attained Nuit and her secret Initiation.

53. The prophet is retained as the link with the lower.

Again the word "assuage" used in a sense unintelligible to me.

54, 55, 56 to the word "child."

A prophecy, not yet (May 1909 O.S.) fulfilled, so far as I know. I take it in its obvious sense.

56 from the word "Aum."

All religions have some truth.

We possess all intellectual truth, and some, not all, mystic truth.

57. Invoke me,—etc.—I take literally. See Liber NV for this ritual.

LIBER LEGIS

Love under will—no casual pagan love ; nor love under fear, as the Christians do. But love magically directed, and used as a spiritual formula.

The fools (not here implying א fools, for III., 57 says, All fools despise) may mistake.

This love, then, should be the serpent love, the awakening of the Kundalini. The further mystery is of פ and unsuited to the grade in which this comment is written.

The last paragraph confirms the Tarot attributions as given in 777. With one secret exception.

58. The Grace of our Lady of the Stars.

59. "Because," etc. This mystical phrase doubtless refers to some definite spiritual experience connected with the Knowledge of Nuit.

60. Nu = 56 and 5+6=11.

The Circle in the Pentagram? See Liber NV.

The uninitiated perceive only darkness in Night : the wise perceive the golden stars in the vault of azure.

Concerning that Secret Glory it is not here fitting to discourse.

61. Practical and literal, yet it may be doubted whether "to lose all in that hour" may not refer to the supreme attainment, and that therefore to give one particle of dust (perhaps the Ego, or the central atom Hadit her complement) is the act to achieve.

62, 63. Again practical and literal. Yet the "Secret Temple" refers also to a knowledge incommunicable—save by experience.

64. The supreme affirmation.

65. The supreme adjuration.

66. The end.

II

1. *Cf.* I. 1. As Had, the root of Hadit, is the manifestation of Nuit, so Nu, the root of Nuit, is the hiding of Hadit.

2. Nuit is Infinite Extension ; Hadit Infinite Contraction. Khabs is the House of Hadit, even as Nuit is the house of the Khu, and the Khabs is in the Khu (I. 8). These theologies reflect mystic experiences of Infinite Contraction and Expansion, while philosophically they are the two opposing Infinites whose interplay gives Finity.

3. A further development of higher meaning. In phrasing this verse suggests an old mystical definition of God : " He Whose centre is everywhere and Whose circumference nowhere."

4. The circumference of Nuit touches Ra-Hoor-Khuit, Kether ; but her centre Hadit is for ever concealed above Kether. Is not Nu the *Hiding* of

Hadit, and Had the *Manifestation* of Nuit? [I later, ☉ in ♎, An VII., dislike this note; and refer the student to Liber XI. and Liber DLV.]

5. A reference to certain magical formulæ known to the scribe of this book. The purification of said rituals is in progress at this time, An V.

6. Hadit is the Ego or Atman in everything, but of course a loftier and more secret thing than anything understood by the Hindus. And of course the distinction between Ego and Ego is illusion. Hence Hadit, who is the life of all that is, if known, becomes the death of that individuality.

7. Hadit is both the Maker of Illusion and its destroyer. For though His interplay with Nuit results in the production of the Finite, yet His withdrawing into Himself is the destruction thereof.

"The axle of the wheel," another way of saying that He is the Core of Things.

"The cube in the Circle." *Cf.* Liber 418, "The Vision and the Voice," 30th Æthyr.

"Come unto me" is a foolish word; for it is I that go.

That is, Hadit is everywhere; yet, being sought, he flies. The Ego cannot be found, as meditation will show.

8. He is symbolised by Harpocrates, crowned child upon the lotus, whose shadow is called Silence.

Yet His Silence is the Act of Adoration; not the dumb callousness of heaven toward man, but the supreme ritual, the Silence of the supreme Orgasm, the stilling of all Voices in the perfect rapture.

9. Hence we pass naturally and easily to the sublime optimism of Verse 9. The lie is given to pessimism, not by sophistry, but by a direct knowledge.

10. The prophet who wrote this was at this point angrily unwilling to proceed.

11. He was compelled to do so,

12. For the God was in him, albeit he knew it not.

13. For so long as any knower remains, there is no thing known. Knowledge is the loss of the Knower in the Known.

"And me" (not "and I"), Hadit was the passive, which could not arise because of the existence of the Knower; "and" implying further the duality—which is Ignorance.

14. Enough has been said of the Nature of Hadit, now let a riddle of L.V.X. be propounded.

15. I am perfect, being Not (31 לא or 61 אין).

My number is Nine by the fools (IX. the Hermit ♍ and ☿).

With the just I am Eight. VIII., Justice ♎ Maat ל, and One in Eight, א.

Which is Vital, for I am None indeed, לא.

The Empress ד III., the King ה IV., are not of me. III.+IV.=VII.

LIBER LEGIS

16. I am the Empress and the Hierophant (ו V.) III.+V.=VIII., and VIII. is XI., both because of the 11 letters in Abrahadabra (=418=חיה= ח =8), the Key Word of all this ritual, and because VIII. is not ♌, Strength, but ♎, Justice, in the Tarot (see Tarot Lecture and 777).

17-21. This passage was again very painful to the prophet, who took it in its literal sense.

But "the poor and the outcast" are the petty thoughts and the qliphothic thoughts and the sad thoughts. These must be rooted out, or the ecstasy of Hadit is not in us. They are the weeds in the Garden that starve the Flower.

22. Hadit now identifies himself with the Kundalini, the central magical force in man.

This privilege of using wine and strange drugs has been confirmed; the drugs were indeed revealed.

Follows a curse against the cringing altruism of Christianity, the yielding of the self to external impressions, the smothering of the Babe of Bliss beneath the flabby old nurse Convention.

23. The Atheism of God.

"Allah's the Atheist! He owns

No Allah." Bagh-i-Muattar.

To admit God is to look up to God, and so not to be God. The curse of duality.

24. Hermits—see *v.* 15.

Our ascetics enjoy, govern, conquer, love, and are not to quarrel (but see vv. 59, 60—Even their combats are glorious).

25. The cant of democracy condemned. It is useless to pretend that men are equal; the facts are against it. And we are not going to stay, dull and contented as oxen, in the ruck of humanity.

26. The Kundalini again. The mystic Union is to be practised both with Spirit and with Matter.

27. The importance of failing to interpret these verses. Unspirituality leads us to the bird-lime of Intellect. The Hawk must not perch on any earthly bough, but remain poised in the ether.

28-31. The great Curse pronounced by the Supernals against the Inferiors who arise against them.

Our reasoning faculties are the toils of the labyrinth within which we are all caught. *Cf.* Lib. LXV. V. 59.

32. We have insufficient data on which to reason.

This passage only applies to "rational" criticism of the Things Beyond.

33. We pass from the wandering in the jungle of Reason to

395

34. The Awakening.

35. Let us be practical persons, not babblers of gossip and platitude.

36-43. A crescendo of ecstasy in the mere thought of performing these rituals; which are in preparation under the great guidance of V.V.V.V.V.

44. Without fear rejoice; death is only a dissolution, a uniting of Hadit with Nu, the Ego with the All, ' with א. (Note 'יo+א ı = ı ı, Abrahadabra, the Word of Uniting the 5 and the 6.)

45. Those without our circle of ecstasy do indeed die. Earth to earth, ashes to ashes, dust to dust.

46. The prophet was again perplexed and troubled; for in his soul was Compassion for all beings.

But though this Compassion is a feeling perhaps admirable and necessary for mortals, yet it pertains to the planes of Illusion.

47. Hadit knows nothing of these things; He is pure ecstasy.

48. Hadit has never defiled His purity with the Illusions of Sorrow, etc. Even love and pity for the fallen is an identification with it (sympathy, from συν παθειν), and therefore a contamination.

49. Continues the curse against the slave-soul.

Amen. This is of the 4, *i.e.* should be spelt with 4 letters (the elements), אמחש not אמן. The fifth, who is invisible, is ע, 70, the Eye. Now אמחש = 741 + 70 = 811 = IAO in Greek, and IAO is the Greek form of יהוה, the synthesis of the 4 elements אמחש.

(This ע is perhaps the O. in N.O.X., Liber VII. I. 40.)

50. *Cf.* I. 60.

51. Purple—the ultra-violet (*v.* 51), the most positive of the colours.

Green—the most negative of the colours, half-way in the spectrum.

The Magical Image of Hadit is therefore an Eye within a coiled serpent, gleaming red—the spiritual red of ש not mere △—at the apex of the Triangle in the half circle of Nuit's Body, and shedding spangles as of the spectrum of eight colours, including the ultra-violet but not the ultra-red ; and

52. Set above a black Veil.

This verse is very difficult for anyone, either with or without morality. For what men nowadays call "Vice" is really virtue—virtus, manliness—and "Virtue"—cowardice, hypocrisy, prudery, chastity, and so on are really vices—vitia, flaws.

53. But the prophet again disliked the writing. The God comforted him.

Also he prophesied of his immediate future, which was fulfilled, and is still being fulfilled at the time (An V., ☉ in 20° ♋) of this writing. Even more marked now (An VII., ☉ in ♎), especially these words, "I lift thee up."

54. The triumph over the rationalists predicted.

LIBER LEGIS

The punctuation of this book was done after its writing; at the time it was mere hurried scribble from dictation.

See the MS. facsimile.

55. Done. See Liber Trigrammaton, Comment.

56. The God again identifies himself with essential ecstasy. He wants no reverence, but identity.

57. A quotation from the Apocalypse. This God is not a Redeemer: He is Himself. You cannot worship Him, or seek Him—He is He. And if thou be He, well.

58. Yet it does not follow that He (and His) must appear joyous. They may assume the disguise of sorrow.

59. Yet, being indeed invulnerable, one need not fear for them.

60. Hit out indiscriminately therefore. The fittest will survive.

This doctrine is therefore contrary to that of Gallio, or of Buddha.

61. At the ecstasy of this thought the prophet was rapt away by the God. First came a new strange light, His herald.

62. Next, as Hadit himself, did he know the athletic rapture of Nuit's embrace.

63. Each breath, as he drew it in, was an orgasm; each breath, as it went out, was a new dissolution into death.

Note that throughout these books death is always spoken of as a definite experience, a delightful event in one's career.

64. The prophet is now completely swallowed up in the ecstasy. Then he is hailed by the Gods, and bidden to write on.

65, 66. The division of consciousness having re-arisen, and been asserted the God continues, and prophesies—of that which I cannot comment.

The ecstasy rekindles,

67, 68. So violently that the body of the prophet is nigh death.

69. The prophet's own consciousness re-awakens. He no longer knows anything at all—then grows the memory of the inspiration past; he asks if it is all.

[It is evidently his own interpolation in the dictation.]

70. Also he has the human feeling of failure. It seems that he must fortify his nature in many other ways, in order that he may endure the ecstasy unbearable of mortals.

There is also a charge that other than physical considerations obtain.

71. Yet excess is the secret of success.

72. There is no end to the Path—death itself crowns all.

73, 74. Yet death is forbidden: work, I suppose, must be done before it is earned; its splendour will increase with the years that it is longed for.

75, 76. A final revelation. The revealer to come is perhaps the one mentioned in I. 55 and III. 47. The verse goes on to urge the prophet to identify himself with Hadit, to practise the Union with Nu, and to proclaim this joyful revelation unto men.

77, 78. Though the prophet had in a way at this time identified himself with the number 666, he considered the magic square drawn therefrom rather silly and artificial, if indeed it had yet been devised, on which point he is uncertain.

The true Square is as follows:

[It follows when it is discovered!]

The House of the Prophet, not named by him, was chosen by him before he attached any meaning to the number 418; nor had he thought of attaching any importance to the name of the House. He supposed this passage to be mystical, or to refer to some future house.

Yet on trial we obtain at once

$$\text{בולשכין} = 418$$

79. So mote it be!

III

1. Abrahadabra—the Reward of Ra-Hoor-Khuit. We have already seen that Abrahadabra is the glyph of the blending of the 5 and the 6, the Rose and the Cross. So also the Great Work, the equilibration of the 5 and the 6, is shown in this God; fivefold as a Warrior Horus, sixfold as the solar Ra. Khuit is a name of Khem the Ram-Phallus-two-plume god Amoun; so that the whole god represents in qabalistic symbolism the Second Triad ("whom all nations of men call the first").

It is the Red descending Triangle—the sole thing visible. For Hadit and Nuit are far beyond.

Note that Ra-Hoor ראהוור $= 418$.

2. Suggested by a doubt arising in the mind of the prophet as to the unusual spelling. But the "I" makes a difference in the qabalistic interpretation of the name.

3—end. This whole book seems intended to be interpreted literally. It was so taken by the scribe at the time.

Yet a mystical meaning is easy to find. Exempli gratia; vv. 4-9.

4. An Island = one of the Cakkrams or nerve-centres in the spine.

5. Fortify it! = Concentrate the mind upon it.

6. = Prevent any impressions reaching it.

7. = I will describe a new method of meditation by which

8. Ye shall easily suppress invading thoughts.

398

9. May mystically describe this method [*e.g.*, Liber HHH, Section 3].

But the course of history will determine the sense of the passage.

10. The stélé of revealing—see illustration.

That temple; it was arranged as an octagon; its length double its breadth; entrances on all four quarters of temple; enormous mirrors covering six of the eight walls (there were no mirrors in the East and West or in the western halves of the South and North sides).

There were an altar and two obelisks in the temple; a lamp above the altar; and other furniture.

Kiblah—any point to which one turns to pray, as Mecca is the Kiblah of the Mahometan.

"It shall not fade," etc. It has not hitherto been practicable to carry out this command.

11. "Abstraction." It was thought that this meant to combine abstraction and construction, *i.e.* the preparation of a replica, which was done.

Of course the original is in "locked glass."

12-15. This, ill-understood at the time, is now too terribly clear. The 15th verse, apparently an impossible sequel, has justified itself.

16. Courage and modesty of thought are necessary to the study of this book. Alas! we know so very little of the meaning.

17. The infinite unity is our refuge, since if our consciousness be in that unity, we shall care nothing for the friction of its component parts. And our light is the inmost point of illuminated consciousness.

And the great Red Triangle is as a shield, and its rays are far-darting arrows!

18. An end to the humanitarian mawkishness which is destroying the human race by the deliberate artificial protection of the unfit.

19. 718 is ὑπομονη, the abstract noun equivalent to Perdurabo. (⊙ in 3° ♋, An VII.)

20. In answer to some mental "Why" of the prophet the God gives this sneering answer. Yet perhaps therein is contained some key to enable me one day to unlock the secret of verse 19, at present (⊙ in 20° ♍, An V.) obscure. [Now (⊙ in ♎, An VII.) clear.]

21. This was remarkably fulfilled.

22. This first charge was accomplished; but nothing resulted of a sufficiently striking nature to record.

The Ordeal "X" will be dealt with in private.

23-25. This incense was made; and the prediction most marvellously fulfilled.

26, 27, 28, 29. These experiments, however, were not made.

THE EQUINOX

30. Not yet accomplished (☉ in 20° ♍, An V.)

31. Not yet accomplished (☉ in 20° ♍, An V.).

32, 33. Certainly, when the time comes.

34. This prophecy, relating to centuries to come, does not concern the present writer at the moment.

Yet he must expound it.

The Hierarchy of the Egyptians gives us this genealogy: Isis, Osiris, Horus.

Now the "pagan" period is that of Isis; a pastoral, natural period of simple magic. Next with Buddha, Christ, and others there came in the Equinox of Osiris; when sorrow and death are the principal objects of man's thought, and his magical formula is that of sacrifice.

Now, with Mohammed perhaps as its forerunner, comes in the Equinox of Horus, the young child who rises strong and conquering (with his twin Harpocrates) to avenge Osiris, and bring on the age of strength and splendour.

His formula is not yet fully understood.

Following him will arise the Equinox of Ma, the Goddess of Justice, it may be a hundred or ten thousand years from now; for the Computation of Time is not here as There.

35. Note Heru-ra-ha = 418.

36-38. Mostly translations from the stélé.

39. This is being done; but quickly? No. I have slaved at the riddles in this book for nigh on seven years; and all is not yet clear (☉ in ♍ 20°, An V.). Nor yet (☉ in ♎, An VII.).

40. I do not think it easy. Though the pen has been swift enough, once it was taken in hand. May it be that Hadit hath indeed made it secure! [I am still (An VII., ☉ in ♎), entirely dissatisfied.]

41. This shall be done as soon as possible.

42. This shall be attended to.

43-45. The two latter verses have become useless, so far as regards the person first indicated to fill the office of "Scarlet Woman." In her case the prophecy of v. 43 has been most terribly fulfilled, to the letter; except the last paragraph. Perhaps before the publication of this comment the final catastrophe will have occurred (☉ in 20° ♍, An V.). It or an even more terrible equivalent is now in progress (☉ in ♎, An VII.). [*P.S.*—I sealed up the MSS. of this comment and posted it to the printer on my way to the Golf Club at Hoylake. On my arrival at the Club, I found a letter awaiting me which stated that the catastrophe had occurred.]

Let the next upon whom the cloak may fall beware!

46. I do not understand the first paragraph.

47. These mysteries are inscrutable to me, as stated in the text. Later

400

MY CRAPULOUS CONTEMPORARIES
NO. V

THE BISMARCK OF BATTERSEA

THE BISMARCK OF BATTERSEA

DANTE perhaps thought when he descended the fifth round of Hell that there was some consolation in the fact that he was getting near the bottom. To us, as we explore the glories of Edwardian literature, such consolation is denied. Abyss after abyss yawns beneath our feet; deep into the gloom we peer and our ears are poisoned with the fetid vapours of the ineffable slime—with the callow crapulosities of a Corelli, the slobbering senilities of a Sims, the unctuous snivellings of a Caine.

But we do not propose to descend so far—there is a limit. But stay! what is that glimmer on yonder ledge? That ledge where the Brown Dog of the Faddist fights its eternal battle with the Yellow Dog of Socialism. The ledge labelled "Battersea," supreme word of malignity in the tongue of the pit? Our laurelled guide quickly lowers us thither.

What is that bloated and beery buffoon who stands upon his head to attract attention? we ask. Bismarck, it appears, is his name. Blood and iron is his motto. 'S death! but I suspect a paradox. Maybe that by blood he means beer, by iron ink.

"Maybe this Nonconformist plum-pudding has been dipped in whale oil—and why have they stuffed it with onions?" How shall I find the key to this mystery? So portentous a sentence —and its meaning? "Christianity is only tenable through Literalism and Ritualism." Not so I read it—and my own secret interpretation sends a guffaw through the black shining sides of the prison. With that I awoke; 'twas all a dream; I must begin again—that opening will never do.

Here, therefore, beginneth the third lesson. How shall we catch the great gray water-rat "That strikes the stars (*sublimi vertice*) on Campden Hill?"

Quoth the famous consort of a famous judge, on being advised to abate the rat nuisance by plugging their holes with a mixture of tallow, arsenic, and brown paper: "Yes, but you've got to catch them first." So we, accepting her wisdom, shall not attempt to suppress the News (plain or illustrated)—we shall rather cope with the stench at its source.

This pot-bellied Publicola must be not only scotched, but killed. This megalomaniac Menenius must be put through the medicinal mangle of criticism—a thing which he has hitherto escaped, for as from the porpoise hides of the portly Monitor the round shot of the Merrimac rebounded, so has the oily evasiveness of this literary porpoise served to protect him from his foes, and now he clumsily gambols through the sea, unaware of the pursuing sword-fish. But a greater than the sword-fish (or shall I say the Sword-of-Song-fish) is here.

Just as a balloon is difficult to crush but easy to prick, so shall it be in these days.

This fellow is simply a trimmer. This seeming porpoise is only a jelly-fish; and the great black curves we saw were but the inkiness of the creature.

We draw out this leviathan with an hook, and he goes conveniently into a beer-mug. We calculate the mass of this brilliant comet, and we find it is not to exceed that of a barrel of butter.

MY CRAPULOUS CONTEMPORARIES

We are appalled by the bellowing of this Bull of Phalaris, and find that it is but an ingenious mechanism worked by the gaspings of an emasculate oyster.

Surely never in all the history of thought—and its imitations—has such a widow's cruse supplied the world with such a deluge of oil. Croton oil.

As a man who orders roast beef and gets hash, so do we look for literature and get mixed dictionary. How do we do it? We stifle the groans of our armchair by continued session and open the Encyclopedia at random. Hullo! what's this? "Schopenhauer, famous pessimist philosopher." (To the stenographer): "The splendid optimism of Schopenhauer—" (Sotto voce) "Let's see what a philosopher is!" (turns it up after a vain search through letter F) "philosopher—lover of wisdom," etc.

(To stenographer) "manifests itself in a positive loathing of all wisdom." (Another turn.)

"Reprehensible—to be condemned."

(Dictating) "and is therefore to be condemned—no! no! please, miss—*not* to be condemned." (Another turn.)

"Catamaran"—a surf-boat used in Madras, hm!—(to stenographer)—"by all Hindoo speculative mystics."

(Speculative mystics—one of our best stock lines.)

We are now fairly started on our weekly causerie, the subject being probably Home Rule.

You see, nobody can get hurt. The invertebrate cannot maul the vertebrate—so we are safe from the chance of their fury. They pay us to defend the doctrine of original sin—so we escape by defending it upon the ground that it is "Jolly." They pay us to attack Free Thought, so we label it "narrow sectarianism," and please the Hard-Shell Baptists—with the purses—without annoying the Freethinker, who is naturally not hit.

The Romans crucified St. Peter head downwards; but it was reserved for this oleaginous clown to offer that last indignity to his Master. We are paid to shore up the rotting buttresses of Christianity, and we begin our article, "A casual carpenter"—

But, let us change the subject!

There was a man—a great man—who some years ago wrote a magnificent philosophical story called the "Napoleon of Notting Hill."

More lucid and a thousand times more entertaining than Bunyan, deeper than Berkeley, as full of ecstasy of laughter as Rabelais, and of mystic ecstasy as Malory, a book of the Chymical Marriage of Christian Rosencreutz with Voltaire.

I think those summits are not unattainable by the subject of our essay—for God's sake, man, forswear sack and live cleanly, and give us something like that!

A. QUILLER, JR.

ARTHUR IN THE AREA AGAIN!

Oh, Allah be obeyed!
How infernally they played!
I remember that they called themselves the Waites.

W. S. Gilbert.

MR. WAITE is at the area door again! It is not altogether unphilosophical to judge a man by the company he keeps, and I have reluctantly decided to dismiss Mr. Waite. He must consider himself no longer my disciple. It has been a painful step, more painful even than when I was obliged to expel him in 1900 from the Hermetic Order of the Golden Dawn. For he shows himself this last time in a quite impossible avatar —that of a Satanic colporteur eating rabbit pie in the kitchens of South Ealing.

I have before me a " Special Catalogue of Occult Books," published by a gentleman giving the name of Foulsham, which I hope shortly to see in " Punch " under the heading " MORE COMMERCIAL CANDOUR."

Item No. 1 is a "talisman." "The key to unlock the mysteries of the Universe." We hear that "charms and talismans ensure success." "This talisman is worn to bring Health, Happiness, and Success," a combination which I regard as remarkably cheap at 4s. 3d. post free.

But if you haven't got 4s. 3d., or are less ambitious, you

may still get a Parchment Talisman for wearing on the breast, from the Great Book by Rabbi Solomon with silk bag and cord for 1s. 3d. There are several; one for honour and riches, one for health, one for " Success in Hazard (betting—cards— games of chance)" which looks to me like cheating, one for Success in Trade, and then a set of three to which I call the particular attention of Professor von Krafft-Ebbing and Sir Charles Mathews. They are:

For Man's Love.
For Woman's Love.
For Love of Opposite Sex.

At the other end the catalogue turns from the psychopath to the servant-girl. All about the mystic meaning of moles, "love signs," and birthmarks, together with works on obstetrics (home-made), cure of Epilepsy, Worms, falling hair, and consumption, Old Moore's gazing Crystals, "Ye Witches Fortune-Telling Cards," and the rest of the rag-bag.

The ham of this exquisite sandwich is Mr. Waite's " Book of Black Magic and of Pacts " as was, " Book of Ceremonial Magic " as is. But for this clientèle of Mr. Foulsham the title is simply " The Book of Magic, including Black Magic, the rites and mysteries of Goethic (sic!) Theurgy, Sorcery, and Infernal Necromancy." Rather tempting for the people who wear talismans " for agricultural prosperity "!

I say fearlessly that this advertisement is a crude appeal to the vilest passions of the most wretched of humanity, to the people who would really love to bewitch their neighbour's cow. It is no reply to this charge to point out that the book is absolutely harmless. It is sold on the pretext that it is poison: if Locusta cheats her clients she is no less infamous: rather more.

If Mr. Waite thought to escape my eagle eye by omitting his name, this note will undeceive him; I repeat that I can no longer consider him as one of my disciples; and if he continues to adopt my ideas and phrases, and to republish them as his own, I shall really be obliged to do something hardly distinguishable from taking public notice of the fact.

ALEISTER CROWLEY.

THE BIG STICK

REVIEWS

THE SECRET TRADITION IN FREEMASONRY. By A. E. WAITE. London.
2 vols, 4to. 1911. 42s.

This is a work of over 900 pages, with twenty-eight plates, and numerous interesting head and tail pieces, sumptuously issued by the publishers. The author may be masonically justified in issuing *ex cathedra*, from his study chair, a new and mystic version of our old rites, but such, to be of value, must be grounded upon historic facts, and not upon the nonsense of garbled masonic histories. In the first volume the author shows an extraordinary lack of knowledge, and hence is unable to fix his theory of an Inner and Secret Tradition upon any solid basis, and the volume, with its inflated diction, and troubled reasoning, is very unsatisfactory. The second volume is much better, and is really an interesting study. In both however he does not seek to hide his contempt, often expressed in uncourteous language, against all who are opposed to his views, or otherwise against those degrees from which nothing could be extracted to support his theorizing, and the writer of this review comes in, with many better men, for a slating.

In September 1910 my attention was called to a Review of my ARCANE SCHOOLS in the London "Equinox," in which I find the following: "It is true he occasionally refers to people like Hargreave Jennings, A. E. Waite, and H. P. Blavatsky as if they were authorities, but whoso fishes with a net of so wide a sweep as brother Yarker's must expect to pull in some worthless fish. This accounts for Waite's contempt of him. Imagine Walford Bodie reviewing a medical book which referred to him as an authority on paralysis!" In spite of this mild castigation he still refers to me with some contempt, and as he has so little regard for the feelings of others, generally, I may be pardoned for following suit. I fancy, to say the least, that I am quite as able to judge evidence as Bro. Waite is; and I may say that for about sixty-five years I have made a constant study of Freemasonry, in my leisure hours, and I conceive that I have forgotten more of real Masonry than Waite ever knew, or is ever likely to know.

In the first place, he seems to be utterly ignorant of the Jacobite Ecossaisism of the Chapter of Clermont, yet it is only in their Pre-grand Lodge Harodim

413

that he could find foundation for his theorizing. My views on this subject occupy about eighty pages, now appearing in "The American Freemason," Salt Lake, Iowa, and to which I must refer my readers.

He cannot find what he seeks in the Hanoverian G. L. of London,—1717; or if he finds anything in the ritual of that body it will be trifling, following the religious training of the two clergymen, Anderson and Desaguliers, who founded it. On the Craft system he ought to have directed his attention to the old York ritual, and that of the Ancient Masons, which in that of York may date from 1726 (see my "Guild Charges").

The Royal Arch degree, when it had the *Three Veils* must have been the work, even if by instruction, of a Kabalistic Jew about 1740, and from this time we may expect to find a Secret tradition, grafted upon Anderson's system; the Arch degree was, undoubtedly, developed out of the Knight of the Sword, or Red Cross, by the Harodim Templars of Clermont, and that out of the operative Harodim.

Any stupid assertion, however historically untenable, but which is supported by a large majority, is a safe stock in trade for all such writers as Bro. Waite; it pays to tickle the palate of the crowd. It would take up too much space to carry this further, but I will ask to point out, first hand, some matters of general interest.

(I, p. 4). The A. and A.S. Rite *was not* invented in America, it was known in Geneva several years before 1802, when Charleston found out that it was of 33°, and began to trade upon it. They had, however, some years before, the *Morinite* Rite of 25° founded at Jamaica in 1767, and not 1761-2, hence anything referring to that date is false.

(P. 10). *Heredom* is a French modification of *Harodim*; even Barruel knew this. It is a term used by the Comicini builders of London, and is still in use with operative Lodges hailing from Durham. It was known to the operative Lodges of the Co. of Durham in 1735, when two of them went under the G.L. of Lodon, and may be ages older than that, and identical with the "Quarter Masters" of Kelwinning, etc., under the Schau Statutes of 1598 and with the "Warden Courts" of Scotland and France, existing in 1622, as Laurie points out. I can provide first-hand light as to the transliteration of the word into Heredomus, or Holy House. Many years ago, or about 1870, I was in correspondence with Mr. J. W. Papworth on the subject, and he put the question to a very learned friend whom he knew at the British Museum, and who suggested to him the above derivation. As he requested that his name should not appear I sent it to the "Freemason's Magazine," under the signature of Δ, and it was at once adopted by Pike; hence the term "Holy House" is about forty years old. I may mention that the Duke of Leinster's "Prince Mason" of Ireland,

414

REVIEWS

which is an amplified version of the London Rosecroix of 1770, but very much older than that, uses the following words in presenting the Jewel of a Pelican, " You are still a Harodim, or Master of the workmen of the Temple,"—a Clermont echo. It seems to be everywhere kept out of sight that the Pelican feeding its young with its blood was the war banner of James III when England was invaded by him in 1715.

(P. 40). Ramsay did no more in 1737, than put his own gloss on what he learned in the Chapter of Clermont. It is true that in 1754 a change was made in the " Illustrious Knight " (Templar and Sepulchre), and an additional degree then added by an unknown de Bonneville, which may be a Jesuit pseudonym, which in 1758 became the 25th degree, by adding the system of the Knights of the East, etc., and later the 32°, and to which some of Ramsay's views were added; he could not have been a member of the English G.L., but was a Jacobite Scotch Mason, and according to his own statement, made to his friend Gensau in 1741, was born in 1680-1681, and not in 1668 as given by Waite; such of these members as were voted Scotch rank by their Lodges, received the Harodim rank of Clermont. Thory says that these Scotch Masons in 1736 had four Lodges, and in ten years received 5,600 members. Personally, I think it likely that the Clermont claims from the Templars (Albigensian) may be just from their own operative Lodges. Fludd, ratherthan Ashmole, may have indoctrinated the London Masons, and I have given my reasons for this view in my American papers.

(P. 295). Waite is mistaken in supposing that the *Ordre du Temple* was not established in England. There was a Convent in 1838 at Liverpool, and its members' names are preserved. The same at London, and Sussex's consent was necessary for Reception; Dr. Robert Bigsby was a member of it, as also of Burnes' revisal of Deuchar's Masonic Knight Templar, which forms the basis of our 1851 ritual, which is not that of Dunckerley who worked the Clermont Templar Kadosh. There was also a Convent under the Duke of Sussex in India.

(P. 312). In reference to Clermont Waite is floating on his own imaginary sea. Between 1688 and 1753, Clermont had three well-known degrees of Harodim, and in 1754 a fourth was added. He quotes a garbled extract from Fratre Kristner, who is reliable, and adds a sneer against me. The Swedish Rite has knowledge that Count Scheffer was received by Derwentwater; Graf von Schmittau; Count Posse, were Received 1737, 1743, 1747. But Waite claims to be the infallible Pope, who is to judge evidence!!!

(P. 322). *Prince Adept* was added to Knight of the Sun at Kingston in 1767, in order that Morin might put in its place, the Prussian *Noachite* to give countenance to his frauds.

415

(P. 409). My view of HRDM-RSYES. is that, as it now stands, it is the French Lectures of Clermont's three grades. I give my reasons for this in the "American Freemasons" papers.

(II, p. 1). This volume, referring as it does, to more recent times, has fewer errors. It might even be extended, and earlier Hermetic details added.

(P. 36). We here read in Waite's words of "*The thing called Co-Masonry.*" I am not a Co-Mason myself, but I occasionaly send things to the independent private quarterly termed "Co-Mason," they are usually articles unsuited to the taste of mentally deficient Masons, or things that better informed Masons desire to hide. Again the system comes in for sarcasm owing to a supposed affinity with the Count St. Germain. We may not like Co-Masonry, for one thing, it affords less opportunity for the convivial Mason, who has no room for the intellectual part; but the system has come to stay, and we may as well treat it with civility.

(P. 92). The reduced Rite of Memphis has never been so numerous as to receive respect, and Freemasons are too ignorant to understand it, and to attack it—as in Co-Masonry—may prove profitable. As a matter of fact, some mistake was made in America as to the alleged reduction, but Egypt always held to the revised system of 1862-1866; at this time the Gd. Orient and the Chief of the Rite revised the whole system, mainly on an Hermetic basis, and gave to thirty-three leading ceremonies the power to confer, at intervals, the remaining sixty-two degrees which are generally added verbally in their relative places, and recently I furnished to America the necessary changes in a MS. of 200 pages. America had the Chapter degrees, 11°-18°, carefully edited, but the higher section was somewhat chaotic, and in 1872 I did not feel justified in making any great change. Bro. Waite thrice gives plates of its 90-95° Jewel—the winged egg—but without identification.

(P. 230). *Rite of Swedenborg.* Of this Kenneth Mackenzie was Grand Secretary from its introduction till his own death. Bro. Waite is quite mistaken in supposing that he had any hand in compiling the ritual; that and the Charter are in my hands as they came from Canada; the Charter is in the engrossment of Colonel Moore, and carries the following names: Colonel W. J. B. McLeod Moore, Gd. Master of Templars, and 33°; T. D. Harrington, Pt.G.M. of the G.L. of Canada, and 33°; George Canning Longley, 33°; The two first names were 33° Masons of the S.G.C. of Canada, then little esteemed, but founded by the Golden Square body of London; but Longley and myself were of the *Martin-Cerneau* body, though I have several 33° Patents of the *Morinite* Sect. Founded, as the Rite is, on a version of Ancient Masonry, carried back to a Feast of the Tabernacles, 5873 B.C., it is most interesting, but too lengthy for general use; under these circumstances I might feel inclined to print it for

REVIEWS

Master Masons, if Freemasonry was an intellectual body, but the needs of English Freemasonry, that in the best and most elaborate of works it is only working for the printer. The Rite was carried from London to the Americas, by Samuel Beswick, a Swedenborgian Minister, who wrote a book on the subject, and he informed me that they had rejected the matter added by Chastannier, and that what was left was the work of Swedenborg. Hence Bro. Waite's description of two secret and unnamed degrees, are of interest at this point.

(P. 368). Knight or *Priest of Eleusis*. I have this skeleton ritual of the Early Grand; and suppose it may be the old 1838 work of Memphis, of which Dr. Morison de Greenfield was an early member. As I look upon it the degree is intended to teach that early christianity absorbed the mysteries of Eleusis, and I mention this because I hear from New York that an eminent scholar, learned in Hermetic Greek, is making a translation in which he will prove that the Gospels and Epistles are pure Greek of the Eleusinian cult, and that the Jewish references are added to give a Semitic colouring. But I must conclude: I could make a decent sized volume in criticising and contesting Bro. Waite's book.

JOHN YARKER, 33°, 90°, 97°.

WEST DIDSBURY,
12/12/11.

SHE BUILDETH HER HOUSE. By WILL LEVINGTON COMFORT. J. B. Lippincott Co.

HEALTH FOR YOUNG AND OLD. By A. T. SCHOFIELD, M.D. Rider and Son. 3s. 6d. net.

KABALA OF NUMBERS. By SEPHARIAL. Rider and Son. 2s. net.

BYWAYS OF GHOSTLAND. By ELLIOT O'DONNELL. Rider and Son. 3s. 6a. net.

IN THE GRIP OF THE WHITE SLAVE TRADER. M. A. P. 6d. net.

CONTEMPORARY BELGIAN POETRY. Walter Scott Publishing Co. 1s.

THE LAIR OF THE WHITE WORM. By BRAM STOKER. Rider and Son. 6s.

A BED OF ROSES.

THE SECRET TRADITION OF FREEMASONRY. By A. E. WAITE.

My previous remark calls for no modification.

MARÉCHAL DE CAMBRONNE.

c

417

A BIRTHDAY

Aug. 10, 1911.

FULL moon to-night; and six and twenty years
Since my full moon first broke from angel spheres!
A year of infinite love unwearying—
No circling seasons, but perennial spring!
A year of triumph trampling through defeat,
The first made holy and the last made sweet
By this same love; a year of wealth and woe,
Joy, poverty, health, sickness—all one glow
In the pure light that filled our firmament
Of supreme silence and unbarred extent,
Wherein one sacrament was ours, one Lord,
One resurrection, one recurrent chord,
One incarnation, one descending dove,
All these being one, and that one being Love!

You sent your spirit into tunes; my soul
Yearned in a thousand melodies to enscroll
Its happiness: I left no flower unplucked
That might have graced your garland. I induct
Tragedy, comedy, farce, fable, song,
Each longing a little, each a little long,
But each aspiring only to express
Your excellence and my unworthiness—

419

THE EQUINOX

Nay! but my worthiness, since I was sense
And spirit too of that same excellence.

So thus we solved the earth's revolving riddle:
I could write verse, and you could play the fiddle,
While, as for love, the sun went through the signs,
And not a star but told him how love twines
A wreath for every decanate, degree,
Minute and second, linked eternally
In chains of flowers that never fading are,
Each one as sempiternal as a star.

Let me go back to your last birthday. Then
I was already your one man of men
Appointed to complete you, and fulfil
From everlasting the eternal will.
We lay within the flood of crimson light
In my own balcony that August night,
And conjuring the aright and the averse
Created yet another universe.

We worked together; dance and rite and spell
Arousing heaven and constraining hell.
We lived together; every hour of rest
Was honied from your tiger-lily breast.
We—oh what lingering doubt or fear betrayed
My life to fate?—we parted. Was I afraid?
I was afraid, afraid to live my love,
Afraid you played the serpent, I the dove,
Afraid of what I know not. I am glad

A BIRTHDAY

Of all the shame and wretchedness I had,
Since those six weeks have taught me not to doubt you,
And also that I cannot live without you.

Then I came back to you; black treasons rear
Their heads, blind hates, deaf agonies of fear,
Cruelty, cowardice, falsehood, broken pledges,
The temple soiled with senseless sacrileges,
Sickness and poverty, a thousand evils,
Concerted malice of a million devils;—
You never swerved; your high-pooped galleon
Went marvellously, majestically on
Full-sailed, while every other braver bark
Drove on the rocks, or foundered in the dark.

Then Easter, and the days of all delight!
God's sun lit noontide and his moon midnight,
While above all, true centre of our world,
True source of light, our great love passion-pearled
Gave all its life and splendour to the sea
Above whose tides stood our stability.

Then, sudden and fierce, no monitory moan,
Smote the mad mischief of the great cyclone.
How far below us all its fury rolled!
How vainly sulphur tries to tarnish gold!
We lived together: all its malice meant
Nothing but freedom of a continent!

It was the forest and the river that knew
The fact that one and one do not make two.

THE EQUINOX

We worked, we walked, we slept, we were at ease,
We cried, we quarrelled; all the rocks and trees
For twenty miles could tell how lovers played,
And we could count a kiss for every glade.
Worry, starvation, illness and distress?
Each moment was a mine of happiness.

Then we grew tired of being country mice,
Came up to Paris, lived our sacrifice
There, giving holy berries to the moon,
July's thanksgiving for the joys of June.

And you are gone away—and how shall I
Make August sing the raptures of July?
And you are gone away—what evil star
Makes you so competent and popular?
How have I raised this harpy-hag of Hell's
Malice—that you are wanted somewhere else?
I wish you were like me a man forbid,
Banned, outcast, nice society well rid
Of the pair of us—then who would interfere
With us?—my darling, you would now be here!

But no! we must fight on, win through, succeed,
Earn the grudged praise that never comes to meed,
Lash dogs to kennel, trample snakes, put bit
In the mule-mouths that have such need of it,
Until the world there's so much to forgive in
Becomes a little possible to live in.

God alone knows if battle or surrender
Be the true courage; either has its splendour.

A BIRTHDAY

But since we chose the first, God aid the right,
And damn me if I fail you in the fight!
God join again the ways that lie apart,
And bless the love of loyal heart to heart!
God keep us every hour in every thought,
And bring the vessel of our love to port!

These are my birthday wishes. Dawn's at hand,
And you're an exile in a lonely land.
But what were magic if it could not give
My thought enough vitality to live?
Do not then dream this night has been a loss!
All night I have hung, a god, upon the cross;
All night I have offered incense at the shrine;
All night you have been unutterably mine,
Mine in the memory of the first wild hour
When my rough grasp tore the unwilling flower
From your closed garden, mine in every mood,
In every tense, in every attitude,
In every possibility, still mine
While the sun's pomp and pageant, sign to sign,
Stately proceeded, mine not only so
In the glamour of memory and austral glow
Of ardour, but by image of my brow
Stronger than sense, you are even here and now
Mine, utterly mine, my sister and my wife,
Mother of my children, mistress of my life!

O wild swan winging through the morning mist!
The thousand thousand kisses that we kissed,

423

THE EQUINOX

The infinite device our love devised
If by some chance its truth might be surprised,
Are these all past? Are these to come? Believe me,
There is no parting; they can never leave me.
I have built you up into my heart and brain
So fast that we can never part again.
Why should I sing you these fantastic psalms
When all the time I have you in my arms?
Why? 'tis the murmur of our love that swells
Earth's dithyrambs and ocean's oracles.

But this is dawn; my soul shall make its nest
Where your sighs swing from rapture into rest
Love's thurible, your tiger-lily breast.

ALEISTER CROWLEY.

THE WINGED BEETLE

By ALEISTER CROWLEY

PRIVATELY PRINTED: TO BE HAD THROUGH "THE EQUINOX"

300 copies, 10s. net
50 copies on handmade paper, specially bound, £1, 1s. net

———◦◇◦———

CONTENTS

d

MR NEUBURG'S NEW VOLUME OF POEMS

Imperial 16mo, pp. 200

Now ready. Order through **The Equinox**, *or of any Bookseller*

THE TRIUMPH OF PAN

POEMS BY VICTOR B. NEUBURG

This volume, containing many poems—nearly all of them hitherto unpublished—besides THE TRIUMPH OF PAN, includes THE ROMANCE OF OLIVIA VANE.

The First Edition is limited to Two Hundred and Fifty copies: Two Hundred and Twenty on ordinary paper, whereof less than Two Hundred are for sale; and Thirty on Japanese vellum, of which Twenty-five are for sale. These latter copies are numbered, and signed by the Author. The binding is half-parchment with crimson sides; the ordinary copies are bound in crimson boards, half-holland.

The price of ordinary copies is Five Shillings net; of the special copies, One Guinea net.

EXTRACTS FROM FIRST NOTICES

" Not every one will care for Mr Neuburg's tone in all the pieces, but he is undoubtedly a poet to be reckoned with, and a volume so original as this is should create no small stir. It is superbly produced by the publishers."—*Sussex Daily News.*

"When one comes to the poems . . . it is evident that they are written in English. . . . In a certain oblique and sub-sensible sense, eloquent and musical. . . . Distinctly Wagnerian in their effects. . . ."—*Scotsman.*

"It is full of 'the murmurous monotones of whispering lust,' 'the song of young desire,' and that kind of poppycock."—*London Opinion.*

"A competent master of words and rhythms. . . . His esoteric style is unreasonably obscure from an intelligent plain poetry-lover's standpoint."—*Morning Leader.*

"A charming volume of poems. . . . Pagan glamour . . . passion and vigour. . . . 'Sigurd's Songs' are commendable for dealing with the all too largely neglected Scandinavian theology. . . . A scholarly disciple. . . . The entire volume is eminently recommendable."—*Jewish Chronicle.*

"A gorgeous rhapsody. . . . Fortunately, there are the police. . . . On the whole, we cannot help regretting that such splendid powers of imagination and expression are flung away in such literary rioting."—*Light.*

"Sometimes of much beauty of rhythm and phrase. . . ."—*Times.*

"Poets who have any originality deserve to be judged by their own standard. . . . A Neo-mystic or semi-astrological pantheist. . . ."—*Liverpool Echo.*

"Love-making appears to have an added halo in his eyes if it is associated with delirium or bloodshed. . . . Mr Neuburg has a 'careless rapture' all his own; the carelessness, indeed, is just the trouble. His versification is remarkable, and there is something impressive in its mere fluency. . . . So luxurious, so rampant, a decadence quickly palls. . . . On the whole, this book must be pronounced a quite grievous exhibition of recklessness and folly."—*Manchester Guardian.*

". . . We began to be suspicious of him. . . . Hardly the sort of person we should care to meet on a dark night with a knobby stick in his hand. . . . This clever book."—*Academy.*

"A vivid imagination fostered by a keen and loving insight of nature, and this allied to a command of richly adorned language . . . have already assured for the author a prominent place amongst present-day poets. . . . An enthusiastic devotion to classic song . . . sustained metrical charm. From first to last the poet's work is an important contribution to the century's literature."—*Publishers' Circular.*

"This [book] contains the answer to a very well-known riddle propounded by the late Elizabeth Barrett Browning. You remember she asked in one of her poems, 'What was he doing to Great God Pan: Down in the reeds by the River?' Well, Mr Victor Neuburg has discovered the answer, for he was obviously wandering near the river if he was not hidden in the reeds. . . ."—ROBERT ROSS in *The Bystander.*

"There is no question about the poetic quality of much of Mr Neuburg's verse. . . . We are given visions of love which open new amorous possibilities."—*Daily Chronicle.*

The Star in the West

BY

CAPTAIN J. F. C. FULLER

FOURTH LARGE EDITION NOW IN PREPARATION

THROUGH THE EQUINOX AND ALL BOOKSELLERS

SIX SHILLINGS NET

A highly original study of morals and religion by a new writer, who is as entertaining as the average novelist is dull. Nowadays human thought has taken a brighter place in the creation : our emotions are weary of bad baronets and stolen wills; they are now only excited by spiritual crises, catastrophes of the reason, triumphs of the intelligence. In these fields Captain Fuller is a master dramatist.

The PHOTOGRAPHS

OF ASANA AND OF PRANAYAMA IN THIS MAGAZINE WERE TAKEN BY THE

DOVER STREET STUDIOS

DOVER STREET, LONDON, W.

To be obtained of

THE EQUINOX, 3 Great James St., W.C.

Crown 8vo, Scarlet Buckram, pp. 64

PRICE 10s. net

Less than 100 copies remain. The price will shortly be raised to
one guinea net

A .·. A .·. PUBLICATION IN CLASS B

BOOK

777

THIS book contains in concise tabulated form a comparative view of all the symbols of the great religions of the world ; the perfect attributions of the Taro, so long kept secret by the Rosicrucians, are now for the first time published ; also the complete secret magical correspondences of the G .·. D .·. and R. R. et A. C. It forms, in short, a complete magical and philosophical dictionary ; a key to all religions and to all practical occult working.

For the first time Western and Qabalistic symbols have been harmonised with those of Hinduism, Buddhism, Mohammedanism, Taoism, etc. By a glance at the Tables, anybody conversant with any one system can understand perfectly all others.

The *Occult Review* says :

"Despite its cumbrous sub-title and high price per page, this work has only to come under the notice of the right people to be sure of a ready sale. In its author's words, it represents 'an attempt to systematise alike the data of mysticism and the results of comparative religion,' and so far as any book can succeed in such an attempt, this book does succeed ; that is to say, it condenses in some sixty pages as much information as many an intelligent reader at the Museum has been able to collect in years. The book proper consists of a Table of 'Correspondences,' and is, in fact, an attempt to reduce to a common denominator the symbolism of as many religious and magical systems as the author is acquainted with. The denominator chosen is necessarily a large one, as the author's object is to reconcile systems which divide all things into 3, 7, 10, 12, as the case may be. Since our expression 'common denominator' is used in a figurative and not in a strictly mathematical sense, the task is less complex than appears at first sight, and the 32 Paths of the Sepher Yetzirah, or Book of Formation of the Qabalah, provide a convenient scale. These 32 Paths are attributed by the Qabalists to the 10 Sephiroth, or Emanations of Deity, and to the 22 letters of the Hebrew alphabet, which are again subdivided into 3 mother letters, 7 double letters, and 12 simple letters. On this basis, that of the Qabalistic 'Tree of Life,' as a certain arrangement of the Sephiroth and 22 remaining Paths connecting them is termed, the author has constructed no less than 183 tables.

"The Qabalistic information is very full, and there are tables of Egyptian and Hindu deities, as well as of colours, perfumes, plants, stones, and animals. The information concerning the tarot and geomancy exceeds that to be found in some treatises devoted exclusively to those subjects. The author appears to be acquainted with Chinese, Arabic, and other classic texts. Here your reviewer is unable to follow him, but his Hebrew does credit alike to him and to his printer. Among several hundred words, mostly proper names, we found and marked a few misprints, but subsequently discovered each one of them in a printed table of errata, which we had overlooked. When one remembers the misprints in 'Agrippa' and the fact that the ordinary Hebrew compositor and reader is no more fitted for this task than a boy cognisant of no more than the shapes of the Hebrew letters, one wonders how many proofs there were and what the printer's bill was. A knowledge of the Hebrew alphabet and of the Qabalistic Tree of Life is all that is needed to lay open to the reader the enormous mass of information contained in this book. The 'Alphabet of Mysticism,' as the author says—several alphabets we should prefer to say—is here. Much that has been jealously and foolishly kept secret in the past is here, but though our author has secured for his work the *imprimatur* of some body with the mysterious title of the A .·. A .·., and though he remains himself anonymous, he appears to be no mystery-monger. Obviously he is widely read, but he makes no pretence that he has secrets to reveal. On the contrary, he says, 'an indicible arcanum is an arcanum which *cannot* be revealed.' The writer of that sentence has learned at least one fact not to be learned from books.

"G. C. J."

WILLIAM NORTHAM
Robemaker
9 Henrietta Street, Southampton Street, Strand

TELEPHONE—5400 Central

MR NORTHAM begs to announce that he has been entrusted with the manufacture of all robes and other ceremonial apparel of members of the A∴ A∴ and its adepts and aspirants.

No. 0.	PROBATIONER'S ROBE	.	.	.	.	.	.	£5	0	0
1.	„	„ superior quality	.	.	.	.	.	7	0	0
2.	NEOPHYTE'S	.	.	.	.	.	.	.	6	0	0
3.	ZELATOR	Symbol added to No. 2	.	.	.	1	0	0
4.	PRACTICUS	„	„	3	.	.	.	1	0	0
5.	PHILOSOPHUS	„	„	4	.	.	.	1	0	0
6.	DOMINUS LIMINIS	„	„	5	.	.	.	1	0	0
7.	ADEPTUS (without)	„	„	0 or 1	.	.	3	0	0
8.	„ (within)	.	.	.	.	.	.	10	0	0
9.	ADEPTUS MAJOR	.	.	.	.	.	.	10	0	0
10.	ADEPTUS EXEMPTUS	.	.	.	.	.	10	0	0
11.	MAGISTER TEMPLI	.	.	.	.	.	.	50	0	0

The Probationer's robe is fitted for performance of all general invocations and especially for the I. of the H. G. A. ; a white and gold nemmes may be worn. These robes may also be worn by Assistant Magi in all composite rituals of the White.

The Neophyte's robe is fitted for all elemental operations. A black and gold nemmes may be worn. Assistant Magi may wear these in all composite rituals of the Black.

The Zelator's robe is fitted for all rituals involving I O, and for the infernal rites of Luna. In the former case an Uraeus crown and purple nemmes, in the latter a silver nemmes, should be worn.

The Practicus' robe is fitted for all rituals involving I I, and for the rites of Mercury. In the former case an Uraeus crown and green nemmes, in the latter a nemyss of shot silk, should be worn.

The Philosophus' robe is fitted for all rituals involving O O, and for the rites of Venus. In the former case an Uraeus crown and azure nemmes, in the latter a green nemmes, should be worn.

The Dominus Liminis' robe is fitted for the infernal rites of Sol, which must never be celebrated.

The Adeptus Minor's robe is fitted for the rituals of Sol. A golden nemmes may be worn.

The Adeptus' robe is fitted for the particular workings of the Adeptus, and for the Postulant at the First Gate of the City of the Pyramids.

The Adeptus Major's robe is fitted for the Chief Magus in all Rituals and Evocations of the Inferiors, for the performance of the rites of Mars, and for the Postulant at the Second Gate of the City of the Pyramids.

The Adeptus Exemptus' robe is fitted for the Chief Magus in all Rituals and Invocations of the Superiors, for the performance of the rites of Jupiter, and for the Postulant at the Third Gate of the City of the Pyramids.

The Babe of the Abyss has no robe.

For the performance of the rites of Saturn, the Magician may wear a black robe, close-cut, with narrow sleeves, trimmed with white, and the Seal and Square of Saturn marked on breast and back. A conical black cap embroidered with the Sigils of Saturn should be worn.

The Magister Templi robe is fitted for the great Meditations, for the supernal rites of Luna, and for those rites of Babylon and the Graal. But this robe should be worn by no man, because of that which is written : " Ecclesia abhorret a sanguine."

Any of these robes may be worn by a person of whatever grade

on appropriate occasions

George Raffalovich's new works

THE HISTORY OF A SOUL

Price 3s. 6d.   Edition strictly limited

THE DEUCE AND ALL

A COLLECTION OF SHORT STORIES

1*s. net*

READY

Through **THE EQUINOX** and all booksellers

READY SHORTLY

THE WHIRLPOOL

BY

ETHEL ARCHER

WITH A COVER SPECIALLY DESIGNED BY

E. J. WIELAND

A DEDICATORY SONNET BY

VICTOR B. NEUBURG

AND

AN INTRODUCTION BY

ALEISTER CROWLEY

Price One Shilling net

A. CROWLEY'S WORKS

The volumes here listed are all of definite occult and mystical interest and importance.

The Trade may obtain them from
  "The Equinox," 3 Great James Street, W.C.   Tel. : City 8987 ; and Messrs Simpkin, Marshall, Hamilton, Kent & Co., 23 Paternoster Row, E.C.

The Public may obtain them from
  "The Equinox," 3 Great James Street, W.C.
  Mr Elkin Mathews, Vigo Street, W.
  The Walter Scott Publishing Co., Paternoster Square, E.C.
  Mr F. Hollings, Great Turnstile, Holborn.
                And through all Booksellers.

ACELDAMA.   Crown 8vo, 29 pp., £2, 2s. net.   Of this rare pamphlet less than 10 copies remain.   It is Mr Crowley's earliest and in some ways most striking mystical work.

JEPHTHAH AND OTHER MYSTERIES, LYRICAL AND DRAMATIC.   Demy 8vo, boards, pp. xxii + 223, 7s. 6d. net.

SONGS OF THE SPIRIT.   Pp. x + 109.   A new edition.   3s. 6d. net.
These two volumes breathe the pure semi-conscious aspiration of the soul, and express the first glimmerings of the light.

THE SOUL OF OSIRIS.   Medium 8vo, pp. ix + 129, 5s. net.
A collection of lyrics, illustrating the progress of the soul from corporeal to celestial beatitude.

TANNHAUSER.   Demy 4to, pp. 142, 15s. net.
The progress of the soul in dramatic form.

BERASHITH.   4to, China paper, pp. 24, 5s. net.   Only a few copies remain.   An illuminating essay on the Universe, reconciling the conflicting systems of religion.

THE GOD=EATER.   Crown 4to, pp. 32, 2s. 6d. net.
A striking dramatic study of the origin of religions.

THE SWORD OF SONG.   Post 4to, pp. ix + 194, printed in red and black, decorative wrapper, 20s. net.
This is the author's first most brilliant attempt to base the truths of mysticism on the truths of scepticism.   It contains also an enlarged amended edition of "Berashith," and an Essay showing the striking parallels and identities between the doctrines of Modern Science and those of Buddhism.

GARGOYLES.   Pott 8vo, pp. vi + 113, 5s. net.

ORACLES.   Demy 8vo, pp. viii + 176, 5s. net.
Some of Mr Crowley's finest mystical lyrics are in these collections.

KONX OM PAX.   See advt.

Collected Works (Travellers' Edition).   Extra crown 8vo, India paper, 3 vols. in one, pp. 808 + Appendices.   Vellum, green ties, with portraits, £3, 3s. ; white buckram, without portraits, £2, 2s.   This edition contains "Qabalistic Dogma," "Time," "The Excluded Middle," "Eleusis," and other matters of the highest occult importance which are not printed elsewhere.

AMBERGRIS.   Medium 8vo, pp. 200, 3s. 6d.   (Elkin Mathews.)
A selection of lyrics, containing some of great mystical beauty.

Household Gods

A COMEDY
By ALEISTER CROWLEY

Privately Printed by the Chiswick Press
and bound in White Buckram with Gold Lettering

PRICE HALF A GUINEA

Copies may be obtained on application to the Author
at the offices of "The Equinox"

Thirty copies of the Sketch of
ALEISTER CROWLEY by AUGUS-
TUS JOHN have been pulled on
Special Paper, and are for sale,
framed, at the Price of One Guinea
Net. Application should be made
at once to the Offices of this
Magazine

OCCULTISM